WHISTLE STOP

WHISTLE STOP

KENNY DORHAM, JAZZ, AND THE JOURNEY OF A TEXAS FAMILY

ROBERT M. PALLITTO
AND JOHN A. MELENDEZ

UNIVERSITY PRESS OF MISSISSIPPI / JACKSON

The University Press of Mississippi is the scholarly publishing agency of the Mississippi Institutions of Higher Learning: Alcorn State University, Delta State University, Jackson State University, Mississippi State University, Mississippi University for Women, Mississippi Valley State University, University of Mississippi, and University of Southern Mississippi.

www.upress.state.ms.us

The University Press of Mississippi is a member of the Association of University Presses.

Manufactured in the United States of America
∞

Publisher: University Press of Mississippi, Jackson, USA
Authorised GPSR Safety Representative: Easy Access System Europe - Mustamäe tee 50, 10621 Tallinn, Estonia, gpsr.requests@easproject.com

Library of Congress Cataloging-in-Publication Data

Names: Pallitto, Robert M., 1964– author | Melendez, John A. author
Title: Whistle stop : Kenny Dorham, jazz, and the journey of a Texas family / Robert M. Pallitto, John A. Melendez.
Other titles: American made music series
Description: Jackson : University Press of Mississippi, 2026. | Series: American made music series | Includes bibliographical references and index.
Identifiers: LCCN 2025054262 (print) | LCCN 2025054263 (ebook) | ISBN 9781496861955 hardback | ISBN 9781496861962 trade paperback | ISBN 9781496861979 epub | ISBN 9781496861986 epub | ISBN 9781496861993 pdf | ISBN 9781496862006 pdf
Subjects: LCSH: Dorham, Kenny, 1924–1972 | Jazz musicians—United States—Biography | Trumpet players—United States—Biography
Classification: LCC ML419.D68 P35 2026 (print) | LCC ML419.D68 (ebook) | DDC 788.9/2165092 [B]—dc23/eng/20251219
LC record available at https://lccn.loc.gov/2025054262
LC ebook record available at https://lccn.loc.gov/2025054263

British Library Cataloging-in-Publication Data available

In memory of Joel Dorham
timbalero increible (R. M. P.)

In memory of Andy Michalec
*Mentor, musician, and friend
we all aspired to be* (J. A. M.)

CONTENTS

PREFACE

McKinley Howard (Kenny) Dorham Jr. was born in 1924 to an African American farming family in Freestone County, Texas, and made his way to New York just as seismic changes in modern jazz were beginning. Dorham's twenty-eight-year musical career saw him performing and touring throughout the United States and Europe with his own groups and in collaboration with every other major figure in jazz. The warmth and expressiveness of Dorham's trumpet sound, as well his sense of swing, technical facility, and graceful phrasing can be heard in his voluminous recording catalogue and in his influence on each generation of trumpeters who followed him. As a composer, he left us nearly a hundred deeply original and powerful pieces that remain fresh and insistent when they are performed today. Whatever celebrity or financial rewards may have eluded him, his body of creative work and the deep and universal respect and affection voiced by everyone interviewed for this book speak to the impact of Dorham's life on American music.

In part, the person Kenny Dorham became actually reflects the story of his remarkable family, who were borne along on the currents of historical change stretching back into the lost history of the antebellum South and continuing through Reconstruction when Dorham's mother's family farmed as landowning freedmen and -women, through the strictures of Jim Crow–era Texas to their dispersal across the United States as they became noted educators, musicians, political activists, and public officials. This book will include extended treatment of the lives of some of Dorham's family members, even during times when he was not with them. A close look at this family's history reveals the multifaceted complexity of Black lives in America and also an intertwining of Black and white social experiences in the Jim Crow South and then in the New York City of the 1950s and 1960s. To be sure, the realities of segregation and racialized economic exploitation are plain to see, but an indomitable strength is also there in the story of Dorham and his family. That strength sustained them through turbulent phases of history and enabled them to enlarge their stake despite bias, hostility, turbulent national events, and brazen injustice.

It is possible to lament the harms inflicted by those macro- and micro-level processes while at the same time celebrating the force of will that Dorham and his family drew upon in order to bear up under them. The earlier family history shaped the person Kenny Dorham became, and his national and international recognition reflected back on his family, affecting their lives.

Telling the story of a life like this, one is confronted immediately by the challenge of relating events that were experienced first-hand by others. This challenge is ever-present for a biographer, but is posed even more starkly when one describes experiences that are particular to another group of people. Writing about the experience of Black Americans from the perspective of a white and a LatinX (in our case) writer poses challenges and may generate skepticism. Will the account do justice to the experience? Will the pain of racism be conveyed? Will the subject emerge as a multidimensional personality? The decision to undertake such a project at all requires a balancing of the importance of telling the story, on the one hand, against evident potential pitfalls on the other. Obviously, we decided that the former outweighed the latter in this case. Fortunately, it was easier to step back and let Kenny Dorham speak for himself because he left us an honest and eloquent—if sadly incomplete—first-hand written account of his meteoric time on the earth. The enduring importance and urgency of some of the themes treated here also enable the telling of this story. Systemic racism, the economic plight of musical artists of color, and Black land loss remain relevant and problematic today for anyone concerned about redeeming the promises of equality and justice that the nation's founding documents proclaim.

Like all of us, Kenny Dorham was a complex person who fought to bring his best self forward and did not always succeed in that effort. He acknowledged a long-term struggle with drugs as he looked back over his own life, and family members similarly mourned his misfortune to have gotten involved in the wrong things. But those aspects of his life have already been publicized by others, and we will not dwell on them here. Instead, what follows is an account of Dorham's rich and momentous time on earth, woven together with the stories of his siblings, children, parents, grandparents, and great-grandparents, recounted with a clear-eyed view of the racism that plagued the wider society and dogged Black lives at every turn, but also portraying the diverse and vibrant existence Dorham and his family lived, with the genuine warmth and joy of family and of living that Dorham himself described as constant through it all.

Highland Park, New Jersey
October 2022

ACKNOWLEDGMENTS

So many people lent their time, expertise, and goodwill to make this book a reality, and we can't imagine how the process would have gone without all of that crucial assistance. We certainly hope we haven't omitted anyone who helped us over the four years that this project was in the works.

First, we would like to thank Craig Gill, Katie Turner, and everyone else at the University Press of Mississippi for their faith in the book and for seeing it through all the twists and turns on its way to publication. The anonymous reviewers also offered helpful suggestions that made for a better book in the end.

Kenny Dorham's family was gracious and generous in sharing documents, photos, and reminiscences of their beloved relative who was born over one hundred years ago. Thanks to Keturah Dorham Holley for sharing memories and photographs, Evette Dorham and LeJuine Dorham Boone for additional family information, Dana Dorham and Michele Barrows Dorham for photos and encouragement, and the late Carolyn Yarbro Smith for her recollections of her cousins and uncles in Texas and New York. Joel Dorham, sadly, did not get to see this biography of his brother in print, but his generosity in filling out the details of his family's history, his brother's career, and his own rich and full life as a musician and activist created a debt that is impossible to repay. For all of that, and for his decades of devotion to preserving Kenny Dorham's work and the music both of them loved, we have dedicated this book to him.

Dorham's friends and fellow musicians were incredibly gracious in sharing stories and details as well as explaining how Dorham influenced their own playing and the work of others. They were enthusiastic to learn that a biography of Dorham was being written, and that it might lead to even greater recognition of his contributions in the eyes of the wider public. We are deeply grateful to Sonny Rollins, Ron Carter, Louis Hayes, Lew Tabackin, Mark Harvey, Bernie Drayton, the late Michael Cuscuna, Joe Magnarelli, David Weiss, Freddie Hendrix, Jason Moran, Ran Blake, John Eckert, and Kal Ferretti. Don and Maureen Sickler deserve special thanks for spending long hours with us at the hallowed Van Gelder recording studio, for connecting us with several people who knew Dorham, and for their work in preserving and promoting the Dorham legacy through creating arrangements and transcriptions of his work and, in Don's case, performing it live and in studio as well.

Our home institutions supported this work in so many ways. At Seton Hall University, we owe thanks to Jeff Togman for helpful advice and feedback on drafts and photographs, Lisa DeLuca for guiding us to nineteenth-century family records, King Mott for setting the scene of East Texas in the last century, Brenda Knight for insights into the Newark/New York jazz scene in the glory years when Dorham was with us, Todd Burroughs for unlocking a treasure trove of newspaper material, Alan Delozier for archival help, Lizi Shcherbakovi for technical help with the manuscript, and David Frank for tracking down hitherto impossible-to-find books. Thanks also to Mike Taylor, Larry Greene, Forrest Pritchett, and Vanessa May for help and support. The University Research Council provided a generous stipend to one of us that funded research, travel, and access to recordings. Additionally, a semester sabbatical allowed temporary release from teaching responsibilities and enabled travel to Freestone County, Texas, to peruse deed and court records and to visit the County Historical Museum.

At Columbia University, we would like to thank Aidan Levy and Jackie Santos for essential interview assistance, Chris Washburne and Ole Mathisen for valuable contact information and several years of musical mentorship, and Don Sickler for an afternoon tour of the Van Gelder studio and for several unforgettable stories that have made their way into these pages and a shared dream of getting KD the recognition he deserves. At NYU, we owe thanks to Dave Schroeder for a few emails and phone numbers, as well as to Alan Broadbent, Drew Gress, and Billy Drummond, whose lessons informed every part of the music-centric sections of this book.

Externally, we are most grateful for assistance from the Hayek Fund for Scholars at the Institute for Humane Studies. A preview of this book was presented at the American Political Science Association's annual conference, where we received helpful feedback that strengthened the final product. Vincent Pelote at the Rutgers Institute of Jazz Studies shared his expansive knowledge of the institute's holdings and of music history in general, and we benefitted from viewing the papers of Abbey Lincoln, George Wein, and May Lou Williams at Rutgers. Many thanks to Arndt Weidler at Jazz Institut Darmstadt; the staff at the Schomburg Center for Research in Black Culture; Morgan Davis at the Library of Congress; Lewis Porter, Sue Mahal, and Frank Alkyer at *DownBeat*; the staff at the Smithsonian; the staff of RIPM at Columbia; the staff at the Austin History Center and the Texas Music Museum; and Harold McMillan, creator of Kenny Dorham's Backyard.

In Freestone County, where it all began, we received invaluable assistance from a number of people. Evelyn Lawson shared her vast knowledge, patiently recounting genealogy and the Black history of the region in response to a multitude of questions over many months. At the Freestone Museum, where a plaque was dedicated to Kenny Dorham in 2012, Patricia Pratt, Mary Cryer Awalt, Don Awalt, Beverly Awalt, and Linda Mullin spent hours with us, providing old maps, photos, stories, and writings reaching back well into the 1800s.

Family and friends helped in every way imaginable—reading drafts, offering encouragement, listening to recordings, sharing meals, attending music performances, talking through ideas, and hearing us talk about Kenny Dorham (a lot). We are forever grateful to Kathryn Motoviloff; Daniel and Isabel Melendez; John, Kerry, and Anne Motoviloff; Christina Pallitto; Ben Smith; and Sophia and Natasha Smith. Thanks to Christina and Natasha for help with French to English translation. Thanks also to Ana Melendez and Diana Devore; Ellen, Roger, and Andrew Miller; Chris and Faith Kotsen; Gerard Byrne and Doris Masse; Shelli Soto and Chris Moyer; Bob and Gwyn Murray; Emily Bregman; Frank Magaletta and Jennifer Evans; Bill Weaver; and Jerry and Karen Wahl.

Thanks as well (from John) to Josh Hasler, Jess Rodriguez, Cory Scarola, Alex Burchfield, Alex Groher-Jick, Seth Benjamin, Charlie Fuertsch, and Henry Litwhiler for asking about the book (and continuing to believe it would come to fruition). Thank you to Rebecca Winterich-Knox for listening to me talk about trumpet solos on numerous occasions with generous interest, recommending just-right revisions to awkward sentences, being supportive through the various ups and downs of this project and being the best partner, writer, and editor I could have asked to be with.

The last bit of thanks is hardest to express. Both of us are deeply grateful to Laura Melendez-Pallitto for always being there to inspire, encourage, educate, extricate, indemnify, gladden, and enrich us. This book would not have been possible without you.

Finally, as the refrain goes, none of the above-mentioned persons are responsible for any errors contained herein.

WHISTLE STOP

INTRODUCTION

NEAR BUTLER, TEXAS, CA. 1934

Young Kenny Dorham sat on the back porch of his family's home, a big white clapboard farmhouse just off old Texas Highway 7. At about ten years old, he took in the post-dinner scene that happened somewhat regularly during the time the Dorhams lived in rural East Texas. Outside, owls, crickets, and whippoorwills called from the darkened woods and fields beyond the circle of light cast by an oil lamp. Moths, beetles, and craneflies crashed into the porch screening, drawn by the lamplight that also attracted wanderers from the Depression-era landscape. Men, mostly white, jumped off the freight trains that crisscrossed Texas and then turned up at farmhouses and town squares looking for food and a place to sleep. On the Dorhams' porch, the night's visitor told stories of his travels. Then he sang a few of the songs collected from boxcars and work camps across the land. The Dorhams had a piano and a guitar in the house, so the performance might take a number of turns as the night wore on. Kenny sat and listened to music that seemed to go in circles, words and riffs coming around like the whistle screech of a train. It stirred him to travel, told of places he hadn't seen, of rail lines stretching across the state and beyond, even into Mexico. These images fueled a lifetime of creative imagination, and he would spend the rest of his days trying to capture in musical terms the moods evoked by those early stories and songs.

As well as visual impressions, specific musical styles and blending of styles imprinted themselves on Kenny's mind. In the 1930s, jazz music was relatively new, and various forms of folk music, including blues, were also circulating in the region of East Texas and the Mississippi Delta. Country blues music was emerging from nearby Wortham and Deep Ellum; barrelhouse saloons had for years incubated a blend of boogie-woogie piano, country dances, and ethnically diverse folk songs. While we appreciate the range of distinct American musical styles that emerged during the twentieth century, the cross-pollination occurring during their development is often overlooked. Kenny Dorham's music is a reminder of those connections. While his musical associations landed him in the center of modern jazz, he brought with him sounds and stories of the West, of country life, and a loose and soulful expressiveness conferred by Texas blues that would give him a unique voice and emotional power.[1]

Twenty-two years later, in the spring of 1956, Dorham could be seen in New York's Café Bohemia, career in full flower, as he recorded a live album with his group, the Jazz Prophets. Dorham painted an autumnal scene with his horn that night as he worked through a familiar ballad with a solo that built out, the seed of one idea blossoming from line to line, held together with long tones and smooth triplets and slides. He was the image of grace as he held the horn, eyes closed, deep in the sound, the metal resonance, his feel endlessly flowing, like the breeze between rustling tree branches. He would return to the melody briefly before executing an elegant turnaround, finally eliciting applause from the crowded nightspot amid chatter and clinking glasses.[2]

BEGINNINGS

Kenny Dorham's story begins in Freestone County, East Texas. Texas is a big place, as so many songs remind us, and it contains varied terrain within its 258,000 square miles. Freestone and its county seat of Fairfield sit in the post oak savannah region of the state, midway between Dallas and Houston, just west of the terminus of the piney woods. It is open country marked by tall oaks that punctuate a prairie covered with bluestem and buffalo grass, yaupon holly, cedar and hickory trees, bluebonnets, and Indian paintbrush. Cattle egrets hop on and off the backs of grazing animals. Red-tailed hawks and turkey vultures ride the warm air currents above the fields. Scissor-tailed flycatchers drop from fenceposts and wires into elegant looping patterns as they hunt insects. Twisted post oaks, some only skeletons of a living tree now, reach skyward with their fingerlike branches. The oaks are so prominent and plentiful, in fact, that they often served as reference points in land surveys. Puffy cumulus clouds skip across the wide horizon, pushed gently by a late summer breeze. The cattle ranches in Freestone County today are smaller spreads, and in fact the country is thicker with brush today than a century ago when larger herds grazed and trampled the land into more open range.[3] Farm roads veer off the main highway to snake through pine and oak woods that once hid moonshine hollows and country cemeteries. The cemeteries remain.

Long before Europeans arrived to begin farming on the oak savannahs, the Caddo people were exploring the area's agricultural possibilities, growing beans, corn, squash, and tobacco in the rich soil of what would later become Freestone County. The Caddo were slowly driven from Texas, first by the French and Spanish and then, after statehood, by Texans. Today the Caddo Nation is based in neighboring Oklahoma, leaving behind in Texas temple and burial mounds, buried artifacts, and a slew of place names, including a namesake town and lake. Spanish names throughout the state recall another part of Texas history: the acquisition of territory from Mexico. The 1848 treaty of Guadalupe Hidalgo ceded large parts of the Southwest to the United States as the price for ending the war with Mexico, and Mexican farmers suddenly found themselves living in a new country. "We didn't cross the border," says a popular Tejano refrain; "the border crossed us." The Spanish and Mexican land grants remained as the popular reference points in land surveys well into the twentieth century, including the Simon Sanchez League grant that spanned a large part of Freestone County and that was home to Dorham's family.

Once white Anglo farmers arrived in the nineteenth century and began carving out farmsteads in the area, modern agriculture grew rapidly, aided by the export routes offered by the Trinity River and the Missouri Pacific Railroad, not to mention the market hub at Dallas and Fort Worth. Cotton in particular thrived here, and could be transported to meet distant demand by use of emerging modern transportation. African American farmers also worked the fertile soil of Freestone County in the late 1800s. East Texas in general contained a large enclave of free Black farmers. Though some worked as tenant farmers, sharecroppers, or laborers, many owned land. In fact, that part of Texas saw a concentration of Black land ownership dating back to the nineteenth century. Even as the number of sharecroppers increased following Emancipation and the end of the Civil War—driven by the mutual necessity of whites who had lost their fortunes in the war, plantation owners who could no longer rely on free labor, and African Americans who were precluded from obtaining land—Black land ownership in Freestone and nearby counties was no anomaly but rather widespread.

Joel Manning (Dorham's maternal great-grandfather), was one Black farmer who acquired title to land during Reconstruction. In 1870, Manning was forty-five years old and living in the new county of Freestone, which had been carved nearly twenty years earlier out of already-existing Limestone County.[4] The decennial census records of that year show that Manning owned land valued at $165 and that he was eligible to vote.[5] Manning and his family lived and farmed in an unincorporated rural community near the county seat and new town of Fairfield. It was a rugged place at that time, still populated by buffalo herds, red wolves, and panthers (mountain lions). Poisonous snakes of four varieties abounded: rattlesnake, cottonmouth, coral snake, and copperhead. The Comanche and Kiowa people controlled the plains and would do so until the army's campaign to vanquish both tribes in the 1870s. Their feats on horseback and fierceness in fighting created a mystique around them that blended with fear in the popular imagination. And the Comanche were an active and powerful fighting force in Texas. In 1836, they had raided near the present-day town of Groesbeck, captured a young girl named Cynthia Parker, and then adopted her into the tribe. Parker later married a Comanche chief, and their son, Quanah Parker, became a much-feared chief himself, leading war parties in Central Texas and the Panhandle until the mid-1870s.[6] Though Freestone County marked the southeastern edge of the Comanche territory, the Caddo nation, specifically its Keechi and Tonkawa branches, also lived in the area until a reservation was established in Oklahoma, where most of the Caddo were living at the time.

It was into this perilous and largely ungoverned situation that Joel Manning arrived, having come west from Alabama sometime between 1853 and 1855 with his wife, Sarah, and sons Henry, Owen, and Alfred. By 1870, eldest son Henry (Kenny Dorham's maternal grandfather) was married and living in a separate home in the same community. Owen and Alfred were twenty-one and eighteen, respectively. Owen, Alfred, and Henry were able, with their father's assistance, to purchase farms of their own on land surrounding the small settlement of Butler, which lay about a dozen miles east of Fairfield on a road that would first become Highway 7 and then Highway 84.[7] The Mannings were not alone in making their trek: There was something of an exodus from Alabama in those years. In fact, historians suggest that the town was named after Fairfield, Alabama, in recognition of the many Alabamans who resettled there.[8] It appears that Joel and Sarah's family was connected to a white family named Manning (A. Manning, Mary Manning, and their son Cale Y. Manning) who also lived around Butler at the same time, having come from Alabama as well. It seems likely that Joel and Sarah and their children had been enslaved by the white Mannings prior to Emancipation. They shared a common surname, and the families' lives were linked in a number of ways. Cale—who went by "C. Y."—and his wife donated land in 1886 to the Butler AME Church, where Owen was a trustee. That acre of land was also the subject of an earlier deed, which described it as the site of the "colored church that was burned down," and the plot would become the Pine Top Cemetery. The reasons for the gift are lost to history, but it establishes another link between the families. And C. Y.'s name appears in a number of land transaction deed records with Owen, Alfred, and Henry; C. Y. is sometimes a grantor and sometimes a witness.[9]

Old deeds and maps provide clues to the roots of Kenny Dorham's ancestors in the Butler area. Henry bought 120 acres on a tract two miles south of Butler that was known as the Gorman farm, adjacent to another hundred acres of Manning land that had also previously been held by the Gormans. Those purchases were financed with promissory notes payable at 10 percent interest. Owen's and Alfred's land lay slightly to the northwest of Henry's, but all of the Mannings' ancestral holdings were clustered around the Butler center, a small group of buildings near a crossroads now marked by the intersection of two farm roads with the east/west highway.[10]

Sarah Manning gave birth to seven more children after she and her husband Joel arrived in Texas. Their farmstead survived the dangers and threats of a wild and unforgiving land and provided the family with sustenance and an opportunity to branch out into separate farming endeavors. Their son Henry married Patsy Redick in 1884 (his second marriage; he was apparently widowed),[11] and their 120 acres on the old Gorman place would become known as the Henry and Patsy Manning farm, which they eventually passed to their children, including Eva Minnie Dorham (née Manning), Kenny's mother. One can only imagine the kind of intense, punishing and dangerous work needed to draw a living from the soil while watching the horizon for anyone who might come along and take the farm and its livestock by force. That threat came from land-hungry whites fueled by racial resentment as well as from Comanche raiders seeking to drive non-Indians from the plains. On one hand, the Manning family's extensive landholdings suggest a prosperity that is not generally assumed for African Americans in the postwar South, but on the other, the retrenchment of racial hierarchy during the Jim Crow era exacted a toll on the family's wealth, as we will see.

In some places, the federal government's Reconstruction-era assistance resulted in increased land ownership for formerly enslaved Black Americans. But with the end of Reconstruction in 1876, when the contested presidential election of that year was settled by a bargain that withdrew federal troops completely from the South, much of that land was confiscated from Black landowners by the states. It is well known that race relations worsened and violence increased in former Confederate states when Reconstruction ended and the Jim Crow era began. But even before that, federal efforts in the South met fierce resistance, and it was especially intense and violent in East Texas. Troops had been removed from Freestone County prior to Reconstruction's end, and the Freedmen's Bureau was not operative in the countryside, functioning instead out of larger Texas cities. The Bureau was aware of the racial violence in rural Texas, though. They took affidavits from victims of that violence in Freestone County and other parts of the state. In one 1868 incident, county resident Mark Walker was driven from his house and shot point blank by the leader of a white mob. Walker escaped the mob with a leg wound and went to Waco and then to Austin for help. His alleged offense was reporting that a Black children's schoolhouse had been burned down by the mob.[12] The same men who captured Walker also broke down the door of his neighbor James Eaton's house and tried to hang him, but Eaton also escaped. A pretext for these attacks was suspicion of the men's involvement with the Union Leagues, organizations aligned with the North that promoted voting and other rights for formerly enslaved persons. According to historian Eric Foner, Black membership in the Leagues was high in the Reconstruction South.[13] League members and leaders were routinely assassinated by the Ku Klux Klan and other white vigilantes. It was amid these conditions that the Mannings forged their homesteads in the Texas wilds.

Despite many obstacles, the Mannings retained control and ownership of their land until the 1930s. They persevered through a hard farming life, and were able to pass on land title to their descendants, including daughter-in-law Patsy Manning, widow of Henry Manning. Nineteenth-century county deed records show multiple land transfers within the Manning extended family, all out near the Freestone County hamlet of Butler. Henry died sometime between 1916 and 1920, and as of 1920 Patsy's household included her daughter Eva (who went by "Minnie" and was born around 1900—Kenny's mother), and sons Alvo, Alfred, and Joel. Five-year-old Eva Lois Manning also lived with the family in 1920, the daughter of Minnie and granddaughter of Patsy.[14] As Kenny Dorham's older sister, Eva Lois would come to play an important role in his musical development.

Like his mother, Dorham's father also had roots in Freestone County. Jasper Dorham came to Freestone during the turbulent years following the Civil War, declaring his birthplace as Tennessee. He worked as a farmer and laborer and also preached. Jasper Dorham married Millie Robey in 1888. They had two sons together (Jasper already had children from a previous marriage). The oldest born to them was McKinley Howard Dorham Sr., who was born on September 2, 1900.[15] McKinley also had a younger brother, Roosevelt. Jasper and Millie divorced, and both went on to remarry. Jasper died in 1919 of complications from diabetes.[16] As of 1920, Millie had remarried, to a man named Stepney Moses, and was living near Fairfield with her children and Moses.[17] In this somewhat insular community, Stepney and his wife Millie would enter into land transactions with the same people the

Mannings were dealing with. Stepney owned his land, and oil and gas prospectors looked to lease from him so they could drill and explore—and they did so. But McKinley Howard Dorham Sr. would soon depart his mother's house to marry Eva Minnie Manning. McKinley and Minnie would remain together until McKinley's death from an aneurysm in 1969, at the age of 69, after a lifetime of hard physical work.[18] McKinley and Minnie raised a family—including son Kenny—in a shared odyssey that took them from unincorporated Butler and Post Oak and other farm locations to Fairfield, then to Austin, then to Oakland, California, then back to Austin.

The early generations of the Manning family, together with many of their descendants, are buried in the small Pine Top Cemetery near the hamlet of Butler, on land first deeded to the AME Church by Henry Manning back in 1879.[19] Nestled in pine and oak woods a few miles off the main east/west road, Pine Top is encircled by a metal chain link fence with a bungee cord holding the gate closed. It bears an entrance arch with Pine Top Cemetery spelled out in metal lettering. Inside the fence are some elaborate nineteenth-century grave markers alongside other stones that are mere crude slabs that are barely legible or not legible at all. What appears to be Owen Manning's name is scratched into one reddish stone, while another old grave marker bears the Manning name without a first name, and some recent graves quickly dug by hand and shovel are barely deep enough to cover the coffins. That the cemetery is still in use and has hosted recent burials adds poignancy to a walk around the grounds, a vivid link to the past. Some of the newer, simple graves attest to the economic straits of the community's current residents, made worse by the COVID-19 pandemic. Joel's Manning's grave is not at Pine Top, or if it is, there is no way to know which of the bare stones marks it. The family matriarch, Sarah, born in 1831, did not die in Butler, but rather in Oakwood in the south of the county. She was living with her daughter Lottie and Lottie's family when she passed, in a house they owned down on Bonner's Ferry Road near Oakwood, where the Trinity River bends.[20] Sarah lived through the early years of the republic, through Emancipation, and through World War I. Andrew Jackson was president when Sarah was born, and she outlasted him and nineteen other presidents. But Pine Top holds generation after generation of Mannings, some of whom share the first names of earlier forebears. A number of them served in battle.

In the evening, as a warm wind rustles the dry oak leaves, history lies particularly heavily on the land. The family's roots and the community that grew up around them beginning in the first years after Emancipation create a presence, a sense of determination to remain, to enlarge their stake, to thrive despite hardship and challenge. It can be seen in the markers and the jars of faded flowers, and felt in the air, as dark descends. Like the day itself, the earlier generations are finally at rest. Kenny Dorham's grave is not there. His journey took him around the country and the world, to the most rarefied levels of the music community, and then to his final resting place in East Austin, a stone's throw from his parents' graves. In the course of that journey, he helped to shape modern music.

CHAPTER 1

POST OAK

McKinley Howard Dorham Jr., who would go by "Kinney" and eventually "Kenny," was the first son born to McKinley Dorham Sr. and Eva "Minnie" Dorham, née Manning. Later, Kenny Dorham memorialized the exact time of his birth: 8:30 a.m. on August 30, 1924, by recording it in a brief autobiographical essay.[1] He confided to jazz historian Phil Schaap that he was named after President McKinley.[2] Dorham's father had been named after McKinley, who was assassinated in 1896, four years before McKinley Sr. was born, and Kenny was named after his father.

Kenny was born in the unincorporated community of Post Oak, which lies a few miles southeast of Fairfield. When Kenny entered the world, East Texas was much changed from the time when his ancestors arrived there, but was still a wild and remote place. The Comanche no longer ruled the plains; they were now confined to a reservation in Oklahoma. Their fearsome war chief Quanah Parker had died a decade earlier, an aging rancher. The buffalo were gone. Yet so much of rural life there remained as it had been. Wolves and panthers still ranged the countryside. Farmers raised cotton, sorghum, and alfalfa. Many of them did so as tenant farmers or sharecroppers. The open country also allowed for cattle ranching, and in fact that part of Texas saw dual land use: cotton farming common to the Southeast and ranching that characterized the Southwest.[3] The great cattle drives were over, but grazing the animals and shipping them to market was still a lucrative proposition. And the stockyards of Dallas-Fort Worth were less than a hundred miles away. Oil discoveries in East Texas beginning at the end of the nineteenth century spurred the creation of new roads and brought wealth to the region. One major oil discovery was made in Wortham, Freestone County, in the year of Dorham's birth.

The nation was recovering from its participation in World War I and was assimilating returning troops back into civilian life. Americans had been spared the devastation and hellish battle scenes that Europeans had endured, but one hundred thousand American servicemembers died in the war. McKinley Sr. and his older stepbrothers duly registered for the draft, but apparently none of them served. The 1918 influenza epidemic did reach North American shores at the end of the war, and nearly three hundred thousand people died from the flu in the United States alone. Cemeteries all over the United States still bear witness to the death toll of the epidemic, with rows of grave markers dating from those years. Prohibition had been in force since 1920 and would last until 1933. Congress had passed the Volstead Act and then empowered the federal government to enforce it with the Eighteenth Amendment. This measure met with opposition as state authorities were often reluctant to enforce it, and the illegal manufacture and transport of alcoholic beverages was widespread, especially in rural areas. A resurgence of the Ku Klux Klan both precipitated and reflected surges in racial violence. The 1921 Tulsa massacre was one particularly horrifying incident in which a white mob, including deputized and armed members, attacked and burned a prosperous Black neighborhood, killing and injuring hundreds of people. In response to high rates of violence against Black Americans, Republican members of Congress introduced a federal anti-lynching bill that contained statistics on the epidemic rates of lynching. However, the bill was defeated in 1922 after Southern Democrats filibustered it.

That same year, racial terror struck much closer to Fairfield. After a young white woman, Eula Ausley, was assaulted and murdered in the nearby Freestone County town of Kirvin, a lynch mob retaliated by burning three African American men alive. A rash of other lynchings of African Americans in the area followed. It came to light eventually that before the lynchings, the Freestone County sheriff had arrested two white men whom he suspected of committing the murder but then released them, allowing time for them to leave the county as the public cast about for someone to blame. It appears that the whites were in fact the ones responsible for the crime, and that there was physical evidence placing them at the scene.[4]

Despite this turbulence and terror in areas around his childhood home, Kenny Dorham's recollections of his early life were happy and peaceful. He recalled the birds, the animals, and the rhythms of rural life, and those impressions would find their way into his music. Near the end of his life, the memories remained vivid as he described them in an autobiographical piece for *DownBeat* magazine: "On a brisk spring morning around the middle to the end of March, while my father groomed the fields, the young plants could be seen breaking through the soil. The chirping of the mockingbirds, jay birds, woodpeckers and flocks of blackbirds could be heard, in contrast to the whippoorwills, the hawks, coyotes, crickets, frogs and rattlesnakes and all the familiar sounds of the big Southwest. And sometimes the lonesome train whistle of the Sunshine Special that traveled across east Texas would join in. A rare combination of musical sounds."[5] This was a description of farm life, and as such, parts of it would be recognizable and familiar to a farm kid anywhere in America. But Dorham conveys something more in his sensitive description of the "familiar sounds of the big Southwest," as he put it. He knew enough to identify and differentiate the creatures he saw and lived with. The coyote and the rattlesnake suggest a Texas flavor, and the whippoorwill lends an element of poignancy for anyone who has heard that secretive night bird. As folk singer Greg Brown suggests, the call of a whippoorwill can give one the chills.[6]

Many other composers have drawn on nature for inspiration, from Dvořak's evocation of the song of the scarlet tanager in his New World Symphony and Messiaen's use of birdsong to W. C. Handy's references to birds and "all the symphonies of their unpremeditated art."[7] In Dorham's case (and Handy's as well), however, the contrast between Edenic scenes of flora and fauna on one hand, and the cruel and vicious practices sustaining the racial hierarchies of the postwar era and the Jim Crow South on the other, is positively jarring. The Freestone County of Dorham's youth had not yet seen interstates, agribusiness, or subdivisions. Life was lived close to nature, and the animals of the fields and woods were not threats but rather inspirations that Dorham would try to capture in various ways later on through his trumpet sound and the way he would attack a note, as well as in direct compositional reference. He could see the beauty of the natural world surrounding him despite the social and political conditions that were also there. Even today, traveling through Freestone County's countryside, the natural features of the landscape are so prominent as to dominate a traveler's impressions. Human habitation is spaced apart between long stretches of woods and fields so that the plants, birds, and animals, rather than the human population, define the landscape.

Dorham was aware of various musical traditions of the region besides jazz, including folk music, church music, country blues, and the work songs people sang as they labored in the fields. He remembered hearing "Shuffle Off to Buffalo" and then learning to play it on piano.[8] Dorham notes that blues pioneer Blind Lemon Jefferson was born nearby, and Dorham even imagined that he might have met Jefferson once, though he later realized he was mistaken:

> We'd also heard of Blind Lemon Jefferson from Wortham, Texas, in Freestone County, and we knew he played guitar. In fact, a man came to our house once who I thought might be him. He was hungry and he asked mama and dad for food. He didn't have any legs. I'm sure of that. He was also blind. At least I think he was. He was real hip, though. I thought he was hip because he wore sunglasses. I'd never seen sunglasses before. How he got there without legs I'll never know. We didn't use the term "hip" back then. We'd say, "He sure is smart."[9]

Kenny Dorham's young imagination was captivated by visitors who stopped off at the farmhouse after "riding the blinds." He would listen as they "sang songs that originated from nearly every part of the Southwest and West."[10] He was especially interested "because they hitched rides on freight trains and went as far west as San Francisco and southwest to the border towns near Mexico. Most of the hoboes were white, I might add."[11]

A traveler in the country learns to look for a lighted place. An electric bulb (or oil lamp, such as the Dorhams had) stands out from afar in a way that lights in the city do not, suggesting that shelter, food, or other aid could be waiting there, particularly enticing prospects for someone just off hundreds of miles in a freight car. The Dorham house drew itinerants from the Texas countryside: "My mom, who was always a most cordial hostess, would run a screen test on the stranger. He'd usually pass the test, and she would feed him, sometimes in the kitchen or maybe on the screened in back porch. After the hobo had eaten, he'd usually tell some tall yarns about his travels and sing some songs that really gave me a hankering to travel."[12] Part of Minnie Dorham's screen test was "How could he not have any money: meaning he was white,"[13] Kenny Dorham recalled. But his parents hosted and fed the visitors they received, an experience that involved crossing the sharply drawn racial lines of the day. In doing so, their gesture contrasted with the many oppressive practices that characterized Jim Crow Texas—racial violence, economic exploitation, and the everyday humiliations of segregated parks, drinking fountains, cemeteries, and passenger trains. One thinks of the generosity of Dorham's parents in opening up their home and sharing their table with white strangers. As for the train-hopping whites who came looking for food, they enjoyed an experience of a communion, out there in the wilds, in which race did not matter. Folk singer Woody Guthrie described his own transracial encounters as he traveled the West and Southwest riding freight trains during the same time period: "I could see folks of all colors bouncing along in the boxcar. We stood up. We laid down. We piled around on each other. I could smell the sour and bitter sweat soaking through my own khaki shirt and britches, the work clothes, overhauls and saggy, dirty suits of the other folks."[14] Dorham further recalls that his father offered the hay room of their barn to strangers needing a place to sleep. The Dorhams' gestures of hospitality—sharing family meals with white travelers and allowing them to stay overnight—bespeak an intimacy similar to the crowded boxcar that Guthrie described. Basic human needs for food, shelter, warmth, and companionship bring people together; compassion reaches across artificial barriers of race as people relate to one another. As we will see, Kenny Dorham was no idealist, but he recalled idyllic moments long ago that reflected his parents' generous humanity during a time when they had every reason to be more guarded. McKinley Sr. and Minnie were religious people, and there was something sacred in their offer to share their food and shelter with traveling strangers.

From a political point of view, one can see a commonality among the participants in this communion-like experience. Perhaps the white boxcar-riding visitors found a connection with Black farmers in their mutual experiences of exclusion: rootless, unemployed white men dodging the railroad bulls, on the one hand, and an African American family sharecropping on land owned by someone else who set the terms for the family's tenancy on the other. At the same time, though, the Dorhams were better off materially than many families during the Great Depression. They had food, a place to live, and still-productive land to farm, unlike the throngs fleeing the Dust Bowl of the plains states. However those interactions are described, they complicate the picture of life during segregation. And they made an impression on young Kenny Dorham that he would later translate into musical terms.

Boredom was another phenomenon of country life. When not working, Dorham needed ways to entertain himself. His older sister married and moved to a nearby town when he was quite young, though she visited her parents often.[15] His brother did not come along until later, when Dorham was thirteen. Even his younger sister was separated from him by seven years.[16] So leisure-time diversions were hard to come by, and Dorham had to be creative. He even remembered picking up cigarette butts discarded by the rail-jumping wanderers and smoking them when no one was looking.[17] Though his family was abstinent, Dorham was a child looking for excitement, and something—anything—different was exciting.

Dorham's inquisitiveness led him to notice and investigate things happening around him. He reminisced at length about yodeling, for example, a form of rural musicality: "Yodeling is the southwestern cowboys' and farm folks' term for a certain type of earlier western folk song-type improvisation. Real western high life. When a cotton picker was taking his last sack of cotton to the scale for the day, one might hear him yodel. . . . A lone cowboy at the end of a day on the range could be heard yodeling. While he unsaddled his mount at the corral, he'd yodel."[18]

Dorham's fascination with yodeling was only a part of his interest in the cowboy's life. Dorham learned to ride a horse early on, picked up the skills of the trade quickly, and even contemplated a career as a cowboy. He earned money herding cattle on a ranch at Ward Prairie, a community outside Fairfield. The other boys he rode with were white, he remembers. Together they drove a hundred head of cattle in from the range so they could be dipped for ticks, fleas, and red bugs.[19] Someone familiar with representations of the American cowboy in popular culture from film to advertising might envision cowboys as exclusively white. In fact, however, there was a long-standing tradition of African American cowboys in Texas reaching back even before statehood.[20] A significant proportion of Texas cowboys were African American or Latino, and in fact it was through Mexico that domesticated horses arrived in the region, horses that later reverted to the wild and needed capture and retraining before they could serve as cattle horses. Even before the Civil War, when slavery was still in force, African Americans worked as cowboys. Bose Ikard, Neptune Holmes, and Ben Kinchlow worked and fought alongside whites and attained renown for their skills and bravery, living out one of so many contradictions of race relations in the prewar and Reconstruction South.[21] To Dorham, then, there was nothing unusual or unprecedented either about his participation in cowherding or his plan to make it a career. He had not succumbed to the myth of the exclusively white cowboy, one of many invented facts about the American West.

Later, as Dorham developed his musical style in composing and improvising, he would incorporate his experiences as a cowhand. He reproduced the yodeling vocalization on his trumpet through bending notes. That effect could be accomplished in a number of ways, such as holding the valves halfway down, swelling the sound by breathing into the note after striking it, or sliding down from one pitch to a lower one. And he heard other players, such as contemporary greats Julian "Cannonball" Adderley and Charlie Parker, yodel on their saxophones.[22] More literal references to the cowherding life would be heard many years later on his album *Whistle Stop*,[23] an homage to his childhood, as well as in his rendition of the popular song "I'm an Old Cowhand."[24]

Dorham's parents were musical. His father played guitar and his mother played piano. Dorham's sister Eva Lois was also gifted musically and was hired to sing and play piano for Dr. Pepper and Coca Cola commercial radio programs. Older by nine years than Kenny, she moved away when he was still a boy to the town of Palestine, some twenty miles distant. She played and sang Duke Ellington's "Mood Indigo" and W. C. Handy's "St. Louis Blues," among other compositions. Eva Lois predicted that her brother Kenny would become a famous musician one day, "like Louis Armstrong," judging from the way he became excited and jumped around whenever he heard music.[25] That was high praise: She had compared Armstrong himself to the angel Gabriel when she first heard him. Armstrong and Gabriel were two musical wonders from far-off lands, and Eva Lois brought news of them to her family in the countryside. And her brother took it all in. The Dorhams had a piano in their home, but locally available music was otherwise limited in variety to church music (Holiness, Baptist, and Methodist), Western music, folk and blues performances by itinerant visitors, and pop tunes on the radio. Nonetheless, Dorham could imitate what music he heard by playing it on the piano by the time he was seven.

In addition to his older sister, Eva Lois, Dorham had a younger brother, Joel (born in 1936, who would later become a musician as well), and a younger sister, Cloteal, who was born in 1931. Kenny was the oldest child at home, and so it fell to him to do farm chores. He sold berries, beans, and other produce in town, walking three miles each way with buckets full of wares. He trapped fox and muskrat for their hides, and would one day write a piece called "The Fox" based in part on that memory.[26] He helped to bale hay, pick cotton, and boil down sorghum and ribbon cane to make syrup. His father worked to build one of the first Texas highways (the "good road," now Highway 84) running east/west through Fairfield and out to the Trinity River, crossing into Anderson County. Before the road was built, the river could only be crossed by ferry, an iffy proposition as the ferry often broke free and drifted downriver. Dorham's father worked on the road and carried other workers to the site by truck in a trip that became shorter by the day as the finished road inched westward toward Fairfield.[27] When the road was finished in 1927, the event was celebrated in a ceremony with state and local dignitaries as a milestone of modernization in Texas. As promised, it changed travel and life generally in the county by linking East and Central Texas. No longer could desperadoes leave their cars on the east bank of the Trinity and disappear; the new bridge took care of that, and the far riverbank was a no man's land no longer.[28] Still, the young Dorham remained fascinated by the stories of outlaws vanishing into the western wilds—a fascination, incidentally, that he shared with fellow Freestone County musician Blind Lemon Jefferson, who sang about Jesse James in his song "One Dime Blues."[29]

For a time, the Dorham family sharecropped for Watt Parker, an auto and truck salesman from Fairfield whom Dorham remembered fondly. Parker owned a team of mules that Dorham's father used for farm work. That work was hard and unrelenting, whether digging wells, planting and harvesting, picking cotton, evacuating by boat when the Trinity floodwaters rose, or rescuing cattle from panthers.[30]

The Dorhams moved to at least three different residences as they worked the land in Freestone County. It was common for families who owned land to farm for shares on someone else's land in addition to working their own. This might seem counterintuitive to an outside observer, but in fact it was often necessary since the land they owned might not be productive enough to yield a crop that would sustain the family. This was the case with the Dorhams: Although they held title to land in the county, they sharecropped on land owned by the Parker and Aultman families. In the later 1930s, the Dorhams actually lived in the Aultmans' large house, as Minnie Dorham worked for the family as a housekeeper.[31] And so while some sharecroppers' cabins during Jim Crow were windowless affairs with unpainted wood slats for siding, the Dorhams' residences were more well-appointed clapboard houses rather than cabins or shacks. One was on the Aultman land near Fairfield, and another was on the Trinity River to the east of town.

Few of the musicians who would become Dorham's contemporaries had childhoods like his, either in terms of the rural setting or the rigors of farm life. Miles Davis was the son of a St. Louis dentist (the family also owned a pig farm, but were wealthy).[32] Julian "Cannonball" Adderley's parents taught college in Tallahassee, Florida.[33] Charlie Parker grew up in Kansas City; Max Roach, Thelonious Monk, and Sonny Rollins spent most of their childhoods in New York City.[34] Dizzy Gillespie's father was a bandleader.[35]

Dorham's early life in Texas stands in marked contrast to his adult years, which were spent mainly living in New York City and traveling to music venues in other American cities and in Europe. He recalled the rhythms and labors of farm life fondly until the end, no matter how different his daily life later became. The early period is notable, though, not only for its link to America's rural agricultural past, but also for distinct elements unique to life in Texas. A remarkable number of early blues and jazz pioneers hailed from the state, and many of their lives overlapped with Dorham's. The 1920s were a watershed period in jazz and blues, with Blind Lemon Jefferson, Henry "Ragtime Texas" Thomas, Sippie Wallace, and Hersal Thomas, among others, moving the music forward with their unique contributions and spreading their influence throughout the region and the entire United States.[36] When Dorham became an adult musician in the 1940s and gained fame for himself working with one leading group after another, he had already spent years absorbing both the images and the impressions of his rural Texas upbringing and also the sounds of his slightly older Texas musical compatriots who infused the Texas blues and territory big band traditions into emerging forms of modern jazz. The story of those contributions, from the early 1900s into the 1930s, is the subject of chapter 3 below.

CHAPTER 2

LAND LOSS AND SHARECROPPING

"FARMING ON THE HALVES"

As a boy, Kenny Dorham remembered asking his father about religion. "He would tell me about God," Dorham recalled. "He was not very educated, but he knew about the Bible and he had some sense about it."[1] Dorham wondered, "If God had all these powers," and "we were supposed to be good people," why was his family poor?[2] McKinley Sr. was a religious man, and he was not about to question either divine providence or the lot meted out to his family. His response to the challenges and injustices facing an African American family in 1930s Texas was simply to work harder. The family raised crops for money and also made use of the abundance of the countryside, gathering berries, beans, sorghum, ribbon cane, and hay. Dorham's father had other skills as well. He led a construction crew on one of the first modern highways in the state, dug wells, and maintained a homestead in Freestone County for twenty years with all the challenges that entailed.[3] Later, he would work as a master carpenter in California.[4] His industriousness, practical knowledge, and reliability earned him respect in his rural community and ensured that he always had work, but these qualities did not permit him either to escape the strictures of sharecropping or to amass material wealth.

Young Kenny Dorham was not satisfied with his father's resignation to a life of hard work without commensurate reward. Compounding Kenny's frustration was his knowledge that "there were people who were bad and were very rich."[5] Contemplating that incongruity, Dorham "sort of lost [his] faith in religion then." He inherited his parents' kindness, generosity, and vast goodwill toward others, but left their religious faith back in Fairfield when he set out on his own in the world. And he began to separate from his family at an early age, though he maintained a close bond with them all his life.

In 1936, at the age of twelve, Dorham went to live with his Uncle Joel in Austin to attend school, returning to the country when classes were not in session and practicing trumpet in the barn, where the wood made a "great resonator."[6] At first, Dorham's family stayed 140 miles away from Austin in Freestone County, in the Fairfield area, but they eventually moved to Austin as well. By 1940, Dorham's parents were living in East Austin, on Twelfth Street.[7] They would move again, to Oakland, California, in the mid-1940s. By then, Kenny Dorham was grown up and out on his own.

For much of the time during their residence in Freestone County, Dorham's father and mother farmed. Dorham's family on his mother's side (the Mannings) had been landowners since the 1870s. Great-grandfather Joel bought land after Emancipation, and his sons Owen, Alfred, and Henry bought multiple parcels themselves. In 1883, Dorham's grandfather Henry bought a hundred-acre tract lying two miles south of the Butler town site where the Mannings were concentrated.[8] Henry purchased the land from C. Y. Manning, a white landowner whose parents had probably enslaved the Mannings and from whom the Manning surname was likely derived. Two decades later, Henry purchased an additional 120 acres from B. J. Parker off a tract referred to in deed records as "the old Gorman place." This property then became known as the Henry and Patsy Manning farm. Simultaneously with the transaction with Henry, B. J. Parker sold the remaining hundred acres of the Gorman land to Henry's younger relative, G. W. Manning.[9] The Manning land (formerly Gorman land) was close to Butler along what is now a farm road half a mile from the current Highway 84. Taken together, the land holdings of the Manning family were significant, and an early twentieth-century deed map shows hundreds of acres under the ownership of the Manning brothers and their descendants.[10]

These purchases were made by promissory notes for all or most of the purchase price. Land transactions in rural Texas in the late nineteenth and early twentieth centuries were sketchy, informal, and often carelessly drawn, and as a result they are confusing to read. Freestone County deed records indicate, for instance, that two deeds were drawn for the 120-acre Henry and Patsy Manning farm, the second deed doubling the purchase price.[11] Whether either deed was valid is all but impossible to say, but since one makes no mention of the other, we can say with certainty that both cannot be valid. Usually, the seller retained a vendor's lien when a buyer gave a promissory note for purchase. Those liens were one swift means for seizing land held by

Black farmers—a judgment could be obtained against anyone who lacked cash on hand and was unable to pay according to schedule. Notes were traded widely, so that the original holder would not likely be the person the landowner would be paying a few years down the road. One of the Manning relatives lost a plot of land in 1913 when a note secured against their property was bought by another creditor and then came due.[12] Probably they did not know the note had been transferred. The written record of payment and note transfer is but a part of the story, as so many transactions were informal and difficult to substantiate at that time.

Even though so many of the Mannings owned land, they were often obliged to farm shares on someone else's land. Not all land in the county was productive, so farming for shares or rent was necessary to make ends meet and to keep food on the table. The options for farming were either tenant farming or sharecropping.[13] The difference between the two arrangements consists in the way that the farmer compensated the landowner for use of the land, whether by paying rent in the former instance, or by relinquishing a share of the year's crop in the latter. This distinction was blurred by the fact that tenants could pay rent either in cash or in crop share. Tenant farmers generally had more of their own equipment than sharecroppers did, which allowed landowners to manage their land and rents from a distance and not be involved in daily farming concerns such as planting cycles or the vicissitudes of weather. For large landowners who increasingly wished to stay out of farm management as the century turned, tenancy arrangements were preferable. Tenants who owned farm equipment generally made out better than sharecroppers because their fixed rent payment, set in advance, decreased the risk of landowners gouging the farmers when it came time to settle up after harvest. In recognition of the large percentage of the share that was lost to them, sharecroppers referred to "farming on the halves" to describe their predicament of realizing only half of what they produced.[14] To make matters worse, sharecroppers had to seek credit, often at high interest due to the speculative nature of farming, in order to purchase supplies for planting. This arrangement left them perpetually in debt, especially in seasons of poor crop yield. This system would exact a particular price from the Dorhams in 1935–36, when they lost their parcel of ancestral land to a debt supposedly incurred by Dorham's maternal grandmother, Patsy, and her deceased husband, Henry.

Kenny Dorham referred to his family's farming arrangement as sharecropping, and it is surprising how detailed and accurate his recollection of the farming operation, which took place when he was a child, remained four decades later. At least some of the equipment and livestock the Dorhams used was owned by someone else. He recalled that when they sharecropped for Watt Parker, they had use of Parker's "four big, young, red, top stock mules."[15] Writing some years later, Dorham took his family's sharecroppers' lot as a given, and focused on his pleasant memories of a youth spent in the country, albeit a youth also spent working hard. It is merciful that children are often shielded from the financial strains their parents are under, and that seemed largely to be the case with young Dorham. He became aware, at some point, of his family's lack of wealth, but that fact does not come across as the predominant reality that he dwelt upon in his later reminiscences. Instead, it was the birds, the horseback riding, and the train whistles that stood out. Still, his parents shouldered the economic woes of a life as sharecropping farmers in Jim Crow Texas.

Often, the owners of general stores that supplied credit for seeds and supplies also owned the land occupied by sharecroppers—a circumstance that was quite advantageous to the former and exploitative of the latter. Store ledgers reveal, moreover, that store credit, in lieu of cash, was typically extended to customers so that their accounts carried a negative balance and outlays of money by the merchant did not have to be made. Moreover, customers did not have access to the ledger books even if they were able to read the notations in them, which they often could not do, given the high rates of illiteracy in Reconstruction Texas, especially among formerly enslaved African Americans.[16] After the Civil War ended, southern planters who'd lost their land when Sherman burned through the South packed up what was left and headed west, intending eventually to reach Mexico and to found a new Confederacy. Some of them stopped in Louisiana and East Texas when they saw the opportunities to grow cotton and rice in those places.[17] Since they could no longer rely on a slavery-based economy to plant, farm, and harvest crops, the displaced planters sought a new arrangement. Farm labor after the war came through the sharecropping system that replaced slave labor, and so sharecropping became a mechanism for sustaining both the agricultural economy and the racialized social hierarchy that had grown up around it.

These similarities between antebellum and Jim Crow social relations were noted by the writers of the WPA-funded guide to Texas history. In 1940, the guide's authors proclaimed, without a trace of irony, that "[g]reat plantations remain intact in the vicinity of Bryan, and here Negroes are still called to and from their fields by means of bells that were in use when their forefathers were slaves."[18] Numerous passages in the WPA text strike the same off note, as the authors seem completely unaware of the stunningly demeaning and dehumanizing tone of their descriptions of Black Texans in statements such as "[t]hey are an important economic factor, as they are in every cotton producing region."[19] A bit later, the authors remark that "[a]mong the contribution of the Texas Negro outside of labor, those to music and folklore are probably most valuable."[20] And even when reporting positive changes in economic fortunes, the WPA guide cannot avoid giving offense: "Counties in east, south and east central Texas have a large proportion of Negro farm owners and tenants. Farm ownership is increasing among them, but living conditions, although steadily improving, are often undesirable."[21] This choice of wording both objectifies African American farm families and blames them for their plight in the 1940s South, as if they had suddenly appeared on the landscape without a history of chattel slavery, and without centuries of legal, economic, and discursive supports for white supremacy. However, the tone and content of these passages from the WPA guide, drafted by prominent Texas writers, is typical of journalistic and public affairs writing of the time and place. Even the Fairfield newspaper barely mentions African American residents, and one would be forgiven for thinking that none lived there, were it not for the occasional reporting of a crime alleged to have been committed by an African American perpetrator.

The Dorhams sharecropped because the land they owned, passed down on Minnie's side from Joel Manning dating back to the 1870s, was not productive enough to support a farming operation. The 120-acre Henry and Patsy Manning Estate is located on what is now Farm Road 489 near Butler, less than a mile from the "good road," that McKinley Senior helped to build, now Highway 84.[22] A sandy two track (a dirt road with two ruts for the tires) leads up a small hill past oaks and sycamores and elders, topping out on a lovely meadow ringed by thick and sturdy pines overlooking acres of flatland. It is a beautiful piece of property, but evidently was not fertile enough to farm profitably. To make ends meet, the Dorhams had to farm someone else's land. At different times, they sharecropped for the Aultman family and for Watt Parker. At the beginning of the growing season, sharecropping farmers typically borrowed money for seed and supplies, and the loan was conditioned on a promise of payment from the yield of that year's crop. Often, a sharecropper had two creditors: the landowner who had claim to a share of the crop, and the merchant who advanced credit for supplies. They could be one and the same entity, but were not always. Either way, the system set up sharecropping farmers to fail; it was almost impossible for them to succeed in the long run.

The Dorhams lost their portion of the Henry and Patsy Manning Estate land in 1936 after years of working to make ends meet by sharecropping. If a year's crop did not turn a profit, thus enabling the farmer to pay off the funds advanced for supplies, the farmer would have to start the next year in debt and was truly squeezed, needing to make twice as much money the following year. Two or three bad crop cycles would be devastating. Sharecropping was hard enough before the Great Depression, but in the midst of the economic distress of the 1930s credit access contracted, supply chains were disrupted, and land foreclosures were rampant. The New Deal policies of the Roosevelt administration discouraged sharecropping in favor of land ownership, a laudable goal but an impractical one without vast financial support. In the end, the administration's stance actually undercut the position of sharecroppers and accelerated the exodus of farmers from the land in the interwar years. The Dorhams' loss of land and their exodus from the countryside replicates an all-too-familiar pattern of their time and place. Federal agricultural policy certainly played a part, but in East Texas there was a more direct and immediate cause.

In the early twentieth century, Freestone County was the site of a massive land grab perpetrated by white landowners, government officials, land agents, and property lawyers. The process started in the nineteenth century, when land was deeded by the Mexican government in large grants to prominent Mexican settlers such as Simon Sanchez and Jose Ygnacio Aguilera.[23] After independence, as Texas joined the United States, those grants were parceled into smaller allotments purchased by American farmers and ranchers. During Reconstruction, some of the owners, like the Mannings from whom Kenny Dorham descended, were African American beneficiaries of land reform who were able to purchase land in the county. By century's end, some 30 percent of Black farmers in Texas owned their land. But over time once Reconstruction ended, white Texans set out to reverse the gains in Black land ownership, driven by the twin engines of racial animus and simple greed. As historian Annette Gordon-Reed put it, "Texans who had enslaved Blacks and been defeated in the Civil War turned on the freed people with a vengeance, seeking to maintain the control they had during slavery."[24] The systematic dispossession of Black landowners in general, and in Freestone County particularly, occurred on a grand scale and has been widely reported. For example, in 1984, Jeanette Willis Adkins and her family filed a federal lawsuit to recover land near Butler that was stolen from their ancestors back in the early 1900s. In an article in the *Los Angeles Times*, Adkins and her family told of a Freestone family member shot dead by a white man in the 1920s over an argument about a horse, and of a disabled relative carried outside in the 1960s and laid on the ground when her property was foreclosed.[25]

The specific tactics utilized to dispossess Black landowners were varied. If a person knew that another community member had unpaid taxes, the tax debt could be paid off by a third party, who then held a tax lien against the property. Eventually that lien could allow foreclosure and land seizure.

(This practice has since been outlawed.) County officials routinely failed to notify Black farmers when taxes were due in order to create indebtedness that enabled foreclosure later on. Fraudulent notes and deeds were common. So many of the old deeds on file at the county clerk's office contain fundamental errors that would likely have rendered them unenforceable. Names of the original land thieves were not always known. Written evidence was difficult to present as it had been created in some cases a century before, and in virtually all instances it was difficult to decipher. Doubtless some of the worst actions were not written down. The Adkins lawsuit detailed the tactics used to reduce her family's vast land holdings of thousands of acres down to a few small parcels. The Willises, whose descendant Jeanette Willis Adkins filed the 1984 court action, were neighbors of the Mannings in the small community of Butler, and it seems likely that the same tactics were used against both families of Black landowning farmers. The Adkins suit was dismissed by the US District Court in Waco because the statute of limitations had passed.[26]

Similarly to Jeanette Willis Adkins, R. T. Kennedy and E. Henderson Lawson have documented the unfolding of the process of land theft in their own family. They trace the family's initial acquisition of land in the area back to an ancestor named Jim Henderson, the son of Irish immigrant farmer Hugh Henderson, and to Zillie Anne Henderson, a woman Hugh had enslaved. Upon Hugh's death, his and Zillie's son Jim inherited Hugh's land and raised his family on it, passing it in turn to his descendants, who farmed and paid taxes on the land for decades. Around 1870, land agent E. A. Mexia (the founder and namesake of the nearby town of Mexia) issued title to the land to the African American farmers descended from the Hendersons who were then living on it. In a sense, this passing of title was redundant since the Hendersons already owned the land, but it also served as further legal support for their claim of ownership. At the turn of the century, however, with Reconstruction over and Jim Crow and its Black Codes in full force, white land speculators saw an opportunity to enrich themselves at the expense of Black farmers in the county. They used the state and federal court systems to create a veneer of legality around their actions. It was thin veneer indeed, as the authors show: an action to quiet, or settle, title to the land was brought in court, and all mention of the Hendersons' rightful claim to the property, including the findings of a judge in a previous case, was excised from the court record.

Land agents who came into the county to settle these claims often took a portion of the recovered land as their fee. This element of pecuniary self-interest explains the vigor with which such suits were brought and prosecuted. It also sheds light on why land agents and lawyers would sometimes fight and litigate with each other: Their interests diverged as suits progressed and judicial findings were more favorable to the partition urged by one rather than another of them, and so their common hostility toward the land claims of Black residents gave way to their own desires for enrichment. Kennedy and Henderson Lawson document the fact that some of the lawyers involved in the controversy switched sides, representing the Black landowners in one case and the white land speculators in another. Whichever side they represented, the lawyers would often obtain an interest in the subject property as compensation, so they gained from the outcome no matter whom it favored. And the schemes were cumulative in the sense that one court ruling paved the way for further dispossession.

Two developments in the Henderson saga are particularly striking. First, attorneys Bonner, Williford, and Ballew represented the Henderson descendants in a 1913 action brought by white land speculators seeking to dispossess them. The Williford family would also be involved in the Dorham/Manning case twenty years later. Here, Williford et al. filed an answer that detailed the Henderson family's long and continuous tenure on the land, as well as the improvements the Hendersons had made. This answer supported the claim that the family had owned, occupied, and cared for the land long before the speculators came along. But the answer was withdrawn in 1915 and stricken from the case record shortly thereafter, with no reason given. That action by the Hendersons' attorneys would seem, at the very least, to violate ethical rules requiring an attorney to maintain fidelity to a client's interest. Moreover, the withdrawal is unexplained, and indeed is inexplicable. The record states only that the answer was filed by "mistake."[27] One can only speculate about what behind-the-scenes negotiation and maneuvering led to the withdrawal, but with that obstacle cleared away by the Hendersons' own attorneys, there was nothing in the record to support the Hendersons' claim of right, title, or interest.

Second, the conspirators were taking no chances. They did not want a contested hearing in open court even if the proofs had been removed. Shortly before the hearing day, each of the Henderson family members and land claimants was arrested and detained for allegedly stealing hogs. Though they were later acquitted, the damage was done. They could not appear in court since they were in jail, and judgment was entered against them by default in the land title case when they failed to appear.[28] They returned from their false imprisonment to find their dwellings boarded and stock gates locked.

The Dorham/Manning case was a bit different in posture but part nonetheless of a larger pattern of fraud, theft, and economic racism relating to land loss. As already noted, the Mannings had bought land as far back as

1870, when forty-five-year-old Joel Manning was farming out near Butler. His holdings passed on to his children, who homesteaded in various eastern parts of the county: near the Stillwell farm, the Prather place, the Word land, and the old Gorman place. Prior to the judgment in October 1934 ordering sale of the Dorham/Manning land with proceeds awarded to their creditors, there was an action for partition, or division of property into shares, filed earlier that year. Titled *H. L. Williford et al. v. Joel Manning et al.*, this was an action seeking partition of shares of land ownership among multiple owners.[29] At first glance, the partition action seems incongruous: Who would want it, and who would bring it before the court? The Henderson family saga sheds light here. Partitioning of jointly owned land makes it easier for claimants later on to know specifically what land shares they can get, especially if the boundaries of those lands have been fixed and approved by a court, as they were here. So partitioning is a prudent preliminary step for a land speculator who knows there will be a future action for title and wants to make that action go smoothly and favorably. In all likelihood, that is what happened with the Dorham/Manning land. Creditors knew they would be seeking title to the estate of Henry Manning shortly, and they wanted to clarify who had an interest in that land so that when they got it, it would be free and clear. In the partition, some of the shares were apportioned to members of the Williford family, including R. L. Williford, the lawyer involved in the Henderson cases. In addition, the 1934 partition of land went part of the way toward the ultimate goal by eliminating some of the parties involved and taking their shares. And the partition itself was made by court-appointed land commissioners, found by the court to be disinterested parties and therefore qualified to act as commissioners in what appeared merely to be a public service for a small fee. One of them, however, J. M. Parker, had a direct interest in the outcome. He was the owner of fifty acres divided from the original Manning estate.

In any event, a judgment was entered the following year ordering sale of seventy acres of the Manning land (excluding fifty acres held by J. M. Parker) with proceeds payable to W. L. Lott in settlement of a $1,184 debt.[30] The circumstances surrounding the purported debt were as follows:

- Patsy Manning, widow of Henry Manning, raising her children (including Kenny Dorham's mother, Minnie) alone, supposedly made several promissory notes to Lott in 1922 that were secured against her property.
- Patsy died in 1927 without a will, and so her children inherited her property under state law.

- Lott alleges in court pleadings that the promissory notes were "renewed and extended" by Patsy's children (her heirs) in 1927.[31]
- In 1928, a claim by Lott to recover payment of the notes was dismissed by the state district court.[32]
- In 1934, upon Lott's request, that dismissal was vacated and the action to recover the debt was reinstated.[33]
- The land (70 acres of it) was put up for auction early the following year. The remaining fifty acres of the Manning estate had been sold to J. M. Parker (one of the "disinterested" land commissioners named above), and Lott disclaimed any interest in that portion of the property now owned by Parker.[34]

Questions arise from this narrative. Why were the promissory notes signed by the widowed Patsy Manning in 1922? Were they valid? Had Henry already paid off the previous notes? Deed records show that several promissory notes were given by Henry Manning going back well before 1922. It seems unlikely that creditors would have left a valid debt alone, without seeking to collect it, for more than twenty years. Also, the earlier deeds to Henry show conflicting amounts, and the purchase amount is stated differently even within one of the deeds.[35] The Mannings also executed multiple oil and gas leases for their farm, some of which stipulated up-front payment of only a dollar and some slightly more. Those, too, are poorly drawn, failing to list Minnie Dorham's name or to show her signature in one case, and reversing the identities of the parties in another. Did Patsy and her children obtain the promised lease and royalty payments as the agreements stipulated?[36] Given the overall climate, one suspects not.

In the Henderson case, land agents asked the Henderson heirs to sign promissory notes promising to pay the agents for the land the Hendersons occupied, telling them they would lose their land if they did not sign, when in fact the Hendersons did not need to sign the notes because they already owned the land. It was a fraudulent and predatory tactic. Did something similar occur with Patsy Manning, a widow with five children? And why were the notes supposedly "renewed and extended" by her children in 1927? If the children (then in their twenties) understood the significance of renewing and extending those notes, why would they sign a document agreeing to that? If they did not understand, what was promised or threatened or misrepresented to get them to sign? Why did the court dismiss a claim for recovery on those notes in 1928? Why, six years later, did the court reinstate the action, at Lott's request? What was the Willifords' involvement in this case, when one of them had been at the center of the Henderson land theft two decades earlier? Finally, the creditor who bought the property at the sheriff's sale—W. L. Lott—was also the Freestone County Clerk.[37] This position gave him inside access to deed and tax records and created an apparent conflict of interest.

One of the consequences of this dispossession was the immediate loss of a valuable asset by the Dorhams. Two years later they moved into the Aultmans' large house near Fairfield, and Minnie worked as a housekeeper for the Aultmans.[38] Just a bit after that, the Dorham family would leave the Fairfield area first for Austin, then for Oakland, California, then back to Austin for the remainder of McKinley Sr.'s and Minnie's lives. This transition marked the end of the family's farming life and the loss of their close connection with the land of rural East Texas that they had worked and improved by farming, road building, and simply being good and generous neighbors. The exact amount of the debt Patsy actually owed, if any, is lost to history, but its origins in a corrupt and exploitative system of sharecropping, backed by a legal system favoring those with greater wealth (who were virtually always white), are undeniable.

The shares held by Patsy Manning's four children (Joel, Alvo, Alfred, and Minnie) were relatively small—less than ten acres apiece. But that is because Henry Manning's original holdings were reduced and divided practically down to nothing over the years. The 1934 partition awarded shares to the Willifords and other parties before the Lott judgment was obtained, such that the Mannings owned only a small share altogether. This legal and transactional history is so convoluted that it is almost impossible to follow, even with the benefit of court records indicating the bigger picture. No doubt it was even more difficult to grasp for Kenny Dorham's parents, who did not have access to those records.

There is also a long-term impact to this story of exploitation and land loss. In Freestone County today, one sees smaller farm and ranch spreads that have stayed viable because of accumulated value over the years as they have remained in the same family for generations. It is no longer boom or bust as it was a century ago. In some cases, too, oil, gas, and mineral deposits have made the land quite a bit more valuable. All of this wealth—legacy wealth—has been available to white families in Texas farm and ranch country, and has been passed on (and grown) from generation to generation to make descendants' lives easier and more secure. But for the Black families who lost their land, like the Dorhams, that legacy was lost too.[39] It would have improved the family's life in many ways. Perhaps it could have helped Kenny Dorham with his final illness that he lacked the money to treat properly, and countless expenses and opportunities would have turned out differently for the family as they grew and spread out across the country. Those consequences, hard as they are to calculate precisely, also stem from the loss of the ancestral Manning land. Nearly one hundred years of legacy wealth was lost to the family as their land fell into other hands. The 1934 judgment was but the last step in a process of whittling down the Mannings' landholdings over a period of decades. Meanwhile, the names of principals in the land theft story are displayed in businesses and street names throughout Fairfield, but the names of the Mannings are lost to history.

The Reconstruction period from the end of the Civil War to 1876 had presented one set of challenges to formerly enslaved Black Americans. For the first time, white Southerners were obliged by federal law (at least in theory) to recognize the rights of people who had been disregarded as legally competent actors before.[40] These included the right to work and to vote. The federal Freedmen's Bureau was the administrative mechanism by which the South was to be reconstructed through settlement of land claims, provision of food and medical care, and establishment of schools for formerly enslaved persons. Expansion of voting rights allowed African American candidates to win elections to national office.

The losing side in any war will chafe at the terms, but the potential changes in race relations made this period especially volatile. Resistance to and resentment toward the Freedmen's Bureau were extreme, particularly in Texas. Arson and murder were common, as noted above in the previous chapters. The federal government itself was divided in its commitment to Reconstruction, as President Andrew Johnson and his fellow Democrats in Congress opposed it while Republicans moved it forward. The contested election of 1876 spelled the end of Reconstruction when Democrats approved the Republican candidate (Hayes) in exchange for an end to federal oversight of the postwar South.

With Reconstruction over, though, the plight of African Americans in the South worsened on numerous fronts. The Reconstruction period saw the passage of the Thirteenth (no involuntary servitude), Fourteenth (equal protection of the laws and due process in the states), and Fifteenth (voting rights) Amendments, but then Reconstruction ended and enforcement mechanisms were dismantled. This change created an unstable situation in which formerly enslaved Americans sought to redeem the promises of the new constitutional amendments, while whites reacted violently to Black Americans' assertions of their rights. In response to that volatility, whites developed elaborate segregationist legal and social codes that would promote a type of stability while also reinstating a racialized caste system like the one that had existed before Emancipation. Consequently, racial segregation from the 1880s onward performed a regulative function by neutralizing the threat of equality. In other words, Southern whites now had to accommodate those legal developments in an environment where white and Black Americans lived and worked in close proximity to one another. Would the change lead to reshuffling of the status hierarchy? Would it disturb white expectations of preferential treatment in resource distribution? The answer was no, and that answer was cashed out through segregation. Civil peace (or a superficial appearance of it) could be maintained through a rigid "color line," as W. E. B. Du Bois put it.[41] Moreover, in white Texans' minds, this constructed need for racial separation justified legal and extralegal punishment when racial lines were crossed.[42] Southern judges and politicians suggested that segregation benefitted everyone by promoting civil peace, and those claims continued on through the desegregation period in the second half of the twentieth century.[43]

The complexity of Southern race relations during this time resulted from a combination of circumstances. White fears of an empowered Black citizenry were at once a pathology and a catalyst for further exploitation and violence. More than four thousand lynchings occurred in the South from 1880 to 1920, over four hundred in Texas alone. The majority of lynching victims were Black.[44] It was common to advertise lynchings in the newspapers before they were carried out, and they could be instigated by the most trifling or imagined occurrence, such as the allegation that a Black man looked at a white woman. This was no faraway threat, as we have seen, since the Freestone County town of Kirvin experienced a horrifying spate of lynchings in spring of 1922, just before Kenny Dorham was born.

Segregation of railroad cars was strictly maintained and enforced by violence well before the practice was enshrined in constitutional law by the Supreme Court in *Plessy v. Ferguson* in 1896. Kenny Dorham felt the effects firsthand when he traveled from North to South by rail in 1946 and was required to move to the back of the car when the train left Saint Louis.[45] The *Plessy* ruling both ratified and facilitated segregation of other spaces and facilities, from parks to drinking fountains to cemeteries. The legendary blues artist Lightnin' Hopkins put the point eloquently in an interview: "Man, I've been places in Louisiana where I tell you I couldn't go in because of my color. I got to be your color. It's true. They used to go in there and break up them joints because it was dignified. They didn't want no dark-skinned person to come in there. You know, the world's been entangled ever since I knowed it was a world."[46]

On the political front, the two major parties competed for the post-Reconstruction Black vote while at the same time devising ruses to take it away. Once again, the Supreme Court provided cover for disfranchisement by ruling in 1898 in *Williams v. Mississippi* that literacy tests for prospective voters were permissible under the Constitution.[47]

In his classic work on the so-called New South, historian Edward Ayers notes the paradox of two groups of Southerners bearing suspicion and mistrust toward each other while also living and working in close proximity. As they did during slavery, white landowners relied on Black labor in order to operate farms. White mine and forge owners benefited from a convict lease system that captured and exploited Black men. White general store owners profited from Black customers who patronized their stores. Moreover, a racialized social system had been operating since the first enslaved Africans were brought to the southern United States. Even as repressive state laws were put in place to preserve that racialized order after Reconstruction, federal constitutional protections outlawing slavery, requiring equal protection, and enforcing voting rights remained in force as well. Litigants asserted those rights in court, even if they seldom won.

And yet free Black Americans were struggling tragically, and heroically, to attain material success and provide a living for their families. After Reconstruction ended, they "could only depend on their own tenacity and hope."[48] Wary of trusting the good intentions of whites to deal with them squarely and respect their rights, Black Americans nonetheless had to interact with white government officials, merchants, landowners, and others in the course of living their lives and obtaining the things they needed. An 1893 letter by A. L. Bailey, a Black man, captures the frustration and anguish of this predicament poignantly. Bailey describes taking his wife to "some secluded spot and . . . read[ing] aloud while she knits." He continues,

> What bitter humiliation I feel when I tell her that I, nor any other colored person, is a *man*, but a *slave*. And if a white man choose he could insult her to my face and I dare not protect her. But before God, if one ever does, I will kill him and pay the penalty, which I well know what will be. I will wipe out the insult with his life blood if I am burned at the stake the next hour. I believe we will never be a people until we rise up like men and die like heroes battling for our rights.[49]

The occasion prompting Bailey's reflection is a peaceful scene where he reads to his wife from *The Inter Ocean*. Bailey is probably referring to a progressive newspaper by that name out of Chicago that was popular among radical Republicans of the time. Bailey is enjoying a basic human activity—relaxing in nature with a beloved companion and reading news of the day—that is possible for him because the era of slavery is past. And yet he knows that the color line is ever-present, even in this world of new possibilities. There is some cruelty in that predicament, which confers a measure of freedom within a still-oppressive social order.

The Dorham story of sharecropping, land loss, and migration to the city for economic reasons parallels the experience of other African Americans in the post-Reconstruction South. Broadly, it corresponds to the Great Migration, in which an estimated six million African Americans left the South for northern and western cities, motivated in part by the work opportunities opening up in manufacturing centers like Newark, Detroit, Chicago, and Gary (and of course to escape Jim Crow conditions). In the Dorhams' case, they did not move as far initially: Austin is only about 140 miles from Fairfield. Their bigger move, though (from Austin to Oakland), was more closely related to the Second Great Migration, which began in the 1940s and drew African American workers west to wartime industries such as shipbuilding. While the Dorhams moved in part to find better prospects, they were also moving away from a place where they had worked, struggled, and lost. A debt of questionable legality supposedly incurred by Minnie's parents caused them to lose the only real material asset they had, one whose value would have increased over time.

Ultimately, though, they did move on for better prospects. Minnie and McKinley Sr. seemed determined to believe that a better life was out there for them, and that their kindness, generosity, and willingness to work hard would bring them good things. And that turned out to be true in many ways. Their children went on to be successful and renowned. Minnie would live to be ninety-two, although McKinley died at sixty-nine of heart disease after a lifetime of hard work.[50] Jazz legends like Lionel Hampton would pass through their house and enjoy Minnie's spaghetti dinners.[51] Their son Kenny would become internationally known during their lifetime for his role in founding modern jazz, America's greatest gift to the world. As the Dorhams prepared to leave the countryside, they had seen their family's fortunes rise and fall along with the those of other Black Americans who had endured slavery, then had rising hopes during Emancipation and Reconstruction, only to have those hopes dashed by the Jim Crow laws.

CHAPTER 3

TEXAS BLUES

Jazz has emerged from a multitude of sources to become
the cosmic ambassador of outgoing music.
—KENNY DORHAM

The roots of the jazz music that Kenny Dorham played reach back into African musical traditions of percussion, string instruments, and vocals. Dorham once said that the connection between jazz and African music was "instinctive": "We learned our tools here, but it probably came from Africa, because we inherited something that goes from tribe to tribe. It has to do with how we are put together. Although we are similar to everyone else on earth, we are still different. We have something that's unique, just as every other race has something that's unique."[1] Here in America, those "African roots underlay the historical evolution of our music, but the rest was developed from our trials and tribulations on the plantation. And we're still on the plantation!" Dorham noted.[2] The American influences on those roots also include the blues, church music, country folk songs and dances, work songs and hollers, and ragtime. Texas, and East Texas in particular, was a prominent source of all of those influences.

The importance of Texas in the history of blues and jazz is partly a matter of geography. Blues historian Alan Govenar notes that importation of enslaved African captives continued after the official end of the transatlantic slave trade, and that Texas was a prime destination for the illegal slave trade because of its remoteness. As a result, the state became home to the most recently transplanted African people with the most vivid recollections of the music of their homelands.[3] Texas also contained many lumber camps, railroad stops, large-scale cotton farming operations, and barrelhouses (improvised bars) where early blues music was created and performed. Additionally, the vast expanse of territory within the state's borders allowed for blending of multiple musical traditions, including African, Mexican, German, and East European, along with folk songs inspired by regional conditions, such as laments about the boll weevil.

But it was not merely geography that put Texas in the forefront of early jazz development. The state had more than its share of prominent composers and performers in early blues and jazz, from Texarkana's Scott Joplin to Wortham's Blind Lemon Jefferson and Centerville's Sam "Lightnin'" Hopkins. And so when Kenny Dorham first appeared on the music scene in the 1940s, he carried with him a rich and distinct regional tradition with echoes of railroad travel, hard-luck farming, problems with the law in the Jim Crow South, wide-open spaces, and a kind of blues worked out at country dances and barrelhouse saloons. His vast musical imagination drew on all of those sources as he helped to create the language of modern jazz. And Dorham himself saw a very wide provenance for the music he loved and made: "From the 14th-century caccia to European-classical sophistication; from the jungle drum of Africa to the New Orleans brass band; from folk-country-western-sanctified, middle Eastern, rock and blues to the Copacabana Beach at the foot of Sugar Loaf Mountain in Rio de Janeiro, home of the last intravenous transfusion into the mainstream of jazz."[4]

Among all of those sources, the country blues of Dorham's birthplace was primary. Govenar points out that the violin, or fiddle, was the predominant instrument in African American music until it was replaced by the guitar in the early twentieth century.[5] The fiddle linked early folk music to rural life, as it was most often played at country dances and was useful for folk tunes, Western art music, and church music. The connection to Africa here was direct, as African stringed instruments such as the *hoddu* had been in use for centuries before the Middle Passage.[6] In order to meet the demands of dances and other social events, fiddlers had to play a variety of musical styles. As evidence for this, Govenar cites interviews conducted by WPA historians with African Americans who had been alive during slavery.[7] The interview subjects recalled fiddles and banjos accompanying various dances, including reels (of Scottish origin) and buck dances, a dance form created by African Americans in the South. The dance melodies played on the fiddle and banjo had to be tied rhythmically to whatever particular dance the musicians were leading, which were, by these firsthand accounts, intricate and patterned. This thread of musical influence, from Africa by way of nineteenth-century Black communities in East Texas, wove string melodies and dance rhythms into blues and then into jazz. Govenar documented the African origins of those traditions by visiting and recording Senegalese musician Barou Sall, a renowned contemporary *hoddu* player, and notes the similarities between his style, developed in Senegal, and the music of American blues musicians.[8]

RAGTIME

Ragtime, a mostly written form of dance-related music played primarily on the piano, developed around the turn of the twentieth century—once again, in Texas—and drew on European classical music as well as on Western formal musical notation. Scott Joplin, the child of East Texas African American railway laborers, is probably the most important ragtime composer. Joplin was born around 1868 in Texarkana, Texas—or near there—and moved to the Arkansas side of Texarkana as a boy. His mother noticed his musical genius early on and supported his musical aspirations. Joplin came under the tutelage of a German American classical teacher and absorbed musical notation and European musical forms as well as classical repertoire and pianistic technique. Joplin put all that he learned into the creation of written ragtime scores. A visit to the 1897 World's Fair allowed him to popularize ragtime on a national level. His most famous composition, "Maple Leaf Rag," was written out in an arrangement people could purchase, so that he received royalties for its sale and use. But he wrote many other ragtime pieces as well.[9]

The word "ragtime" developed from the idea of ragged, broken, or uneven groups of notes, which created a different kind of dance rhythm.[10] Syncopation, or patterned accents on certain parts of the beat in a measure, moved the music along, as did punctuating notes in the left hand played against right hand melody runs. Some commentators describe ragtime as consisting of straight (rather than swinging) eighth notes, suggesting that later stride and boogie-woogie piano styles had more drive, or swing, to them. Even if we accept that characterization as correct, though, it is undeniable that ragtime featured accented notes as perhaps its most prominent characteristic.

Joplin suffered financial and medical problems and died at the age of forty-eight (the same age as Kenny Dorham, incidentally). Some of his music was confiscated to satisfy a debt, and although he did receive remuneration to a degree for his copyrighted works, it did not approach a level that allowed him to live comfortably, and certainly this compensation was disproportionate to the fame that the new genre, ragtime, attained during his lifetime. As Joplin lived most of his life in the Jim Crow South or on its fringes, race certainly circumscribed his life chances. He was a brilliant African American composer living during a time of great racial strife and injustice, and he was creating a musical form that was new and popular (read: that whites wanted to profit from). His story is a tragic one, but his accomplishments long outlived him.

New Orleans-born pianist Jelly Roll Morton took inspiration from ragtime, played some ragtime pieces, and even called his own compositions "rags." But he put a swing feeling to them by emphasizing the second and fourth beat in a four-beat measure. That innovation allowed the music to move around and flow in a way that ragtime did not permit, with its more abrupt and even jerky melodic movement. Ragtime piano also underwent a transformation when it was played in barrelhouses, which were roughly improvised bars created by lumber camp operators to provide entertainment for their current laborers and to attract additional workers, and which were venues that often featured live music.[11] Barrelhouse music was looser and less restrained than ragtime or country dances—not surprising since the camps and the barrelhouses themselves were wild, sometimes violent places where heavy drinking was the norm.[12] Boogie-woogie piano, with its tremolos and rollicking bass-line arpeggios, flourished there. While claims that Jelly Roll Morton invented jazz are certainly an exaggeration, the transition from ragtime to boogie-woogie was a crucial moment in the development of jazz. And there is a Texas connection here, too, in the composition by Fort Worth–born Euday Bowman titled "Twelfth Street Rag."[13] Bowman's ragtime piece served both as a Rorschach test and as a blank canvas for early jazz musicians. It was recorded by a number of prominent artists in the 1920s and 1930s, including Louis Armstrong, Duke Ellington, Lester Young, and Mary Lou Williams, each of whom put their own individual stamp on the piece and inflected it with their own jazz sensibilities.[14]

THE EMERGENCE OF THE BLUES GENRE

Blues music was developing at roughly the same time as ragtime. While the first blues recordings were not made until the 1920s and 1930s, early versions of blues music were already being played at the turn of the twentieth century. The great blues singer Ma Rainey claimed to have heard blues for the first time in 1902.[15] Music researchers have also unearthed early blues verses, written in highly racialized language, from the 1890s.[16] And so by the time Charley Patton (late 1920s), Blind Lemon Jefferson (1920s), and Robert Johnson (1930s) made their soon-to-be classic records, blues music was already known to the publics of Texas and the Mississippi Delta.

But turn-of-the-century Black music was fluid and diverse. As one historian puts it, the music "was evolving rapidly, forms blurring and bending, experimentation becoming the expectation. Genteel dances became ragged tunes, hymns became secular songs, commercial hits became folk ditties. The music was so diverse and changing so quickly that it was not codified into fixed forms, its notes transcribed to paper and disseminated through the channels of the marketplace. Key figures worked on their own in those early years, generally unknown to each other."[17] It bears mentioning that seemingly disparate musical styles were connected in different ways. Barrelhouse music, for example, shared an affinity for the piano and was played close to rail lines, while also drawing on some church music.[18] In fact, East Texas blues musician T-Bone Walker said he first heard boogie-woogie piano in church.[19]

Early Texas blues pioneer Blind Lemon Jefferson, who lived from 1893 to 1929, developed a blues style that was distinct from other early practitioners. He played arpeggios (chord tones up and down in a rhythmic pattern) and blues chords on the guitar like other blues artists, but his melodic approach was unique. He sang in a high-pitched voice and interjected growls and squeals into his lyrics. He played long runs of notes, often on a single string of the guitar. He left spaces between sections of the melody and limned them with his unique, virtuosic guitar runs. Jefferson was creating a Texas blues sound that others would imitate and extend. Texas blues in its earliest form could be identified, in part, by long, single-string guitar runs and the sparse accompaniment delivered by a single musician with a guitar, rather than the fuller instrumentation that would later be associated with Chicago blues: piano, saxophone, and other horns in a full and blended sound.[20] 1920s Texas was a rural place, and the blues it produced were a rural music—country blues, rather than the city blues that would develop elsewhere.

Though Jefferson was well known to other musicians and to local audiences during his lifetime, he attained iconic status after his early and untimely death. His recorded output was limited because he died not long after record producers discovered and became interested in his music. Nonetheless, the records he made in the 1920s are virtuosic, groundbreaking, and hauntingly beautiful. His high-pitched voice still sounds mysterious all these years later, beckoning from the wilds of East Texas with a strange insistence as he sings about the weird apparitions of country life, from snakes in the house and magic charms to trains that ride off into nowhere.[21] There is one known photograph of Jefferson, and it has been reproduced countless times. Blind from birth, he made his way around venues in the Deep Ellum section of Dallas and other places and lived on his music earnings. Keenly attuned to the world through his other senses, he could tell the sound of a penny from other coins dropping into his cup, according to Mance Lipscomb.[22] Jefferson played long solo passages on the guitar and riffs in the spaces between vocal statements that built a complexity into blues and made his style difficult to imitate. It is no surprise that even before modern communications, and in a wild and sparsely populated region, the Dorhams had heard of Blind Lemon Jefferson, as he lived much of his life in Freestone County, between Couchman and Wortham. Only in recent times was his final resting place in Wortham (eighteen miles west of Fairfield) marked in a recognizable way, with a cemetery that bears his name. It lies next to the main cemetery with Jefferson's grave at the back, overlooking a cleared field. Among the numerous items left on the gravestone by visitors is a scrub-brush, apparently honoring Jefferson's final wish, written on the stone, to "see that my grave is kept clean." And of course a train whistle blows just outside the cemetery, announcing a colorful string of freight cars not much changed from the ones that ran through Wortham during Jefferson's lifetime.

In terms of subject matter, Texas blues drew on local concerns such as the blight on the cotton crop caused by the boll weevil. Slightly younger Texas blues singer Leadbelly sang about the boll weevil to a folk melody.[23] In fact, much of Leadbelly's repertoire related to folk traditions both formally and topically. His association with folk singer Woody Guthrie attests to his interest in folk themes and melodies, as well as social justice concerns. Leadbelly exemplified the melting pot aspect of Texas blues, where the ingredients combined in a way that gave the state's musical products a regional flavor.

Music draws upon experiences, and the blues is particularly dependent on the store of impressions, images, struggles, and calamities that make up a life. Blues musicians traveled widely and sang about the places they'd been. Much of that travel, early on at least, involved trains, and so the romance and adventure of railroads runs deep in American culture. In fact, blues songs are a source of the romance with trains in the popular consciousness. Watching a string of freight cars named and labeled for rail lines from all over the continent gets the imagination going and starts the mind yearning to travel. The sight of a train running along a desert bluff or paralleling a river course quickens the pulse, and the sound of a train whistle at night can bring on an acute loneliness or an abiding sense of peace, or both. So many blues songs—"Mean Old Frisco Blues," "Alabama Bound," "See See Rider," and "Sunshine Special," to name just a few—are also train songs. Kenny Dorham's connections to the Texas railroads were quite direct. He was captivated by the boxcar-riding travelers who visited his childhood home, and he remembered the very same Sunshine Special train passing through East Texas in his youth, a train that Blind Lemon Jefferson hoped would "run me away from here."[24] Operated by the Texas and Pacific Railway, the Sunshine Special was an east-to-west passenger train that originated in St. Louis and ran through Texarkana and Dallas/Fort Worth all the way to El Paso, with connecting service to Mexico City—a far more cushy ride than a freight car for someone seeking a train to "run me away from here."

One can see train motifs running (to torture a pun) all through jazz as well, a phenomenon that underscores both jazz's indebtedness to the blues and the affinities between musical and geographical movement. Somehow, the locomotive feeling of such disparate pieces as Blind Lemon Jefferson's "See See Rider," Duke Ellington's "A Train," and John Coltrane's "Blue Train" and "Locomotion" connect them.[25] And this is to say nothing of Kenny Dorham's "Whistle Stop," the title track of his 1961 homage to his Texas roots. It is easy to disappear down the rabbit hole of making train-related connections across American music. "Orange Blossom Special" and "Wabash Cannonball" have been recorded by musicians across musical genres of blues, bluegrass, country, and jazz, suggesting the intertwined presence of trains in American musical traditions and the common sources from which multiple American styles developed.

Texan Henry "Ragtime Texas" Thomas, born in Big Sandy in 1874, is a transitional figure in the development of blues out of traditional nineteenth-century musical forms.[26] Thomas played the quills, a wind instrument made from cane reeds, while simultaneously playing guitar, and his early songs were not blues but folk melodies. He came to blues, and recorded them, in the 1920s. Nonetheless, elements that would become prominent in country blues could be heard in his music early on, such as the yearning to escape the hard life of Texas cotton farming.[27] Oliphant suggests that the multi-instrumental techniques Thomas employed (albeit with both instruments played by Thomas himself) prefigured the interplay between solo and rhythmic accompaniment that is one of the foundations of jazz.[28] Moreover, blues historians have noted that Thomas's guitar and vocal techniques helped to define Texas blues: "faster, lighter" melodies, and use of the thumb to strike the tonic (root) note of the chord rhythmically, "the sound light and insistent."[29] His vocal imitation of country sounds, such as a train whistle or brake, were also formative.[30] In several respects, then, "Ragtime Texas" Thomas was crucial to the development of regional blues style and, more broadly, of jazz music itself.

Similarly to Henry Thomas, Mance Lipscomb came to the blues through Texas folk and dance music. He was born a bit later than Thomas (1895) and lived into the 1970s. Lipscomb grew up in Navasota, Texas, and his father was a country fiddler who performed at dances. Lipscomb played a variety of music (dance tunes, church hymns, country ballads, and blues) and developed his own guitar techniques.[31] He was discovered by the public much later in life, in his sixties, but had been playing those songs since he was young. He encountered Blind Lemon Jefferson when Lipscomb was in his early twenties, as Jefferson performed in an area of Dallas known as "Deep Ellum." Bounded by Deep Elm Street and Central Track, Deep Ellum was a popular place for blues musicians to play, and it has remained an arts hub ever since. Lipscomb's diverse repertoire recalls Mississippi John Hurt (1893–1966), who was not from Texas but who also played hymns ("I Shall Not Be Moved," "Here I Am Lord, Send Me") and traditional folk songs ("You Are My Sunshine," "Chicken") as well as blues ("Monday Morning Blues," "Coffee Blues"). Like Lipscomb, Hurt was rediscovered later in life, in the 1960s during a period of folk and blues revival, and he played before larger audiences after that, with greater remuneration. Sam "Lightnin'" Hopkins (1912–1982) also recorded later in his life, when he was in his thirties. But he'd met Blind Lemon Jefferson when Hopkins was only eight, and played guitar for Jefferson. Hopkins was born in Centerville, Leon County, just south of Fairfield where Kenny Dorham lived, and quite close to the land owned by the Mannings. Though Hopkins's performing career lasted further into the twentieth century and saw him playing with fuller instrumentation as well as by himself, the store of rural East Texas impressions from which he drew to make his music was remarkably aligned with Kenny Dorham's. Here, for instance, is a blues lyric he sang during an interview later in his life:

> When I first started hoboing, I taken a freight train to be my friend.
> When I first started hoboing, I taken a freight train to be my friend.
> Yeah, you know that train is gone,
> I just standing there wondering, would it ever come back again.[32]

Dorham played a different style of music, modern jazz, but his roots were similar to these musicians', and he found a way to weave the images and moods of rural life into his own music, even without words. When Kenny Dorham began to compose and improvise, he showed immediately that he could draw many textures from the blues. Listening to him perform his compositions that are blues by form, one discovers variations from racing ("Philly Twist") to frolicsome ("KD's Blues") and from dark and funky ("Blue Friday") to lush and contemplative ("Blue Spring"). And they can be simple blues "heads" (melodies) that flow into stretched-out soloing, or else intricate arrangements featuring multiple layers and colors. When Dorham recorded "Blue Spring" with a small group featuring Cannonball Adderley on alto sax, he voiced the ensemble parts in a way that suggested a much larger orchestra and also accentuated the gently contemplative feel of the piece.[33] Somehow the other soloists tap into the tune's essence so that their solos on blues chord changes stay true to the deep wistfulness of the melody. It is a distinctive facet of Dorham's musical personality that he was always mindful of—and steeped in—the Texas blues tradition he encountered in his childhood but at the same time able to develop and extend that tradition with so much variation and nuance. This is not to say that other jazz soloists failed to incorporate the blues into their solo conceptions: To the contrary, the wellspring of blues feeds so much of jazz improvisation by so many jazz artists, from Louis Armstrong and Duke Ellington to Miles Davis, Horace Silver, and John Coltrane. The point here is not that Dorham was the only jazz artist to reflect the blues in his work, but rather that the Texas blues tradition inflected his playing and composing in a particular way.

The music of early twentieth-century African American country blues musicians was diverse, eclectic, and innovative, and it spread from East Texas and the Mississippi Delta across the nation and the world. Govenar notes the phenomenon of "white crossover," in which white Texas musicians picked up on blues stylings and even specific lyrics. Jimmie Rodgers and Bill Neely, to take two of Govenar's examples, heard blues as they worked in the fields alongside Black farm laborers. Interestingly, Neely's and Rodgers's performances were not marketed as "race records" the way Black blues musicians' work was.[34] In some way, blues became palatable to white audiences when sung by white artists. Rodgers was known for yodeling which, as we have seen, was a preoccupation of Dorham's. Dorham heard cowboys and farmers yodeling and took it as a mark of country authenticity, and he found ways to yodel on the jazz trumpet as well.

The crossover between Black blues artists and the white musicians who imitated them is only one facet of a complex racial dynamic present in early twentieth-century Texas. Black musicians played for all-white or all-Black audiences at some times and for mixed audiences at other times. The demeaning minstrel shows of the nineteenth century were appropriated in different ways by different listeners, and musicians could take an ironic or detached stance as they performed music that indulged racial stereotypes. None of this, of course, should suggest that the shows were anything less than offensive; rather, the point is that Black performers had to navigate the assumptions and expectations of listeners as they plied their musical trade. Racist assumptions on the part of whites were part of the social milieu in which African Americans lived. W. C. Handy's recollection of his time playing with Mahara's Minstrels is a case in point. The band played rigidly segregated towns, often in the employ of white politicians and merchants, and withstood insults, threats, and demands for racially stereotyped comedic roles as part of the act, all the while maintaining high levels of musicianship and pride in their abilities.[35]

THE BLUES FORM: CHARACTERISTICS

Blues is a word that is used so often and so casually that it can be difficult to pin down its usage. In music, it can refer to a mood or to a specific song structure. The word *blues* connoted a melancholic state of mind long before it was used in reference to a musical form.[36] When blues as a distinct style of music emerged at the turn of the twentieth century, an element of sadness or suffering was usually associated with it. Blues songs referenced lost love, betrayal, persecution, and natural disasters, among other themes. Formally, the music developed certain common characteristics that remained constant as blues musicians honed their individual styles. One prominent element is the use of major chord harmonies against minor note melodies. A blues tune in the key of F, for example, begins with an F or F dominant chord sounded on the guitar. The melody sung against that chord often substitutes an A-flat for the A-natural in the F chord, which creates a tension between that sad, minor, sound and the major chord beneath it. It is not difficult to imagine how that structural innovation of creating tension between happiness and sadness mirrors the spirit of the blues as a struggle between hope and despair.

The canonical blues form is either eight bars (measures) or twelve bars. When the singer reaches the eighth or twelfth bar, respectively, a new chorus begins. Of course, blues musicians played with this form and varied it, but nonetheless the vast majority of blues songs are recognizable as having eight or twelve bars per chorus, and blues musicians always extend the performance of a song by singing or playing multiple choruses.

The twelve-bar blues consists of three four-bar sequences, as Western music in general is made of four-bar segments. After the first segment, the melody is repeated against a chord that is a fourth higher than the first one. The third and final segment of the song is sung or played against a chord that is a fifth higher than the first, and then the form concludes. Sometimes blues are compared to the haiku form in poetry, as both contain three related lines that resolve in some way on the final one. They have also been likened to modern poetry for their elevation of mood and image over linear narrative.[37] The eight-bar blues is more condensed, featuring only two segments, and its shorter form has generated more variants. Here is an example of a blues lyric by Blind Lemon Jefferson titled "Matchbox Blues":

> Well, I'm leavin' town, but that cryin' won't make me stay
> I'm leavin' town, cryin' won't make me stay
> Baby, the more you cry the further you drive me away.[38]

And here is an eight-bar blues by Jimmy Rushing by the name of "How Long, How Long Blues":

> Baby how long, baby how long
> Has that evening train been gone
> Baby how long, baby how long, baby how long.[39]

These lyrics reflect the call and response tradition of field hollers and work songs, in which one singer would respond to another. The folk music documentarians John and Alan Lomax recorded many call and response performances as they traveled through the South collecting blues and folk songs in the first half of the twentieth century.[40] Some of these recordings featured prison work gangs, but that type of singing could also be heard among Texas and Louisiana field laborers, even well past mid-century. The singing enlivened an otherwise silent environment in the cane and cotton fields, where there was no conversation outside of the music, and a certain freedom was to be found within those songs and the singing of them.[41] In blues music, even if only one singer is performing, the call and response still can be heard, as the initial lament is first stated and then repeated in a different register. In the twelve-bar variety, the third line often provides a resolution to the preceding lines, or a twist on them.

Beginning with W. C. Handy and Ma Rainey, jazz composers and performers adopted blues into their music, both in terms of form by writing songs in either the eight- or the twelve-bar form, and by inflecting written and improvised melodies with blues figures including the blues scale, which contains the minor third described above and other altered notes. There are many, many blues compositions in the jazz repertoire, and they are played at every tempo from very slow to impossibly fast. Improvising jazz musicians do not always use so-called blue notes (found in the blues scale) either. Charlie Parker played fast-tempo, happy-sounding twelve-bar blues, such as "Au Privave," "Relaxing at Camarillo," and "Cool Blues," and Kenny Dorham learned many of them during his time with Parker.[42]

Fast or slow, happy or plaintive, blues compositions in the jazz vein took on a Texas flavor when Dorham played them. His trumpet style, especially in its fully developed form, reflected Blind Lemon Jefferson's long runs of notes and deeply blues-inflected figures. Dorham also displayed a freer feeling of time in his solo construction, varying the length of phrases and the time value of individual notes while always maintaining a sense of swing. These facets of Dorham's musical style will be discussed further in the chapters on his career as an adult musician, but these connections with the early Texas blues greats of the preceding generation are important to emphasize. In the words of contemporary trumpet master Freddie Hendrix, Dorham always played "bluesy as all hell."[43]

Just as jazz compositions structured as blues are often played fast or joyfully, some popular, non-blues jazz standards are performed with blues inflections. In other words, they are not blues in form, but the blues scale or parts of it are used by soloists to strike a particular emotional tone. The great trumpeter Clifford Brown recorded "Parisian Thoroughfare" in 1954 when he was with drummer Max Roach, and although this is an upbeat, thirty-two-bar song form that suggests bustling traffic in the European city, Brown uses notes from the blues scale at multiple points in his solo.[44] Similarly, Kenny Dorham can be heard on many of his recordings using a blues scale or blues phrases when soloing on standards. One good example is his 1956 rendition, also with drummer Roach, of the Cole Porter show tune "Just One of Those Things."[45] Dorham and company take the piece at an absurdly fast tempo, about 300 beats per minute.[46] After tearing at a breakneck pace through the melody and long solos by trumpet, tenor saxophone, and piano, followed by restatement of the melody, Dorham and the rest of the group conclude with a rubato ending in which they play much more slowly and more loosely, using drawn-out blues scales until the final held note.

THE BLUES MEET JAZZ

W. C. Handy was one of the first composers to incorporate blues into big band compositions. His famous "St. Louis Blues" is one example, and it is in fact blues by form. A bit later, Duke Ellington also used blues forms as well as blues melodies in his compositions for orchestra. But Ellington began his career as a professional musician in the 1920s. In the early 1900s, W. C. Handy traveled with his band through the South and Southwest. They played venues such as store-opening celebrations and political rallies, and their audiences were both Black and white.[47] These were trained, professional musicians who played from written scores in their programs. But Handy had encountered blues musicians whose music interested him, and audiences were interested too. They requested that the band play blues-related compositions, or what we would refer to as blues today. Those encounters were the impetus for Handy to write early jazz scores that left room for improvisation but that also voiced horn parts and had to be read by his band.

In New Orleans, cornet player and bandleader Buddy Bolden was already playing at dances and other events around the turn of the twentieth century. He experimented with faster tempos and long stretches of improvisation.[48] To some, improvising was an illegitimate practice, referred to as "faking."[49] Looking at this development with the benefit of a century of hindsight, a listener today might find the criticism strange, given the familiarity and popularity of jazz today. But echoes of that bias against improvisation can be heard even today as jazz is distinguished from European classical music in some circles—in fact, the word *legitimate* is sometimes used synonymously with *classical*. Regardless of criticism from some quarters, Bolden continued to experiment and to make his own impression on the development of music. He had received formal musical training, but he used it to develop and play a new style that was just as demanding as classical music in its technical aspects, and that also required a spontaneity and flexibility of its own. Incidentally, Bolden was unrivaled in his popularity among Black audiences in New Orleans.[50] In a development that foreshadowed an all-too-common pattern among jazz musicians in the coming century, Bolden's mixed public reception probably contributed to the mental and physical problems that ended his career. As Ayers points out, the white newspapers ignored him until the day he attacked his mother in a rage. They covered that incident, calling him simply "a deluded colored musician."[51]

Sippie Wallace, who grew up in Houston in the early 1900s, was another central figure in early jazz. She came from a musical family: Her brothers George and Hersal both played piano, and George was a composer as well. Sippie Wallace was known as a blues singer, and she met a number of jazz musicians in New Orleans and maintained musical associations with them.[52] She recorded with Louis Armstrong, Sidney Bechet, and King Oliver in the 1920s, making records that contain early examples of improvised solos, the foundation of jazz.[53]

The next important association between Texas and the development of incipient jazz styles was the formation of territory bands by Texans moving through Missouri and the Southwest in search of musical associates and performance venues.[54] Texas trumpeter Lammar Wright, for instance, joined Bennie Moten's band in Kansas City and toured and recorded with them from 1921 to 1927.[55] Like Bolden, Oliver, and Armstrong, Wright pioneered improvisation on the trumpet and expanded the expressive potential of the instrument using mutes, growls, and screams.[56] The Blue Devils group, a counterpart to Moten's band, featured Texans Oran "Hot Lips" Page, Buster Smith, and Eddie Durham (no relation to Kenny).[57] These bands traveled the Southwestern territories of the United States in the 1920s and 1930s, playing for dances and other functions. Since Texas itself is eight hundred miles wide, the bands traveled vast distances from one venue to another, and had to string those appearances together in order for the band to remain commercially viable. Some of the work was in Kansas City (hence the draw of that city for Texas musical talent), but the bands traveled far and wide in the region, transplanting musical influences as they went.

The 1920s, 1930s, and 1940s saw an exponential increase in bands, styles, and sheer musical output. It is striking to think that the timespan from the first blues recordings in the mid-1920s until the time when Kenny Dorham began writing arrangements for jazz bands was only twenty years. Quite literally, Dorham grew up along with jazz: He was born in its early years and was already composing and arranging jazz compositions himself when barely out of his teens. And Lionel Hampton, an important musician and bandleader whose career began when Kenny Dorham was a child, would hire Dorham just a few years after the Hampton band formed in 1940. These musical stirrings, signs of things to come, can be sensed in Dorham's recollections of childhood as his sister Eva Lois brought home recordings and news of jazz bands she had heard, and as she performed some of the music herself.

Kenny Dorham was in the midst of revolutionary changes in music in another way as well: He spent his childhood in a region of the country where a distinct blues style was forming. And the creators of this new music shared many of Dorham's childhood experiences: hard farm labor, rural sights and sounds, Jim Crow social norms, unemployed workers traveling the countryside, a growing rail network, and increasing modernization. The Dorham family would leave the countryside for Austin when Kenny reached his teens, in response to large-scale changes in agriculture and economic conditions, but his childhood in Freestone County shaped him, and memories of it would stay with him for a lifetime.

CHAPTER 4

AUSTIN

Whenever I wanted to do a little extracurricular stuff like jazz, I did it in our barn.

—KENNY DORHAM

Kenny Dorham moved to Austin in 1936, at the age of twelve, and stayed with his uncle Joel Manning (Minnie's brother) at first.[1] Kenny's parents eventually joined him, and by the time he was finishing high school in 1940 the Dorham family was living at 1218 East Twelfth Street.[2] Austin is divided by Highway 35, and the Dorhams lived on Austin's segregated East Side, not far from the sprawling University of Texas facilities and a short distance from the capitol but separated from both by a color line. The Supreme Court case that allowed African American students to attend UT Law School would not be decided until 1950, by which time Dorham was grown and gone. His parents would later return to Austin from California and spend the remainder of their lives in the same neighborhood where Kenny passed his teen years. Summers and breaks took Kenny back to Fairfield, and even while away from home he remained in close contact with his parents and siblings.

Austin musician and activist Harold McMillan emphasizes the vibrancy of segregated East Austin in the 1940s and 1950s. Segregation prevented Black Austinites from participating in the social and political life of the larger city, but at the same time it made East Austin a close-knit and thriving community with Black-owned businesses, Black-run schools, neighborhood cafés, and a string of rocking jazz and blues clubs along East Twelfth Street. The names are evocative: Harlem Theater, Charlie's Playhouse, Ernie's Chicken Shack, the Victory Grill.[3] Nearby Huston-Tillotson University (then called

Tillotson) drew African American students in the years before the *Brown* decision. Tillotson boasted a renowned, elite stage band that attracted eminent visitors such as Nat King Cole, Adam Clayton Powell, and W. E. B. Du Bois.[4] The Dorhams were in the thick of things as they lived at various times at 1218 or 1415 East Twelfth Street and at 1006 East Thirteenth Street.[5] McMillan traces Austin's current reputation as a preeminent music hub back to the early jazz and blues scene of the 1940s and 1950s. He notes that even in later years, white musicians like blues legend Stevie Ray Vaughn came to East Austin to develop and hone their style because that was where the best music in town was being played. McMillan also points out that East Austinites crossed the I-35 color line in very few instances, as musicians playing for UT fraternity parties and as domestic workers at the university.[6]

Dorham attended L. C. Anderson High School (formerly E. H. Anderson), an all-Black institution on the east side of Austin whose history reflected the complex dynamics of race and education in the twentieth century. The school's first location was a one-room schoolhouse built in 1889. The school moved to another building in 1909, and then to a third location at Pennsylvania Avenue and Comal Street in 1913. Comal Street was the site of Anderson High when Kenny Dorham was there. The school would move twice more, including once in 1953, when a new building was created to meet growing demand as segregated East Austin's population increased and as equalization of facilities was undertaken in an attempt to preserve a separate but equal schooling regime prior to the *Brown* ruling. In the late 1960s, as districts across the country faced enforcement suits seeking to desegregate their schools, the city enacted a policy by which students could choose which Austin high school to attend. When that failed to work, a federal judge ordered all students—Black and white—living in nearby communities to attend Anderson. The Anderson students took the initiative to clean and organize the facility in order to welcome the new students properly and to show their pride in Anderson and its traditions. But their hospitality was not enough to overcome white parents' resistance to sending their children there. Increasingly by the day, parents withdrew their children, choosing to forego education entirely rather than integrating. Seeing that process beginning to unfold, Judge Jack Roberts decided to close Anderson High entirely and to distribute its students elsewhere. In 1973, the new Anderson High opened to reflect a different demographic mix that included both Black and white students. But the still-living alumni of the original Anderson High remain proud of the original school with its caring teachers, strong civic spirit, and elite music and sports programs.[7] The band and football teams were perpetually in the running for state championships, though they could compete only against other all-Black schools. During Dorham's youth, the school was a few blocks from his house. On the way there each day, he would pass the Twelfth Street house of Isaiah Quit Hurdle, a noted educator and activist who taught science at Anderson. Hurdle's house, and the beautiful, historic Southgate-Lewis house across the street from the Hurdle home, still stand today.

Anderson certainly changed Kenny Dorham's life. In 1939, when he turned fifteen, Dorham got his first trumpet. His sister Eva Lois had urged her parents to buy it for him. She'd already seen musical promise in her younger brother, and as an accomplished musician herself, she wanted to encourage him. The fourteen-dollar trumpet wasn't suitable for a serious music student, though, so his parents bought him a better one—a Conn trumpet—at the Anderson bandmaster's suggestion. Things were rough at first, Dorham recalls: "It took me a half hour just to get a sound out of it."[8]

The trumpet differs from piano, percussion, vibraphone, and guitar in that producing any sound at all takes practice. The correct embouchure (application of the lips to the mouthpiece) is needed to get the lips to vibrate enough for any sound to come out of the horn. Once a student learns how to make a sound, the next challenge is to control the tone, and there a beginning trumpeter resembles a beginning violinist: Tonal control is a difficult goal, and some of the notes played on the way to attaining that control are not pleasant to hear. But Kenny Dorham got there right away, moving quickly through etude books and starting to memorize, by ear, music he heard in other places. The Anderson band director, B. L. Joyce, was "very stern about music. He didn't allow you to play jazz or anything until you had learned all the fundamentals of music," Dorham remembered.[9] Joyce was a stern-looking man who ran the unit with military-type discipline and who himself wore a uniform complete with hard-brimmed hat. One day during band practice, Dorham mischievously began playing "Dipsey Doodle" by Larry Clinton's orchestra, which he'd heard on a record: "I was stomping my foot, and the guys were behind the curtain urging me on. The bandmaster looked over his glasses, pointed at me and hollered, 'Leave the bandstand! Leave the music room and don't come back.' I was out of the band for three or four days, and I was really itching to get back. He spoke to my parents, and I got my discipline together for the music room. From then on I was just a student and not trying to do anything special."[10] On the one hand, this is a story about a band director trying to keep order in the rehearsal room, and any bandleader (or teacher, for that matter) working with kids can sympathize with Mr. Joyce. But this separation between jazz and other forms of music echoes W. C. Handy's comments and the attitudes of all of the preceding critics and audiences who derided what they called "faking" in incipient jazz efforts. On the day he drew his teacher's ire, Dorham was not playing from a concert band or marching band score, but imitating a record by ear, even if he was not improvising. After that incident, he learned to go home to the barn when he wanted to do "any extracurricular stuff like jazz."

Anderson High graduates remember only one time when Mr. Joyce deviated from his "no jazz" policy. The band was playing at a football game against Wheatley High from San Antonio, an archrival in the segregated Prairie View Interscholastic League. Anderson was losing, and the opposing band played one swing number after another. Dorham's friend and fellow musician Alvin Patterson (who eventually succeeded Joyce as Anderson's band director) recalls the moment: "Mr. Joyce called me over and said, 'What was that swing thing you were playing the other day when you thought I was out of listening range?' I said that was 'Tuxedo Junction' and he said, 'OK, let's hear it.' The band also did Cab Calloway's 'Fat Foot Flewzy.'"[11] The crowd responded. They "went nuts when the precise, militaristic Yellow Jackets of marches and grand overtures turned to swing and jazz."[12] The enlivened crowd in turn energized the football team to mount a comeback, and Anderson eventually won the game.

In bandmaster Joyce, Dorham experienced the bias against improvisation that was held by many professional Black musicians who came of age in the early twentieth century. W. C. Handy expressed a similar view before he began incorporating jazz and blues influences into his musical palette. Trumpeter Buddy Bolden, one of the earliest jazz stylists, felt that criticism directed against him as well, even if his audiences applauded his innovations. It was certainly an understandable sentiment, given that classical music during that time was both the standard for serious music and almost exclusively white.[13] Bandleaders like Handy were foreclosed from many musical opportunities despite their vast training and abilities, and Handy took pride in his own precision, reading acumen, and technical prowess and that of his bandmembers. They were more than equal, in many cases, to the white musicians of their time. Dorham's later friend and bandmate Lou Donaldson spoke of the same anti-jazz bias that he experienced while studying at North Carolina A&T in Greensboro. Even playing jazz in the practice rooms could get you in trouble, he said.[14]

Similar to Handy, B. L. Joyce was proud of the Yellowjacket band, and that pride unfortunately moved him to keep jazz music at a distance as much as he could. But his pride also moved him to design and construct their uniforms: He was a tailor as well as a bandleader.[15] They looked sharp and played in a disciplined manner. One Anderson student, Bo Rhambo, wrote arrangements for the band. Trumpeter Martin Banks would go on to play with such jazz notables as tenor saxophone great Dexter Gordon.[16] Pianist Teddy Wilson was another Anderson graduate who became a leading figure on the New York jazz scene.

Outside the band room, the horn players experimented with jazz. Alvin Patterson lived on Washington Street on the East Side, and he hosted jam sessions in his backyard. Along with Patterson, Dorham got to know Buford Banks (trombone) and Paris Jones and Warner "Rip" Ross (trumpet). Gil Askey, who went on to fame in Motown, and Hermie Edwards ("the baddest horn player in East Austin") were also part of the Washington Street sessions. Patterson remembers Dorham deferring to the (slightly) older musicians; he describes Kenny as "quiet," "deep," and "[v]ery thoughtful and perceptive."[17] Dorham copied Erskine Hawkins, fellow trumpeter and composer of the aforementioned "Tuxedo Junction."[18] He most admired Bix Beiderbecke, Roy Eldridge, and Bunny Berrigan at that time: "Bix *sounded* like a piano player, because he knew all the changes. However, Roy had more happening than anyone else."[19] He was probably referring to Eldridge's rhythmic and harmonic complexity and sheer brilliance of musicianship.

Dorham was absorbing influences, and like all jazz musicians before and since, learned other people's solos on the way to creating his own sound and style. It is sometimes assumed that jazz improvisation requires nothing more than spontaneous creativity, and that is an understandable assumption because its practitioners are inventing, on the spot and in real time, new melodies within the chord structure of the piece they are playing. But in order to improvise spontaneously and in sync with the rest of the group, the improviser must be free and comfortable. Part of that freedom and comfort is technical mastery of the instrument, and part of it is feeling the swing or drive of the music. To get there, musicians often practice patterns or phrases (and even entire solos) until those passages emerge spontaneously on the bandstand. Dorham was learning and practicing the solos of his trumpet idols at a very early time in the development of jazz when that kind of imitation was a very new thing. In fact, jazz itself was a very new thing then. Of course, studying others' styles was a step toward becoming a mature and individualistic soloist with one's own sound, technique, and idiomatic improvisational language. Later, Dorham's sound would be immediately recognizable, so unique and creative that listeners could say after hearing a few notes on the radio, "Oh, yeah, that's Kenny Dorham."[20] And it is almost as easy to hear Dorham's influence in the playing of later trumpeters who followed him.[21]

The rapidity of Dorham's musical progress is remarkable. Receiving his first trumpet at fifteen, he was immersed in the crucible of the talent-rich Yellowjackets high school band within a year and playing professionally with big bands just a few years later, after graduating high school in 1942. When Dizzy Gillespie hired him into his big band in 1945, Dorham had only been playing trumpet for six years, and a stint with Texas saxophonist Russell Jacquet's band was already in his rear-view mirror. Perhaps most incredibly of all, Dorham had not even been playing trumpet ten years when Charlie Parker hired him to join his immortal quintet. Even with the stimulus of his regular rehearsals with Patterson and friends, this learning curve is incomprehensibly steep. During this time, Dorham had to learn not only the rudiments of the trumpet, reading music, and written brass band repertoire, but also a different form of music—jazz improvisation—that was still in its early stages. And yet Dorham absorbed it all, never looking back.

Immediately after high school, Dorham took the lessons learned from Joyce and his fellow Yellowjackets with him when he graduated Anderson in 1942 and enrolled at Wiley College in Marshall, Texas.[22] Wiley is a still-existing historically Black college founded in 1873 by the Freedmen's Aid Society of the Methodist Episcopal Church (as was Tillotson). Founded during Reconstruction, the school survived the withdrawal of the federal presence from Texas and the retrenchment of segregation and racial terror that followed during the Jim Crow period. Wiley's music programs of the 1940s were vibrant, offering a range of opportunities, including an all-women jazz band. These institutions represent what historian Henry Louis Gates Jr. has described as a parallel society. Shut out of the aspects of civil society that whites controlled, Black Americans elaborated their own social structure with supporting institutions, and rightly felt pride in the quality of output, musical and otherwise.[23] Wiley band director Bertrand Adams was anxious for Dorham to come: He knew even that early on that Dorham would contribute on the level of Wiley alums like Wild Bill Davis, Roy Porter and, later, Harold Land.

Although Dorham entered too late to join any band and only stayed a short time, he made musical contacts at Wiley, including alumnus Henry Coker, for whom Dorham wrote a composition titled "Malibu" in 1945.[24] Dorham began as a chemistry major but was at Wiley less than a year before he was drafted into the army, an interruption in college plans experienced by many during the war, but nonetheless this was detrimental to Dorham's attainment of credentials that would have allowed him greater employment opportunities later in life. In one of his final interviews near the end of his life, he talked about a desire to teach outside of music and about his plans to finish his degree, though that never happened because he simply ran out of time. Although the war in Europe and the Pacific was raging, Dorham did not see action. He boxed while in the service, but came home in 1943 to continue his musical career, a turn of events that was fortunate for American music history.[25]

After his military discharge, Dorham pursued big band opportunities in earnest, first out on the West Coast from October to December of 1943. Early 1944 saw him in Houston with Russell "Illinois" Jacquet's band. Dorham estimated that he was hired by more than twenty big bands in those first years of his musical career.[26] He didn't stay in Houston long because he had already heard what was happening musically in New York. Not yet twenty-two years old, he found the center of it all at Minton's Playhouse in Harlem. He sat in with tenor sax legend Eddie "Lockjaw" Davis, who extended Dorham a standing invitation to the session. He accepted the invitation and encountered tenor players Wardell Gray and Dexter Gordon, and Florida-born trumpeter Fats Navarro.[27] Navarro in particular took a liking to Dorham, and the feeling was mutual. Fats Navarro was another bebop pioneer whose precise and balanced solo lines foreshadowed Clifford Brown's, and who also shared with Dorham an ability to execute complex ideas. Dorham's and Navarro's playing differed, though, in the former's looser and more fluid rhythmic conception. Dorham's was rooted in the rubato fills and runs of Texas blues guitarists like Blind Lemon Jefferson, an early musical influence that stayed with him all his life. Navarro was more likely to play long lines of eighth notes, sometimes scalar and other times in arpeggios, up-and-down chord tones that flowed and swung by their evenness, weaving through the chord changes with fluent execution and precise timing. Dorham could do that as well, and critics described his playing as a "running" trumpet style for his use of extended runs.

Late in his life, Dorham explained that he developed the running style after listening to Charlie Parker's records before he'd ever met Parker. Translating Parker's ideas to trumpet, he said, required him to move away from the high, screaming trumpet notes of big band style to lines that moved up and down the staff as Parker's saxophone playing did—"like a rollercoaster," Dorham said.[28] Especially on faster, bebop-oriented tunes, Dorham used runs of notes so long as to be breathtaking to the listener, sometimes in double time using sixteenth notes rather than eighth notes, fitting twice as many notes into a line as the eighth notes would have taken. But he utilized space more than Navarro did to punctuate a line, along with jagged offbeat accents. Two good examples of this technique are "Blue Spring Shuffle" from the *Quiet Kenny* album and "Basheer's Dream" from *Afro-Cuban*." His running lines of notes are punctuated by pauses and accents that work against each of the very different grooves of the two pieces to create tension and release. Even early on as he was honing his style, Dorham favored expressive melodic ideas in his improvisation that were composed of difficult intervals, especially for a trumpet player who had to navigate those intervals with only lip movement and breath control. When those lines are written out in musical notation, it is clear how tough they are. Playing through them cleanly requires excellent technique, but for Dorham, technique was never an end in itself. Rather, the ability to play jagged, uneven intervals allowed him to produce expressive ideas that did not sound like anyone else's. A music student can appreciate the technical difficulty of these solos, but any listener can feel the emotion and hear the colors of those distinctive lines.

Navarro told Dorham, in what was something of a backhanded compliment, that he was anxious to hear Dorham once he "straightened out his style." The two men remained friends until Navarro's death in 1950, at the age of twenty-seven. At one point, Dorham gave Navarro the literal shirt (a jacket, actually) off his back by selling it to pay for Navarro's dinner, but then lost the money left over by betting on Navarro in a game of pool.[29]

Dorham actually recorded with Navarro during this early part of his career, at a studio in New York in September 1946.[30] While the recording is in no way revelatory, bearing as it does the hallmarks of a hastily assembled date, it is fascinating to hear Dorham go toe-to-toe with Navarro, who was regarded as the gold standard bebop trumpeter above even Dizzy Gillespie, according to some critics and musicians, and who would go on to be Clifford Brown's primary influence. Likewise, it is exciting to hear Dorham gel with pianist Bud Powell and drummer Kenny Clarke, who were held in equivalent esteem on their instruments. While Dorham was not yet at his technical and artistic peak, this recording shows that he could hang with the heavyweights.

Another trumpet colleague in those days was Henry Boozier, whose big sound made him ideal for first trumpet parts, which are typically higher in range. Dorham's soloing ability generated a demand for him to play second trumpet in the big bands—the solo chair. Dorham and Boozier traveled together through a number of bands as something of a package deal. Dorham's generosity led him to seek out and create spots for Boozier, most notably when they both auditioned in 1945 for Dizzy Gillespie's big band and Dorham insisted that Gillespie hire both of them.[31]

1945 was an important year in Kenny Dorham's life for another reason: He had met Rubina Corbin, and they married on February 16 in New York. They were living in Harlem along with Rubina's mother when their first child, Keturah, was born. Rubina's mother had come to the United States years before, from Trinidad. She would eventually provide the young couple with an elegant home in Brooklyn, and she lived with them for a long time.[32]

Eldest daughter Keturah Dorham-Holley remembers her father warmly as a kind man, "someone you could always talk to." She met one musical luminary after another at the family's home in the Sugar Hill section of Harlem, and later in Brooklyn, as they were always coming by to visit, rehearse, or prepare to go on the road. Dizzy Gillespie was a frequent visitor, noting how much Keturah had grown between visits.[33] One Easter Sunday, Dorham took Keturah and his next-oldest daughter, Leslie (born in April 1947), to meet Dinah Washington, a memory that has stayed fresh for Dorham-Holley over the decades.[34] After Leslie, the Dorhams had three more daughters over the next thirteen years: Evette, LeJuine, and LaMesha. Evette (born in 1950) shares a birthday with her father on August 30. LeJuine was born in November 1952, and LaMesha, the youngest, in March 1960.[35] Dorham was on the road a lot when his girls were young, but doted on them when he was home. Keturah remembers his banana cream pudding as a particular favorite homemade dessert.[36]

Evette remembers meeting many jazz luminaries who were always coming by the house. These memories refer to the period when the Dorhams lived at 1499 President Street in Brooklyn, where Kenny Dorham had set up a rehearsal studio downstairs. Thelonious Monk regularly came for dinner and often had a camera with him, with which he took candid photos of family members.[37] Dorham was known for being generous with his time and music theory knowledge. The occasion for many musicians' visits was to workshop a piece of music or to fix issues in a musical composition, a kind of problem-solving that revealed both deep music theory knowledge and a practical turn of mind reminiscent of Dorham's father's many skilled pursuits. Dorham did not work with tools, but with his mind, taking in other people's repair projects that were written on music manuscript paper.

He practiced piano a lot while at home and used the instrument for arranging and composing as well. Incidentally, Dorham thought all jazz musicians, regardless of instrument, should study piano in order to grasp theory and chord structure, and he practiced what he preached, to the point where others noticed his skill level.[38] Rehearsals were held at the family home, but calls to travel were (and are) an accepted reality for working jazz musicians. Dorham's daughters remember him traveling a lot, but faithfully bringing back presents and always supplying them with books. He insisted that his children be studious and inquisitive, a trait that carried over from his own active intellectual pursuits while he was growing up. His return from the road was always an exciting affair, as a taxi would pull up and Dorham would deposit his suitcases in the vestibule of the family home, generating excitement over his arrival.

One time in particular stands out: his trip to Rio De Janeiro later in Evette's childhood. Before he came home from that trip, Dorham sent a wooden crate all the way from Latin America. The mysterious container turned out to be filled with fabrics, books, and "all sorts of exotic things."[39]

Long before the Rio trip, Dorham set his career on a fast track as a big band trumpeter and arranger. In 1945, at the age of twenty-one, Dorham made his earliest recording appearance on a Mercer Ellington record featuring the singles "Metronome All-Out" and "Pass Me By." Later that year, he appeared with trumpeter Frank Humphries's orchestra on two tracks, "Lonesome Mood" and "After You've Gone."[40]

In 1946, Dorham recorded with Mary Lou Williams on her original compositions "Kool" and "Mary Lou." On "Kool," Dorham plays with a mute, covering the melody and taking a short solo with graceful turns. It is a nascent demonstration of his style, showing his development towards a more assured sound. He reaches for ideas he can't quite execute yet, having not entirely unscrambled his language. "Mary Lou" likewise features another short solo from Dorham, as well as some tentative backing vocals on the song's chorus. Dorham's ideas are somewhat hesitant, not yet untangling into the substitution runs that would become his trademark. A contemporary *DownBeat* review of the recording praised Williams's pianism as "sparkling," but dismissed Dorham's trumpet playing as "unforgivably sloppy."[41]

While Dorham's time in Williams's band was relatively brief, it would mark the beginning of a pivotal association with a leading light of the music. A young prodigy, Williams began performing at clubs at the age of six and touring at the age of twelve. Williams rose to prominence as a performer, arranger, and composer in the big band era, writing charts for Andy Kirk and his Twelve Clouds of Joy band in Oklahoma City.[42] After nearly two decades of touring, Williams found more regular employment at Café Society Downtown and began mentoring the star figures of the bebop scene, including Dizzy Gillespie, Charlie Parker, Thelonious Monk, and Tadd Dameron. In an interview with the music publication *Melody Maker*, Williams reflected the vibrant scene happening at her apartment: "During this period Monk and the kids would come to my apartment every morning around four or pick me up at the Café after I'd finished my last show, and we'd play and swop ideas until noon or later. Monk, Tadd Dameron, Kenny Dorham, Bud Powell, Aaron Bridges, Billy Strayhorn, plus various disc jockeys and newspapermen, would be in and out of my place at all hours, and we'd really ball."[43] Perhaps most notable among Williams's accolades was Monk's designating her as a compositional mentor. He would frequently visit her house and play his compositions repeatedly for her to see whether they might be hits. It is likely that Dorham gleaned similarly valuable lessons from his time with Williams.[44]

In 1946, Dorham was ghostwriting arrangements for Walter "Gil" Fuller because Fuller had more work than he could complete. That year, bandleader Billy Eckstine summoned Dorham to fill the trumpet chair previously held by Fats Navarro. Dorham was following Navarro from Gillespie's band to Eckstine's. Gil Fuller bought Dorham a train ticket from New York to Monroe, Louisiana, where he was to meet the Eckstine band. Dorham was still living with his family in Sugar Hill—not yet in Brooklyn—when he made the trip south. He noted wryly that he rode in the forward section of the train from New York to St. Louis, but then had to move to the back as he entered the South.[45] This moment was significant for someone who had grown up in segregated Texas, then moved to New York where racism took more subtle, less overt forms. In 1946, at twenty-two, newly married and starting a career as an in-demand trumpeter and arranger, he found himself thrown back into the same racial milieu where he began his life. But in 1946, that was the reality in the American South. After all, it would be eight years before segregation was struck down by the Supreme Court in *Brown v. Board of Education*, and a lot longer than that before the court required implementation of its ruling. Its promise of complete desegregation has never been realized, even today.

The train ride was notable in other ways as well, not the least of which was Dorham's traveling attire: "[B]rown alligator on brown suede shoes ('hustler shoes,' Lou Rawls called 'em); a tailor-made $60 F&F suit; a brown silk sport shirt with a Mr. B collar; black mascaraed mustache; brown horn-rimmed glasses (bebop glasses, they were called); and a bebop cap. It's pretty hard to describe the cap, except to say that on top there was a little one-half to one-quarter inch cloth nipple one quarter-inch in diameter. That was really considered chic—then."[46] With that postscript, Dorham seems amused looking back on his sartorial style of the mid-1940s, and at the same time he offers a clue about the culture of music performance in early jazz.

Robin D. G. Kelley notes the political significance of fashion choices like zoot suits in the 1940s and 1950s, which reflected some of the first stirrings of pride movements among previously marginalized groups of Americans.[47] Bebop jazz, created and developed further by Black musicians, generated a fashion sense that rejected business suits, tuxedos, and other formal attire while presenting an elegant formality of its own. Bebop culture was emulated by beatniks seeking to affect the same hipness and countercultural sense as the musicians themselves. Dorham himself maintained an individual sense of style all his life with finely tailored suits and carefully chosen shirts and ties, as well as an array of hats and scarves. Saxophonist Benny Golson and others recalled Dorham's attention to fashion, even if they did not always salute his choices. In his autobiography *Whisper Not*, Golson wrote with amusement, in fact, about one of Dorham's suits in particular that created a look that he himself could not have pulled off.[48] In the 1950s, Kenny knew an expert tailor in Brooklyn named Ellie Clark. Clark was renowned for his skill, and he maintained a clientele of style-conscious musicians, including Max Roach and Kenny Dorham. Dorham's friend Bernard Drayton actually met Dorham for the first time at Clark's shop. Drayton was there installing audio equipment, and Clark introduced him to Dorham. They remained friends, incidentally, for the rest of Dorham's life. Drayton remembers the double-vented, tailored jackets and custom slacks that Dorham and Roach favored.[49]

But back in 1946 in his then-fashionable suit, Dorham was in a train car with less elegantly attired passengers. He shared the segregated rear of the train with an increasing number of country folk and their burdens as the train rolled south: "cotton sacks, cooking utensils, and what smelled like lunches in pails with perforated holes in the lid for air and ants. Further down, as I reached the state of Louisiana, they were bringing on live chickens in burlap sacks, and squealing pigs. Also rabbits, squirrels, some dead possums, and a couple of live ones, correctly called opossums."[50] Though Dorham had come a long way from rural life since leaving home for Austin as a preteen, the folkways and subsistence strategies of the countryside were familiar to him from his upbringing in Freestone County. Even at the end of his life, he remembered farm life vividly and reflected his East Texas childhood in his musical compositions. But the slick urbanity of the jazz world returned abruptly when he arrived at the date and met Art Blakey and his new boss, Billy Eckstine. Eckstine and some others carried guns, Dorham recalled, but "that didn't bother me too much, being from Texas."[51] On Dorham's first night with the band, drummer Art Blakey's press roll catapulted the trumpeter into the four-measure solo break on "Love Me or Leave Me." "That was *really* stepping," Dorham recalled.[52]

As always, Dorham impressed his new bandmates and held down the solo chair for a tour through the South and Southwest. His close friend Sonny Rollins acknowledged learning a lot from the records the band made during Dorham's tenure. Dorham remained with Eckstine until the night he called one of his bandmates an Uncle Tom, and Eckstine fired him.[53] Bandleaders faced the challenge of holding the unit together in the face of discord, and when conflict arose, someone had to go, even someone as talented as Kenny Dorham.[54] Somehow it was understood that a zero-tolerance policy, as it would be called today, was in place for traveling jazz bands that already faced formidable economic, political, and practical challenges to their existence because fighting bandmates could put the unit out of business. As for Dorham, his laid-back, easygoing personality evidently found its limits in people who showed servility in the face of racism. His charisma and gregariousness were apparent, but he had a tough side too. Later, friends would remark on how he could be mysterious, how no one fully knew him. Perhaps that observation reflects the complexity of all human personalities, and most especially the deepest, most creative and thoughtful ones.

This early phase of Dorham's career also reveals the difficult predicament of innovators in the arts. It is an old and oft-repeated story that artists seeking to break new ground face forces of resistance and reaction from the public and even from within the artistic community itself. Manet faced criticism for the way he depicted the female nude. Jackson Pollock's break with representational painting undermined the very definition of art itself according to some critics, provoking controversy. Bob Dylan's electric turn led audiences to boil with rage and to call him "Judas," and these are only some of many examples.[55] Dorham himself didn't start as an innovator: He began learning jazz by listening to established swing bands of the 1920s and 1930s, and his trumpet idols were Erskine Hawkins, Louis Armstrong, Bix Beiderbecke, Roy Eldridge, Bunny Berrigan, Harry "Sweets" Edison, Ziggy Elman, Buck Clayton, and Count Basie's brass.[56] Dorham only later broke with the swing tradition by venturing into bebop. He was not the first to play bebop jazz—that distinction is often given to Charlie Parker. But Dorham entered the music world in the early years of jazz and then aligned himself with the bebop revolution in the mid-1940s, when bebop was in its infancy.

Dorham was uncompromising in his commitment to this branch of jazz music, to the point where he declined to participate in the free jazz movement in the late 1960s. While bebop was popular with a core audience, not all in the listening public embraced it. There were a variety of explanations for that resistance: Some Americans feared subversive influences from the bebop counterculture, while others found the music harder to access and understand than dance band numbers. The smaller groups onstage playing bebop did not always court the audience in the manner of entertainers as did the big bands, which was alienating to some. And then, as noted previously, some musicians in the African American community feared further alienation from the white-dominated music world. It was a bit of a double bind for some—W. C. Handy's minister father forbade him to play music at all, and even after he became a professional bandleader, Handy struggled to gain full acceptance in the (white) music world.[57] Part of the artistic innovator's path has always been to fight through public and critical opposition, and that struggle has been compounded for Black artists by structural racism, which undermines, discredits, appropriates, and steals.

Dorham had faced those kinds of opposition from the time he was a student of B. L. Joyce back in Austin. Despite these obstacles, he was unwavering in playing his own way and in forging a style of improvising and composing within the bebop tradition while moving the tradition forward through hard bop in the 1950s and modal jazz in the 1960s. Thoroughly grounded in reading and theory, Dorham was straightforward about his intention to stay the course, vowing in an interview to "keep playing. That's where the basic satisfaction is at."[58] In 1948, that course was just being set. Dorham's growing reputation would lead to an historic association with one of the greatest jazz musicians of all time at the end of that year.

CHAPTER 5

AN INVITATION FROM CHARLIE PARKER

I knew all the tunes Bird played and just how he played them.

—KENNY DORHAM

Just before Christmas in 1948, Kenny Dorham received a message that Charlie Parker wanted to see him. The messenger was singer Harry Belafonte, who was on the bill with Parker at the Royal Roost. Belafonte came to Dorham's home on 157th Street in the Sugar Hill section of Harlem to tell him, and Dorham went immediately to see Parker. This was no idle social call: Parker wanted Dorham to join his band at the Roost the following night, Christmas Eve.[1] Dorham related these events in an interview near the end of his life.[2]

One can only imagine how thrilling and terrifying the invitation was, on multiple levels. Charlie Parker, nicknamed "Bird" or "Yardbird," was already considered a popular phenomenon by the public and a revolutionary innovator by the musician community. Together with Dizzy Gillespie, Parker had forged an entirely new way of playing jazz, and he was at the forefront of the bebop movement along with a small group of other New York musicians.

Bebop was rooted in Gillespie's and Parker's intensive study of modern harmony, repurposing the octatonic scale (famously popularized by Igor Stravinsky in compositions such as *The Rite of Spring*) to daringly navigate chord progressions. Most of Parker's compositions were contrafacts of popular standards, meaning they used the same chords but featured new melodies, often serpentine and played at blazingly fast tempos. Listening to his music now, one hears a surprising amount of overlap with the Bach Inventions in that Parker's melodies resemble Bach's in shape and density while showing an almost unparalleled conception of harmony. Beyond the scalar stunt pilotry, Parker also showed a remarkably advanced rhythmic concept by making impossible runs with difficult-to-notate beat groupings, only to then land squarely on the downbeat of a measure. The ability to shape phrases with this level of freedom was something Dorham studied intensely as a prerequisite for the opportunity to play with Parker; it is legible in all of Dorham's solos as he moves through song forms with comfort and ease, sidestepping his way through chord changes before reaching a natural resolution point.

In his biography of Bud Powell, music historian Guthrie Ramsey writes that bebop improvisers relied not only on a unique instrumental tone to distinguish themselves, but on an entirely new harmonic concept:

> Bebop musicians introduced a rich harmonic vocabulary into black popular music. While the basic chord progressions of most bebop compositions were based on the American popular songbook and twelve-bar blues forms, the musicians continually enriched these standard structures by brushing them with ninth-, eleventh-, and thirteenth-scale degrees in the melodies and supporting accompaniments. Use of the flatted fifth-scale degree became a signature gesture within this new harmonic approach. Timbre in bebop underscored the notion of individuality within the collective. Although earlier idioms of jazz had certainly produced highly individualized approaches to "quality of sound"—Coleman Hawkins, Sidney Bechet, and Bubba Miley come to mind—bebop pushed this aesthetic to the limit. Charlie Parker's acerbic tone and Dizzy Gillespie's streamlined bite became models for similar experimentations in timbre among jazz musicians.[3]

The innovation of a new harmonic vocabulary was a key aspect of Dorham's development as a musician. Not only did he develop a specific tone and approach to note placement, but he also incorporated Parker's harmonic vocabulary as a means of going beyond previous idioms that were solely tied to quality of sound. This new approach to scales gave players a wealth of variations to put into their solo lines. And the rhythmic palette of bebop was just as revolutionary as the melodic and harmonic palettes:

> Bebop musicians deployed rhythm in flexible and dynamic ways, and when it was executed within the typically fast tempos of bebop performances, this specific brand of rhythmic virtuosity made the music a dazzling sonic display, one that some listeners found disorienting.

> Though bebop's continuing influence has trained our contemporary ears to hear this rhythmic conception as logical, Russell claims that as late as 1948, some listeners still believed that bebop had "no beat" and that it was "rhythmically incoherent." In tempo, accentuation, subdivision of the beat, and articulation, bebop's rhythmic innovations were the style's most fundamental and dramatic quality and rupture with the past.[4]

Casual audiences' inability to dance to the music's complex rhythms made them assume that the music was formless. However, more astute listeners recognized that the music was actually so rhythmically advanced it was almost superhuman. Improvisers were able to manipulate time in such a way that they could fly through a harmonic sequence and still land comfortably on the first beat of a measure, pulling away from the form only to lock back into it with virtuosic ease. Like Parker, Gillespie, and Powell, Dorham had honed this ability, coupling a harmonic conception based around diminished substitutions with a nimble time feel, as evidenced by his playing on the 1948 live recordings of "Half-Nelson" and "Little Willie Leaps" from The Royal Roost. The best analogue to Dorham's and Parker's technical artistry is the way certain athletes (particularly in basketball and tennis) describe the game as moving at a slower pace for them than it does for real-time spectators, allowing them to make split-second choices with incredible fluidity. In his solos, Dorham is able to pull off harmonically information-rich lines at fast tempos while keeping his place in the song and sounding melodic, the equivalent of having a fiery backhand or a graceful floater that is both beautiful and game-clinching.

Parker's songs, whether entirely original, standards, or contrafacts of standards, became the proving grounds on which Dorham could place his unique stamp, demonstrating not only a mastery of the building blocks of the bebop language, but his own individual melodic turns of phrase and instrumental tone. He signified on these song forms, forging a musical identity that made use of Parker's vocabulary while staying distinct from Gillespie and Davis, Dorham's predecessors.

In addition to the musical changes that bebop introduced, this new genre of jazz also changed the musician/audience dynamic in a way that would influence music from the 1940s on. As noted above, bebop was not a musical form suited to dance halls. Solos often extended through multiple choruses and explored dissonance and rhythmic tension. Leaders did not always announce tunes or joke with the audience. In a way, this modern form of jazz demanded more attention from the audience, and thus it diverged from the big band performances that Dorham had become accustomed to. Parker was of course a master of the new musical form in which he worked, which routinely featured absurdly fast tempos and unexpected harmonic leaps.

When Dorham got the invitation to join Parker's group, he had already played bebop, of course, but with Parker he would be doing it alongside the leading figure in the genre, in front of a large in-person and radio audience in the center of the jazz world, memorialized by a live recording. And he was barely twenty-four years old. To prepare for this daunting moment, Kenny Dorham had exactly one day.

He would be replacing Miles Davis, who was leaving Parker's group to form his own band. Davis had already attained his own level of notoriety, and anyone attempting to replace him would face the challenge of meeting the expectations of bandmates and listeners who'd been hearing Miles Davis each night. To make matters worse, it was Davis himself who had suggested Dorham as his replacement.[5] If Dorham flopped, he would be damaging Davis's credibility as well as his own reputation.

Though the job with Charlie Parker was a new experience for Dorham, he had been around modern jazz innovators for a few years. He was familiar with Minton's Playhouse, where he'd auditioned successfully for Dizzy Gillespie's big band in 1945. After that, he frequented small-group sessions at Minton's, where he encountered Parker regularly. "[H]e was so great," Dorham recalled, "that everyone would leave the bandstand when he played. Dizzy would usually play with him, or sometimes Miles or Fats. Dizzy, Lorraine Gillespie, Sarah Vaughan and I used to hang out at Minton's and play a lot at that time."[6] Dorham had met Miles Davis before then, at Fifty-Second Street, a club in New York. The New York scene, at least in its upper echelons, was relatively insular in the mid-1940s.

In December of 1948, then, Dorham was poised to make a leap from informal jam sessions into high-visibility stage appearances. Ramsey notes the divide between the experimental jam sessions at Minton's Playhouse and the more selective performances in the clubs on Fifty-Second Street:

> Wonderful times with rooms and audiences, compared to respect among peers and the real thing—a distinct dichotomy produced in two very different cultural spaces. Harlem was a woodshed. It was a rite-of-passage experience in which bebop musicians came of age. Fifty-Second Street, on the other hand, represented the larger marketplace, the media, and commercial industry. With proper exposure on the Street, an artist could gain access to record contracts and prestigious concert bookings in halls that previously had been off-limits. A

> bebop musician's career soon depended on having others manage or navigate this move. Thus, bebop's journey to 52nd Street represented another important rite of passage: it became a mainstream business. The economic reality that bebop musicians could not sustain careers in Harlem is an important point to keep in mind while reevaluating the notion that bebop was somehow exclusively anticommercial.[7]

Ramsey here observes something essential about the nature of the optics surrounding the music: To be recognized, musicians had to be seen by certain figures, almost exclusively white, within New York's cultural landscape. Even if the real feats of musicianship were occurring elsewhere, and even if the critics didn't have the vocabulary or background to understand what they were hearing, this was a central aspect of the scene. Ramsey's comment also serves as a useful framework for understanding Dorham's latter-day critical neglect in record guides and conservatory classes. To be canonized like Gillespie and Parker, a musician usually required the recognition of the white critical establishment. Regardless of his talent, Dorham's performances not being seen and not receiving a certain critical assessment over the years hindered his career significantly.

Dorham's absence from the supposed jazz canon is evident in any number of critical texts. The mystery of his relative absence in landmark biographies and anthologies becomes easily explicable when one reads the dismissals of his playing. In his book, *Living with Jazz*, critic Dan Morgenstern places Dorham in the second tier of Parker's collaborators: "Fats was the ideal trumpet for a Parker quintet. He had the ear, speed, execution, and sound to match Bird's flights of fancy, and Bird's music was in his soul. Only Dizzy equaled him among Bird's trumpet mates—with all due respect to Miles Davis, Kenny Dorham, and Red Rodney."[8]

Morgenstern makes a sweeping claim that groups together three shockingly unlike trumpet players to reinforce what is ultimately a taste-based observation, one that is not especially surprising given Morgenstern's general focus on early-period jazz. He makes a similar dig later in the book, depicting a scene in which Dorham played after Coleman Hawkins, who was then viewed as a respected elder statesman of the music. Comparing Dorham to Hawkins, Morgenstern states that "[i]n contrast, Dorham, a tall, well-built young man who once boxed in the Golden Gloves, seemed to be a little in awe of his trumpet. He handled it gingerly, a little cautiously, as if it were a strange chick."[9] With this odd comment, cushioned in strangely ornate prose and containing an observation about Dorham's body that reads with uncomfortable racial overtones to the modern reader, Morgenstern makes his unfavorable opinion of Dorham known. In Morgenstern's estimation, Hawkins and Navarro are worthy of study and reverence. Dorham is not.

In their book *The Penguin Guide to Jazz*, British critics Richard Cook and Brian Morton have similarly harsh words about Dorham's later work: "Despite the sustained energy of *Una Mas*, the title-track of which is one of Dorham's finest moments, and of *Trompeta Toccata* (both of which paired the trumpeter's brightly burnished tone with the muscular tenor of Joe Henderson) Dorham seemed to be running out of steam in 1963; 'one more time' was beginning to sound like once too often."[10]

Morton, Cook, and Morgenstern are in the business of making categorical claims, not so unlike the fixedly numerical rankings and ratings of a *Pitchfork* or *Rolling Stone*. Ultimately, and surprisingly, it is Miles Davis, quoted later in Morgenstern's book, who offers a biting pushback on this point of view. Asked how he would rank other trumpet players after himself, Davis replied:

> *After* me! Hell, it's plenty great trumpet players don't come *after* me, or *after* nobody else! That's what I hate so about critics—how they are always *comparing* artists . . . always writing that one's better than another one. . . . That bugs the hell out of musicians. It's made some damn near mad enough to want to hang up their horns. . . . The thing to judge in any jazz artist is does the man project, and does he have ideas. You take Dizzy—he does, all the time, every time, every time he picks up his horn. Some more cats—Clark Terry, Ray Nance, Kenny Dorham, Roy Eldridge, Harold Baker, Freddie Hubbard, Lee Morgan, Bobby Hackett—a lot of them.[11]

Davis, in a moment seemingly incongruous with his famously abrasive public persona, offers a crystal clear summation of the jazz landscape. The trumpet players do not need to be placed into contentious rankings, a construct, Davis notes, of the white critical establishment. Instead, they can coexist as unique entities, with their own sounds, vocabularies, and approaches to their lineage within the music. Davis and Dorham can be appreciated next to Gillespie and Navarro and Rodney; they don't need to be placed in contention.[12]

Whereas critics have sidelined Dorham, as noted elsewhere, musicians have not. Ramsey's framework is a helpful one in outlining the outward-facing reasons more provocative figures gained career traction and accolades while Dorham's workmanlike attitude did not. Cultivating an intriguing stage persona and creating visibility in the right venues were not of interest to Dorham, and so he did not pursue those activities.

This critical appraisal process was only beginning for Dorham in 1948, and the job with Parker was a big spot. At the time, Sid "Symphony Sid" Torin was doing radio broadcasts from the Royal Roost for WMCA radio. Symphony Sid would announce tunes and personnel and occasionally chat with the musicians onstage. Though Sid's reputation among musicians was complex, he was credited with introducing Black artists to a wide radio audience, and some musicians dedicated songs to him: One example is Lester Young's "Jumpin' with Symphony Sid."

Sid broadcast Dorham's opening night with Parker on WMCA, and it lasted from Christmas Eve into the early hours of Christmas morning. Fortunately, the broadcast was preserved on record, so we can hear it today, and it is one of Parker's better-known live recordings, whether people know Kenny Dorham is in the trumpet chair or not. At one point, the band plays a jazz version of "White Christmas" in homage to the season, and Parker soars to lyrical heights, bringing out colors from the tune's chord structure that no one could have imagined before. Kenny Dorham follows him with an equally inventive and colorful solo using notes that are not in the song's written harmony, such as a flatted ninth and a minor third resolving to a ninth. Those figures, along with the triplets Dorham uses in his solo, foreshadow improvisational techniques that would become part of Dorham's unique style as it matured in the 1950s. Though perhaps his nervousness shows through at certain points, he rose to the occasion on his opening night with Parker. The best evidence for that judgment might be the way Parker's and Dorham's solos fold into one another seamlessly. Dorham reaches the level of the master with whom he is sharing the bandstand, a feat that is almost incomprehensible when one considers the circumstances under which it took place.

The format of Parker's groups was one that would become a mainstay of jazz thereafter: two horns (trumpet and saxophone) and a piano/bass/drums rhythm section. The musical repertoire was diverse, consisting of popular standards including ballads and up-tempo pieces, and of course blues. Some were original compositions by Parker and his associates, based on the chord structures of well-known standards, such as George Gershwin's "I Got Rhythm" and Ray Noble's "Cherokee."[13] In this session and in his other work with Parker, Dorham drew on his early exposure to blues as well as his ability to write arrangements in order to keep pace with Parker and his rhythm section. After all, it has often been said that jazz improvisation is composing in real time. Someone who can visualize "how two horns sound together," as Dorham once said, is at an advantage when trying to fit in with a new group or playing a new melody over known chord changes.[14] As one of only two horns in the Parker ensemble, Dorham could expect to play a solo on each piece the group performed, following Parker's solos, which varied widely in length. Kenny Dorham passed yet another audition on that Christmas Eve/Christmas morning, and he remained with Bird through 1949 as the group toured the US and made their way to Paris in late spring.

Kenny Dorham's spring 1949 trip to France under Charlie Parker's leadership marked a resumption of European touring, which had been interrupted by World War II. Jazz historian Phil Schaap notes that US musical groups did not play overseas during the war for obvious reasons, with the exception of the occasional concert for the troops, and that after the war's end in 1945 it took a few years for things to settle down before American promoters were willing to book performances there.[15] And of course Dorham himself was actually serving in the army at the start of the US involvement in the war. Schaap suggests that Parker's 1949 tour was the first major postwar engagement of a US musical act, followed, of course, by a spate of others.[16] There were already expatriate American musicians living in France at this time, but Parker's name recognition and artistic reputation enabled him to command star treatment. To cite Schaap again, Parker was able to bring his own working group rather than relying on promoters to pull together locally available musicians. This arrangement involved paying for travel and accommodations for the Charlie Parker Quintet, which included Dorham, drummer Max Roach, pianist Al Haig, and bassist Tommy Potter—a cost not previously assumed as part of such bookings.[17] As so often happened in his life, Kenny Dorham landed in 1949 at a conjuncture of historic events, forging a new style of music alongside perhaps the best-known figure in jazz as a new European social and political order was taking shape and transatlantic mobility was increasing dramatically. But Dorham's experience of this world-historical moment did not appreciably change Dorham's outlook, as he recounted the events of that spring with typically modest amusement, keeping the focus on Parker and the warm reception conferred by the Parisian audience.[18]

The Paris trip also resulted in a recording session and yielded some incredible demonstrations of the beboppers' capacity for blazing speed. On May 15, Dorham played with Roach, Haig, and Potter at Studio Technisonor alongside tenor saxophonist James Moody. On a solo over the tune "Maximum," a contrafact of the Dizzy Gillespie tune "Bebop," Dorham plays two impeccably swift choruses, practically flying off the click of Roach's ride cymbal as they clock in at about 345 beats per minute. In addition to "Maximum," the group recorded the songs "Prince Albert," which is Dorham's contrafact on the Jerome Kern standard "All The Things You Are"; "Yesterdays"; "Maxology"; and the bebop classic "Hot House." Few details about the session are available, but it is remarkable to imagine the band taking time from a full touring schedule to lay down these burning tracks. A review of the recording appeared in *La revue du jazz* that August, complimenting the mournful and saxophone-like quality of Dorham's playing: "Kenny Dorham's trumpet could, if you did not listen closely, be mistaken for an alto saxophone and one in mourning at that: his sequence of connected notes brings sounds that come and go and are never brought to conclusion."[19]

The year with Parker generated a host of memories. Dorham recalled a night in Milwaukee, before the Paris trip, when they played for nearly five hours; Parker arrived late wearing his famous black pinstripe suit. He was happy. "Although we had missed him," Dorham recalled, "we had been having a lot of fun, and we had everything rolling. This was in early spring, and it was a little warm that night."[20] Parker called a tune Dorham had never heard titled "Painting the Town Red." Dorham's memory of the performance was vivid: "He played that for about half an hour, and each chorus was more fantastic than the one that had preceded it. After he had been playing for about ten minutes, I said to myself, what is he going to do next? Because everything was flawless; it was perfect. I sat down in a corner of the bandstand, crossed my legs and just listened to him play. Max Roach, Al Haig, and Tommy Potter were in the rhythm section, and it was beautiful. Bird really painted Milwaukee red that night!"[21] Next, Charlie Parker asked for a suggestion, and Dorham called a tune named "Circus." Parker gave him the first solo, which "kind of triggered my feeling for the song," Dorham said. They had never played it together, but after Dorham's solo, Parker "just played his can off on that."[22]

When not on the bandstand with Parker, Dorham did not see him. He was mysterious. They never rehearsed. They did not need to because Dorham "knew all the tunes Bird played and just how he played them." On "nights when [Parker] didn't feel well and might falter a little," Dorham could "hold the group together."[23] Phil Schaap notes one particular example of Dorham picking up Parker in a January 1949 recording session that included "Groovin' High," where Dorham's strong and upbeat solo recovers the swing of the performance after a weak solo by Parker.[24] Undoubtedly, Dorham's compositional and arranging abilities helped him to become the de facto leader as a stand-in for Parker when necessary. At the age of twenty-four, Dorham took an early but long step toward musical maturity by necessity, as he was obliged to take over occasionally for Parker. This was a mere ten years after the first time he'd picked up a trumpet, back in Austin as a schoolkid.

The next big musical step for Dorham was the trip to France in May of the year. Parker's same working group of Haig, Potter, and Roach played a week of official performances—a sort of week-long festival in Paris, Marseilles, and Roubaix—with Left Bank jam sessions in between. According to the concert announcements, the group had a full schedule:

May 8–9: Salle Pleyel, Paris (Festival International de Jazz)
May 10: Rex Theatre, Club Martinez et Christera, Marseilles
May 11: evening jam session at Cité Universitaire, Paris
May 12: Colisée Movie Theatre, Roubaix
May 14: Salle Pleyel, Paris
May 15: Salle Pleyel (two concerts, including closing all-star jam session)[25]

The war had ended four years earlier, and Black American musicians enjoyed a warmer and more welcoming reception in Europe than they got back home in the States. As Dorham tells it, "In 1949 Bird had all Paris at his feet. He was playing a concert and there is this part in 'A Night in Tunisia' where the break comes and Bird had to fill it in—well he does, and the whole place cracks up. Bird, in all his life, never witnessed such enthusiasm. He just stood there with a look of exuberance on his face. I said to him, 'Gone Bird.'"[26]

During the course of the tour, Dorham was singled out for praise by the French press. A review of the May 14 show in *Jazz News: Blue Star Revue* complimented Dorham's playing, writing that Dorham "has an astonishing ease on the trumpet" and that his "velvety but always inspired phrases are followed by dizzying silences and, at times, delightful gags."[27] Another review observed the contrast between Davis's and Dorham's playing concepts, writing that "Kenny Dorham, who ensured the succession of the great Miles Davis, seems to be more a disciple of Gillespie."[28]

At the end of their brief Paris tour, the group participated in a closing jam session where they were joined by a variety of jazz musicians then present in the city, including Miles Davis, Sidney Bechet, and Oran "Hot Lips" Page.[29] Page was a fellow Texas trumpeter from an earlier era, whom Dorham admired. After the war, so many Black musicians and other artists took refuge from Jim Crow conditions stateside by sojourning in Paris and other European cities. Some stayed an extended period, and some never went back to the US. Dorham himself would return to Europe later and perform extensively in Denmark and Sweden, as well as in Latin America.

Dorham had a deep appreciation for Parker's genius: "I had heard Bird long before I came to New York, and right from the start he was my favorite soloist. His speed especially influenced me, but even today I can't get anywhere near it."[30] And Dorham knew how far ahead of his time Parker was. "Today," Dorham said in a 1962 interview, "Bird would be as much out in front as he ever was. You'd have to change the sax before anyone could play it like he did."[31] Though Dorham never saw Parker practice, "he was always able to hit the bandstand like a ball of fire."[32] And he'd constantly challenge his bandmates. "He'd play themes from [Stravinsky's] *Rite of Spring* (just a quarter or a half-step off) on the twelfth chorus or so. The musicians dug it, but I don't think the audience knew what was going on."[33]

As someone who spent an extended period of time with Charlie Parker and heard him create on the bandstand each night when he was at the peak of his powers, Dorham had the chance to understand Parker in ways that the general public could not. In the decades since Parker's death, many musicians, historians, and critics have tried to probe the complexities of his personality and his life. Not surprisingly, many of Dorham's observations had to do with Parker's musical creativity. But Dorham's assessment of Charlie Parker as a person is also quite illuminating. "Bird was a real happy person," he said. "[I]t never seemed like he had any acute traumatic grievances. He knew our society wasn't right, and he would talk about it sometimes. His thing was like he'd just get high and blank that other part out. I guess he saw it wasn't going to get together in his lifetime."[34] Dorham's reflections about Parker as a "happy person" must be read in the light of later events in Parker's life: multiple marriages, loss of a child, psychiatric hospitalization, struggles with drugs, and a premature death at the age of thirty-four from various health complications. At the same time, though, Dorham saw him as a fellow collaborator and bandmate. By Dorham's own account, the other parts of Parker's life—the more troubled ones—unfolded in other places, away from Dorham. Like so many artists, Parker was at his best when he was creating. Even his last recordings, which show the physical and mental strain he was under, also convey a range of feelings, including tenderness, joy, and nostalgia. Dorham remembered the best parts of Parker. And like Dorham himself, Parker was not naïve about the state of American society in the postwar years. Both musicians persisted with their artistic quests despite what they saw and lived through.

It also seems clear, from both Dorham's accounts and others, that Parker could be witty, mischievous, and intellectually probing, like Dorham himself. "He knew a lot about the strangest things, like how a car engine is put together and how it functions." And then there was his sense of humor: "Bird would become inspired by a person in the audience, and direct his playing accordingly, whether humorous or sarcastic or whatever. We called those things he did nursery rhymes. Once, back in the spring of 1949, at the Royal Roost, a real beat-looking chick yelled, 'Play "My Wild Irish Rose."' Bird glanced at her and threw in an out-of-key phrase from *The Lady is a Tramp*. We all broke up."[35]

In reflecting on his time with Parker, Dorham invoked the concept of the fourth wall—the invisible curtain separating performer from audience—and explained how he learned from Parker how to navigate it. "You're aware of the audience and yet you have to preserve a sense of detachment so you can create a piece of music or a role internally."[36] This may have been one of the most enduring lessons Dorham took from Parker. Dorham was always aware of his audience, whether in a live setting or in a recording studio. He knew how to convey emotion, he avoided repetition of ideas, he spoke through the blues in his solos. These artistic traits persisted even as Dorham transitioned from swing-era big bands to bebop quintets.

Dorham continued to play with Parker for about a year after Paris, appearing with him for several dates at the Three Deuces alongside Haig, Potter, and Roach the November following the tour.[37] "Then he started doing things with strings where he didn't use a trumpet," Dorham remembered, "so I started to play with various people again."[38]

Another unfortunate byproduct of Dorham's time with Parker, himself a tragically famous drug user, was a lingering addiction to heroin, something Dorham struggled with, off and on, until the end of his life. Kahron Spearman writes, "By the late Sixties, Dorham worked day jobs for sustenance—food and sometimes heroin. The addiction, picked up during his sessions with Blakey, Navarro, Hank Mobley, and others, wreaked havoc on his organs. With a wink and a slow nod, Dorham hinted at the dependence in 'Fragments.' 'Of course, we all belonged to Local 802, but I'm speaking of union in union, or our union.'"[39]

It is impossible to know exactly—and unproductive to speculate about—Dorham's personal reasons for drug use. Systemically, there were a number of reasons that drugs insinuated themselves into the performance settings and social milieu of the music. Guthrie Ramsey describes the unfortunate ubiquity of drugs, particularly heroin, on the scene, depicting Times Square, particularly Fifty-Second Street, as an "entertainment district teeming with young people and many others in search of good times." Drawing on the work of Eric Schneider, Ramsey notes that

> [i]n the immediate postwar years, these were fairly few—specific jazz and after-hours clubs, bars, and cafeterias that catered to a crowd of pimps, hookers, drug dealers, jazz musicians, and their hangers-on."[40] This subcultural element of the jazz scene had precedents in the 52nd Street clubs (whose predecessors were the clubs catering to marijuana users when using the drug became illegal). Indeed, 52nd Street clubs such as "the Onyx, the Downbeat, the Three Deuces, and the Spotlight—all lost

> their cabaret licenses for a time in 1945 because of narcotics trafficking on the premises."[41] The jazz occupation took place in an atmosphere rife with opportunities to abuse alcohol, marijuana, and more.
>
> When heroin became a part of the scene in the late 1940s, the structural elements to foster and support a conducive environment already existed: a combustible mix of "musicians, hustlers, dealers, and fans; a hipster subculture based in this social setting that valorized heroin as part of its rejection of square America; and the music itself (with the related influence of Charlie Parker) together account for the spread of heroin among bebop-playing musicians."[42]

Ramsey attempts to debunk the myth of jazz having some sort of inherent criminality and instead points to the unique set of financial, legal, and locational elements that allowed drug use to flourish in the club environment. Likewise, Ramsey manages to strip away the cultural narrative around the relationship between jazz and drug use, rejecting ideas about its lurid glamor or essential contribution to the sound of the music. Many early portraits of famous jazz musicians indulge in this part of the story, offering tell-all accounts of the musicians' addictions in graphic detail; reducing Dorham's story in that way would be factually incorrect and editorially irresponsible, but altogether ignoring the drug and the extensive harm it did would be equally wrong.

Saxophonist Gary Bartz, another Art Blakey alum, offers a more musician-centric explanation for heroin's prevalence in the jazz community, describing his own struggles with addiction:

> I was a drug abuser and drug addict at one time. . . . I wasn't using needles, but you know we were snorting and we would just do that on the weekends because it was prevalent. It was everywhere. You'd go somewhere and say you want to hit, and you do a hit, and then eventually it would become a habit. . . . [W]hen I joined Art Blakey, I was really around it with him because he was very loose about it. He would do it in front of anybody, and I remember sometimes he would ask me to help him do it. Now, he knew I wasn't doing it, but he would ask me to help him, so now it got to be like, "Oh, what is done." He's doing it. It looks easy. It looks like there's not the problems that people say. But of course there were the problems.[43]

Bartz goes on to explain how drug-using musicians formed their own clique and how his own relationship with drugs allowed him to connect with them off the bandstand:

> I would not, probably, have gotten to know many of the great musicians if I hadn't been doing that, which—there's no reason to do that. But Philly Joe Jones, you know, we became good friends, Kenny Dorham . . . lots of lots of the greats who were doing that. It was more like a community, and so you see the guys that weren't doing it, you know, you wouldn't hang with the guys that were doing it, and the guys that were doing it were the most visible and, I think, the greatest. People like Joe, people like Art, people like Lee [Morgan], people like Kenny Dorham. I mean I could go on and on. So it became like it was a part of the community. So they would, if they knew you were doing it, then you were part of it. It was almost like a gang or something, so I think that had a lot to do with the community itself.[44]

Bartz acknowledges how the drug's social component allowed it to insinuate itself into the music. Musicians who used heroin became part of an in-group scene, rarely recognizing how dangerous it was, given its prevalence and the nonchalance of its users. Later, in the same interview, Bartz describes how his perspective shifted after seeing how crippling heroin's aftereffects were, a fact that Parker's life would illustrate in the years to come as he grew increasingly ill in the throes of addiction.

Dorham would reunite with Parker some five years after the tour of France, under dark circumstances. His final appearance with Parker, in the lead-up to the latter's death, was grim. Critic Leonard Feather's *DownBeat* article about Parker's death, "Parker Finally Finds Peace," paints a sad scene:

> The final night, Charlie [Parker] was playing at Birdland for two nights only, with Bud Powell, Kenny Dorham, Art Blakey, and Charlie Mingus. One set was too much for anyone who had known and respected this man. He refused to take the stand, quarreled with Powell, stalked off after playing a few desultory bars, and a few minutes later was seen by a friend around the corner at Basin Street, with tears streaming down his face.
>
> "You'll kill yourself if you go on like this," said Mingus, who loved Charlie and was mortified at the spectacle of his imminent self-destruction.
>
> A week later, Charlie Parker was dead.[45]

Another (somewhat overwritten) account from *DownBeat* adds some detail to Parker's final days: "Bird's last appearance at Birdland was not a happy one. In March, 1955, he played a two-night gig with Bud Powell,

Charlie Mingus, Art Blakey, and Kenny Dorham. There was friction in the group and after an argument with a water pistol. [*sic*] But during the last days of his life, he sat in his room at the Alvin hotel, across the street from Birdland—a broken and half-forgotten man, in lonely contemplation of the scene of some of his successes."[46]

The loss of Parker was obviously a difficult one for Dorham, as Parker had been his musical hero and central influence and then eventually became his mentor and boss. Their time together was key to Dorham's development as both a trumpeter and an artist. The year and a half with Parker was a watershed period in which Dorham traveled the world, filled in as a part-time bandleader in one of the most important ensembles in music history, and shared the stage each night with the very best musicians around. The constant pressure to perform must have been enormous, but from all appearances he took it in stride. The association with Parker seemed like it would be a springboard into a busy decade as the 1950s approached.

CHAPTER 6

THE UNCROWNED KING

I feel you play the way you live. The different things that happen come out in your playing. If you're sad, you play minor.

—KENNY DORHAM, INTERVIEW WITH *DOWNBEAT*, 1959

Following his time in Charlie Parker's quintet, Dorham found himself in consistent demand as a sideman. Dorham by this time was widely known on the scene in New York, receiving calls from the most vaunted bandleaders for club dates and recording sessions. While some of his essential albums would come later, in the early 1960s, it is the music from the 1950s that most listeners are familiar with. In part, this public familiarity resulted from Dorham's many musical associations during the 1950s. He appeared on so many records and performed in so many clubs that it was difficult for listeners and critics *not* to cross paths with him. Name a major figure in jazz, and Dorham most likely played with them at some point during that decade. Keturah Dorham-Holley recalls that her father was constantly rehearsing and traveling when she was a child.[1]

At the same time, as Dorham himself noted in his "Fragments of an Autobiography," he was not always working in music full-time, although it would be difficult to tell from the quality of his recordings. Referencing a brief period between his living in Harlem and his eventual move to Brooklyn, Dorham regards this time as something of a liminal period. Musical work, frequent as it was, did not pay enough by itself, and he had a young family to support. So he took a variety of factory jobs: "During the '50s, I worked for Republic Aviation, at the U.S. ammunition depot in Vallejo, Calif., and at the U.S. medical depot in Oakland, while living out there with my wife and two daughters, Keturah and Leslie."[2] The ammunition depot job left a vivid recollection that he recounted in detail two decades later. It involved assembling large artillery shells by compressing the explosive material into them, a redundant and soul-destroying process that seemed antithetical to Dorham's artistic goals. He referenced the "destructive side of society," seemingly in realization of the contrast between bomb-making and music. Fortunately, before too long and with encouragement from drummer Art Blakey (who also worked for a time in industry), Dorham was able to make a more definitive return to music. It was this relationship with Blakey that would prove to be one of the most pivotal of Dorham's career. Their connection would eventually lead to a handful of seminal recordings:

> In 1954 and part of 1955 I was working at the Jack Frost Sugar Refinery [in Long Island City, New York] to get away from the regular scene while Art had formed the famous group with Lou Donaldson, Horace Silver, Clifford Brown and Curly Russell. Prior to that, Art and I had made a classic date with the high priest, Thelonious Monk (*Carolina Moon*, etc.) for Blue Note. I made my own first date for Debut records—Charles Mingus & Company—with Kenny Clarke, Walter Bishop, Percy Heath, and Jimmy Heath there, and one for Blue Note, called *K.D. Plays Afro-Cuban*, with Art propelling the forces, Horace Silver, Oscar Pettiford, Cecil Payne, Hank Mobley, J.J. Johnson, and myself, plus Carlos (Potato) Valdez on conga and Richie Goldberg on the side with a cowbell.[3]

There will be more to say about those early recordings, but Dorham's summary of them indicates just how much music he made with Blakey, and how varied it was. He had first met and worked with Blakey in the Eckstine band in 1946, but Blakey's urging him back into the jazz world in the 1950s may have been the difference between the artistic life he lived and a series of industrial jobs that would have consumed his energy from early adulthood until retirement age. Dorham chose the former, and this would be one of several pivotal points in his artistic career where he rededicated himself to the music: "After being encouraged to resign from my job in industry by Art, I started to work in the Jazz Messenger group. I suppose it would be called No. 2, since Clifford Brown had been in the group before me."[4]

Dorham's first record as a leader, *Kenny Dorham Quintet*, was released by Charles Mingus's Debut Records. Recorded on December 15, 1953, the album is primarily made up of short cuts, with middling recording quality. It showcases Dorham's melodic phrasing but little else; it is a scattered effort, consisting mostly of ballads with very few solos. This may have been a result of Mingus's decision to release only a small selection of the tracks for the first vinyl pressing. Other albums from the period give a better sense of Dorham's technical capability and artistic intuition. The standout track of the record is "I Love You," in which an observant listener can hear a number of Dorham's unique turnarounds. Dorham made repeated use of certain musical figures that acted as both hinges between and endpoints for different ideas: "An improviser's own recurring vocabulary patterns are most apparent when they're isolated by rests or otherwise exposed within the context of surrounding material. Examples abound. . . . In the A section of Dorham's performance of 'I Love You,' he uses an ascending minor arpeggio as a catalyst for his improvised phrases three times and repeatedly features a descending melodic pattern as a cadential figure."[5]

In contrast to the Debut Records association, Dorham's collaboration with the Jazz Messengers would be more long-lasting. Pianist Horace Silver met Dorham shortly after arriving in New York and they quickly fell in together. Silver recalled the warmth and generosity with which Dorham welcomed him into the fold:

> After the concert was over and all the musicians were waiting onstage to get paid, I walked over to the piano and started playing à la Bud Powell. All the musicians came over and stood around the piano and listened to me play. Kenny Dorham said, "Man, this kid plays the tenor like Lester Young and the piano like Bud Powell." Kenny gave me his address and phone number and told me to call him. He invited me down to New York some Sunday to hang out with him. He wanted to take me to the Audubon Ballroom on a Sunday night, where he played with a big band called the Messengers, led by Art Blakey. This band consisted primarily of musicians who were of the Muslim faith and who had changed their names to Muslim names.[6]

After Dorham and Silver became acquainted, they began to move in the same clique as Blakey. These relationships were the nucleus of a number of the most prominent hard bop albums of the period.

On November 13, 1954, and February 6, 1955, Silver cut his second record as a bandleader, *Horace Silver and the Jazz Messengers*. Silver describes the sessions fondly, taking particular note of the group cohesion:

> When Alfred asked me to do a fourth trio session, I said, "Alfred, if you don't mind, I would like to use some horns on this session."

He said, "Okay, who would you like to use?" I said, "Kenny Dorham on trumpet, Hank Mobley on tenor, Doug Watkins on bass, and Art Blakey on drums." We got together and rehearsed and did the session. It came out great. Alfred decided to record us a second time. After making these recordings, all the cats in the band said, "Man, we sound good together. We should try to keep this band happening." These recordings were first released on two different ten-inch vinyl records under the name of the Horace Silver Quintet. They were later compiled and released on a twelve-inch vinyl called Horace Silver and the Jazz Messengers. Some of the tunes included were "Doodlin,'" "The Preacher," and "Room 608." Out of these sessions in late 1954 and early 1955, the Jazz Messengers were born, most definitely one of the greatest groups I've ever had the privilege of working with.[7]

Dorham also looked back on these sessions with a similar degree of appreciation: "Art asked me to make a date with him in 1955, and I was honored, of course. The group had Doug Watkins, Horace Silver, and Hank Mobley. We made tunes like *The Preacher*, *Doodlin'* and *Room 608* (which was Horace's room in the Arlington Hotel on W. 23rd St., I think)."[8] Dorham flies on these tracks, with solos full of graceful sixteenth-note runs, propelled by Silver's driving left hand and the sturdy backbeat of his gospel-infused compositions. Dorham's playing on Silver's hit tune "The Preacher" is particularly noteworthy, full of blues licks and punctuated phrases. "The Preacher" is another example of the deep connection to the blues in Dorham's solo conception. He fits in perfectly with the overall blues and gospel feel of the album. Silver's overwhelming respect for the trumpeter is palpable in his remembrance of their time together: "Kenny Dorham and Hank Mobley are two of the most underrated musicians in jazz. They worked so well together. They were both giants. They sure played some slick shit when they improvised. I remember baritone saxophonist Charles Davis asking Kenny to show him some of that slick shit that he played. Kenny's reply was, 'Man, it's all on my records. If you can cop it, go on and get it.'"[9]

Silver's album would prove to be a cornerstone for the music, establishing the sound of hard bop, bebop's rhythm-and-blues inflected successor. In *The Oxford Companion to Jazz*, writer Gene Seymour describes Silver's album as the boilerplate for the genre:

As with the sessions recorded earlier that year at Birdland, the music on this album is melodically simple and rhythmically aggressive. The

> beat was large and heavy enough to support any tune and its myriad variations, propelling the "narrative" of the instrumental performance without yielding to unnecessary flash. Silver's companions were likewise uncomplicated. In their simplicity however, there was infectious energy and warmth similar to the satisfactions delivered by an earthy blues singer. The well-rounded, riff-inflected design of such Silver tunes as "Doodlin" and "The Preacher" made them both accessible to pop audiences and admired by jazz aficionados. The tunes were easy to grasp, hard to forget.[10]

Silver's writing found a kind of middle ground between the intricacies of bebop (Silver was an avowed disciple of Bud Powell) and a sturdy backbeat. Silver's writing also balanced radio playability and harmonic artistry, a formula he continued to pursue throughout his long career. This style of jazz would become a fixture of the Blue Note record label's releases from the 1950s to the mid-1960s.

On November 23, 1955, Dorham cut a live recording with Blakey's second Jazz Messengers lineup (the first featuring star trumpeter Clifford Brown), at the renowned Café Bohemia jazz club.[11] As Dorham noted, he had played with Blakey a number of times before this live recording. Still, it is a valuable document of Dorham's development. It is audible how Dorham has worked through and synthesized Charlie Parker's bebop vocabulary onto the trumpet. While that rhythmic foundation is audible in those earlier recordings, on these sets he comes off as a player who has studied hard enough to comfortably experiment. Dorham's chemistry with Silver and Blakey here is crackling, even stronger than what is heard on the prior studio dates. His interplay with saxophonist Hank Mobley is also particularly strong, as they chase close harmonies on ending tags. This chemistry was forged on the bandstand, something that came shining through in live performances. In July of that year, Dorham had played a notably sizzling set at the Midway Lounge in Pittsburgh as a part of Blakey's Jazz Messengers.[12]

In November, Dorham appeared at the Monday night "Jazz in Jersey" sessions at Andy's,[13] a club in Philadelphia, sharing the bill with Mobley, and on December 3, The Jazz Messengers played at Far Rockaway High School,[14] headlining a series of jazz concerts organized by Harold Celomby, a high school teacher and jazz fan. The music was undeniably impressive, but tensions in the band indicated the beginnings of an eventual splintering. In a 1990 interview with music critic Gene Lees for his publication, *Gene Lees' Jazzletter*, Silver was candid about some of his frustrations with the group, adding contrast to the largely positive comments in his memoir:

> It was a cooperative group in the beginning. We didn't go to a lawyer and have papers drawn up. It was a gentleman's agreement that the group was to be a cooperative. So nobody was the leader. We got the idea from the Modern Jazz Quartet. They did it, and they did it successfully. People in the group weren't taking care of the business, and so it fell apart on a business level.
>
> Several times I was dissatisfied with the business aspect of it, because the guys were goofing off. Sometimes the guys would show up late for the gig and we'd get docked money. Several times, I told myself I'm gonna quit. But I couldn't quit! Every time we'd hit a gig, the band would be cookin' so tough, I said, "Oh shit. I can't go nowhere. Where'm I gonna find guys like this to play with?"
>
> The thing that made me leave was the drug problem. Art and myself and Nica's [Baroness Pannonica de Koenigswarter's] daughter, we got arrested in Philadelphia.[15]

Silver goes on to describe the encounter in hair-raising detail. The police pulled them over on the way back to New York, presumably because they were two Black men with a white woman in the car. The police found a gun in the glove compartment and Benzedrine tablets in Koenigswarter's purse, then arrested all three of them and held them first in a precinct jail and later in the local jail for about three days. Silver added that the FBI questioned them each individually, pulling them from their cells in the middle of the night as a scare tactic. Eventually, Silver's father came out to Philadelphia and bailed him out, but the experience made him want to leave the organization:

> Some of the guys in the group were into drugs. I said to myself, "I love these guys, they're all beautiful guys, and they're great musicians, and where else can I go to play with guys of this calibre? Long as I'm clean, if they bust them, they're gonna let me go. I got no track marks on my arms, I'm not in possession, they'll let me go."
>
> But when I got busted, and I had to spend three days in the jail, and had to go to a hearing and hire a lawyer to defend me to make sure they didn't send me up for nothing! My father had to pay this money, and then I had to pay him back. It cost several hundred dollars. I said "I gotta leave these guys now, because as much as I love them, they're just too hot."[16]

Silver's conclusion of the anecdote is haunting: "Doug Watkins is dead, Kenny Dorham is dead, Hank Mobley's dead. They're all gone except Art and myself."[17] The logic of this comment is not necessarily airtight. Watkins died tragically in 1962 crossing a busy highway (another victim of the perilous road life jazz musicians endured) and Blakey was a notorious heroin user, but Silver's essential point stands. Drugs ravaged the community, and even for a sober musician like Silver, law enforcement run-ins like the one in Philadelphia were common.

On January 30 and March 29, 1955, Dorham recorded his sophomore release, *Afro-Cuban*. The album would prove to be a meaningful display of his approach to both composition and improvisation while also bearing an unusual assurance of concept, gliding between driving Latin polyrhythms and propulsive swing. Blakey's volcanic playing, along with Silver's percussive piano comping, is bolstered by the Afro-Caribbean percussion patterns of conga player Carlos "Potato" Valdez and cowbell player Richie Goldberg on several tracks. Dorham also shows off his arranging chops, with layered horn parts orchestrated among his trumpet, Hank Mobley's tenor saxophone, Cecil Payne's baritone saxophone, and J. J. Johnson's occasional trombone.

Dorham himself goes full tilt here with some of his fiercest playing, fresh ideas springing up at the top of each chorus, driven by his powerful time feel. On these tracks, Dorham's linear concept sounds the most assured and fully formed of his work up to that point. It is not an exaggeration to say that no single note falls out of place. The compositions feature strong hits, weaving countermelodies, smooth transitions between Latin and swing rhythms, and written basslines that accentuate both the melodies and the clave-based groove of the Latin sections. These features would all become trademarks of Dorham's writing style, further developed on subsequent compositions, but already developed on this date. On this album, "Minor's Holiday" and "Basheer's Dream" feature some of Blakey's most flaring accompaniments.

Branching off from these dates, Dorham played in two of Hank Mobley's recording sessions on July 27, 1956, and August 18, 1957. The resulting releases were *Mobley's Second Message* and *Curtain Call.* These albums were, along with Silver's work, template setters for hard bop: bebop harmony cooled to a more relaxed temperature. The almost-shuffling swing of the songs was as fashionable and chilled as a shaken martini. A highlight of *Mobley's Second Message* is Dorham's treatment of the ballad "I Should Care." He caresses the melody, playing at a slow and contemplative pace that maintains its pulse and never drags. He employs favorite techniques, such as swelling a held note without vibrato simply by breathing more air into it. His solo attains something very difficult and elusive even for jazz greats: creating new melodic passages that convey as much emotional urgency as the original melody, and sometimes more. In jazz, playing a flatted ninth or a chromatic neighboring note is a means to create a specific mood or feeling. Dorham's solo suggests colors that are hidden within the harmonic structure of the song but that remain unexpressed until he finds them. Somehow he taps into a wordless language that conveys nuances of emotion through carefully chosen notes and intervals. Many improvisers strive for this level of expression but few attain it, and none better than Dorham. It is easy to get lost in the performance, something that often happens when he plays ballads.

Curtain Call sounds loose in comparison to *Mobley's Second Message*, with the relaxed mood occasionally falling into lethargy. While both are Mobley's dates and Dorham is in strong form, the real star of these records is drummer Art Taylor. Taylor subtly curates the feel on each track, from tipping to burning, careful not to overstep on heads and solos. His ride cymbal has gravitational pull. Taylor would later appear on Dorham's record *Quiet Kenny*.

African American newspaper adverts indicate an uptick in Dorham's club engagements in 1956.[18] The *Chicago Daily Defender*,[19] *New York Amsterdam News*,[20] *Los Angeles Sentinel*,[21] *Pittsburgh Courier*,[22] and *Philadelphia Tribune*[23] carried reviews, commentary and performance announcements regarding African American musicians and musical groups, as well as material on actors and socialites in the Black community. Historian Larry Greene has noted that a different representation of Black public consciousness—one that was more fine-grained and more accurate—could be gleaned from those mid-century periodicals as compared to the white newspapers of the time that also covered some of the same events.[24] And some of the venues advertised in those newspapers were owned and operated by Black businesspeople, so they would not have received notices in white newspapers anyway.

Early in the year, Dorham toured with the Birdland Stars of '56, an ensemble that included Sarah Vaughan, Bud Powell, Lester Young, and Count Basie. They played venues in Norfolk, Cleveland, Chicago, and at the Syrian Mosque in Pittsburgh.[25] The promoters put together a large and prestigious group of musicians, which may have been one reason why they ran into legal trouble with the Birdland name.[26] This tour resulted in the release of a two-volume live album of select recordings from the thirty-five shows they played across twenty-seven cities. Dorham's band consisted of John Simmons on bass, Kenny Clarke on drums, Hank Jones on piano, Al Cohn on saxophone, and Conte Candoli doubling on trumpet with Dorham. Dorham is at the height of his early period playing here, his tone polished and his lines fleet.

During the mid-1950s, Dorham also deepened his friendship with saxophonist Sonny Rollins, which dated back to the late 1940s. Both men would make regular trips out to Thelonious Monk's house, seeking to get lessons from "the old master painter," as Rollins called him.[27] Rollins recalled their initial kinship being almost immediate: "Kenny was such a gentle person. We became friends right away when he moved up to an area where I was living at in New York with his family. We both were playing music, of course, so we had that interest in common."[28] Rollins emphasized the esteem other musicians held Dorham in: "We used to listen to Kenny as one of our teachers. [Especially] on all the records he made with Billy Eckstine. Kenny was quite renowned."[29] Rollins goes into more detail, describing how his relationship with Dorham went beyond just music: "Kenny had played with Charlie Parker down at Birdland. And I remember we used to always be hanging out waiting for him to come back uptown, after the gig. And you know, we'd joke about it, he'd tell us all about playing with Bird. It was really more like a familial relationship I and a couple of other people had with Kenny."[30]

Within the Sonny Rollins Archive at the Schomburg Center in New York, there is a collection of Dorham's sheet music, written for Rollins. It features some individual lead sheets and big band arrangements of "Ol' Folks" and "Lotus Blossom." Various line notes suggest the close informality between Rollins and Dorham: One note reads, "Sonny this is you going out here, you can play one chorus with just the rhythm (opt)."[31] At the same time, this as-yet unplayed arrangement shows Dorham's eye and ear for harmonic detail, as the harmonies are carefully laid out with the same subtlety shown in his writing for Dizzy's band and on larger ensemble albums like *Afro-Cuban* and *Blue Spring*.

Dorham collaborated with Rollins on two of his records. Recorded on October 5, 1956, *Rollins Plays for Bird* has the relaxed quality of a blowing session, with long solos and a list of common standards. The momentum occasionally flags a bit in the transitions between songs in the medley at the top, but the quality of the playing is consistently high. The songs are not Parker originals, but rather are standards associated with him. Dorham also recalled this session as being fruitful, a particular display of Rollins's softer side. Of the second record, Dorham says, "Then there was a date made with Sonny Rollins for Prestige called *Moving Out*, which had Percy Heath, Art Blakey, Elmo Hope, and myself, Sonny played a beautiful *Silk and Satin*, a ballad with accompaniment by the other three."[32] In slight contrast to the Parker tribute, *Moving Out*, recorded on August 18 and October 25, 1954, is off to the races from its opening track. The players sound energized, navigating the harmonic passageways between chords with dexterity. As he had with Mobley, and as he would later have with Joe Henderson, Dorham clearly had a near-telepathic musical understanding with Rollins. Rollins also emphasized the depth of their personal connection: "I almost cry when

I think about him because he was such a swell guy."[33] Rollins's bond with Dorham was so strong, in fact, that he would later provide financial support to Dorham's family in the wake of his untimely passing.[34]

On June 26, 1956, the jazz world was rocked by the death of young trumpeter Clifford Brown. En route to a gig in Chicago, Brown had been travelling with pianist Richie Powell (brother of Bud Powell) and Powell's wife, Nancy. Brown and Richie Powell had each taken turns at the wheel before asking Nancy to take over. Caught in the rain on the Pennsylvania Turnpike, Nancy went off the road and crashed the car near Bedford, Pennsylvania, presumably having lost control of the vehicle.[35] The crash killed Brown as well as both Richie and Nancy. Musicians across the country were devastated, especially Max Roach, Brown's co-bandleader and closest friend. Roach reportedly locked himself in his room with a bottle of cognac upon hearing the news in an attempt to numb the pain.[36]

Brown's meteoric development as a musician captured the attention of many musicians. From a shockingly young age, Brown was known for his incredible speed and grace on the trumpet. With a polished, quicksilver tone and fully developed melodic concept, he was, and still is, the technical gold standard for most trumpet players. Brown united with Roach in 1954 to form a quintet that recorded and toured extensively during Brown's short career. Together, they released several seminal albums together, including *Clifford Brown and Max Roach* (1954), *Study in Brown* (1955) and *Clifford Brown and Max Roach at Basin Street* (1956).

Shortly after Brown's tragic death, Dorham was hired by Roach to fill Brown's now-empty trumpet chair. This was in part a byproduct of Dorham's friendship with Rollins and also of Roach's search for a new trumpet player. Roach and Dorham had also played together in Charlie Parker's 1949 quintet. Dorham recorded with Roach on September 17 and 19, 1956, in New York, and again on March 18 and 20 of the following year at Capital Tower Studios in Hollywood, California, participating in sessions that would eventually be released as *Max Roach + 4*. In October 1956, Dorham played in Philadelphia as part of a large benefit concert for Powell.[37] And as noted, Dorham and Rollins were friends. So when Dorham joined Max Roach's group following Clifford Brown's death, Dorham already had multiple connections to the group's members.

Max Roach + 4 cast Dorham in an interesting role—stepping directly into Brown's shadow after his untimely death at twenty-five. Roach was, in many regards, Brown's double on another instrument. Admired across the jazz scene and beloved by drummers as different as Tony Williams and Bill Bruford, Roach was known for the speed, precision, and control of his drumming. Alongside his elder, bebop maestro Kenny Clark, Roach was one of the first players to innovate four-limb independence on the drum kit. Prior to Roach and Clarke's trailblazing efforts, most big band drummers aligned the entirety of their playing behind simple, driving bass drum quarter notes. After Roach and Clarke, a drummer might play four separate rhythms on the ride cymbal, snare drum, high-hat, and bass drum. Roach had a particularly strong chemistry between his high-hat and ride. This style pushed rhythmic emphasis away from the bass drum (a sound still prominent in most popular music today) and toward the ride cymbal (around which every jazz drummer built a distinct, fingerprint-like pattern) while utilizing the snare and bass drum for offbeat accents or "bombs."

The strength of the bond between Brown and Roach and their joint pursuit of blazing tempos and impeccable phrases made Brown's spot an undesirable position to fill. The uncredited liner notes to the album make this observation a little over-bluntly: "Kenny Dorham, who plays trumpet on these sides, is one of the few musicians who could satisfy the exacting tastes of a Max Roach, or for that matter, of anyone who had spent every night for a couple of years listening to the creative soul of Clifford [Brown] at work."[38] But Rollins offered a similar, though more subtle, take, in his remembrance of the group's transition: "After Clifford Brown's tragedy, Max had been auditioning other people to fill [that] chair in his band. He had several people, but Kenny was the guy that really filled the bill, as much as possible. Clifford Brown was sort of a phenomenon. But Kenny would certainly [have been] a person of his own renown."[39] The choice is doubly interesting in that Dorham doesn't sound much like Brown. Though they both shared a mutual admiration for Fats Navarro and Dizzy Gillespie, Dorham has a darker, harsher tone and makes more use of space between phrases.

Max Roach + 4 was the first album Roach released as a leader following Brown's death, and it carries with it a fitting intensity. On some of the fastest material ("It Don't Mean a Thing," "Just One of Those Things") the band soars to dizzying heights. Three hundred beats per minute blaze by, as if Roach is trying to push the band to a breaking point, though Rollins and Dorham remain unflappable. Roach's solos (which are frequent) are furious, with the sound of his exact sticking, perfectly smoothed rudiments, and snare rolls as crisp as a starched shirt collar. Still, though it is impossible to know exactly what Dorham was thinking at the time of recording, it is difficult not to hear him really pushing on the first record. In particular there is a sparkling quality to some of his leaps into a higher register and an acrobatic element to his double-time runs. There is intensity on every track (even the slower ones) ignited by the insistence of Roach's time.

Also on display is Dorham's comfortable mastery of bebop. On "Woody N' You," Dorham slides in and out of the chord changes, using dominant and diminished chords to leap through chromatic runs, broken up with simpler, three-note motifs. Dorham's use of substitutions and the bebop scale usually entailed constructing lines that included passing notes that create harmonic tension that then resolves on a chord tone in the measure that follows. In this solo, for instance, he hits an E-natural on an E-flat seventh chord, creating a momentary clash in the harmony, before continuing down to E-flat and D-flat, the root and seventh of the chord, respectively, before finally landing on C in the next measure, the third of the A-flat major seventh chord that the sequence begins with. The speed at which Dorham executes this idea makes it seem tossed off, but a closer inspection reveals his study of Parker.

Dorham's own appraisal of Brown was no less than glowing. He describes a performance at a Syrian mosque in which Brown came on the bandstand:

> Max and Art went into their percussion battle royal each playing accompaniment for the other while the other soloed, bringing the house to a standing ovation. As they kept playing, the King, the real acknowledged king of the trumpet (or the other king) Mr. Dizzy Gillespie, strode front and center and started revving up some of his classic abundance and genius. A full three-man rhythm section was on stage by now.
>
> Then Clifford Brown, the young king—and I do mean king, probably the youngest player in trumpet history to achieve musical maturity—came onto the stage.
>
> There were now two drummers, piano, bass, and the trumpets on stage, and John Lewis, music director of the Modern Jazz Quartet, said to me. "You'd better go out and get some," suggesting my participation in the trumpet "scream along."[40]

Not that things were all gloom in those subsequent years after Brown's passing: Bassist George Morrow recounted a comic story from Dorham's early tenure in the band:

> We started out again [in New York] and used Donald Byrd and Barry Harris and then Kenny Dorham took Donald Byrd's place. Brownie [Clifford Brown] had a way of playing "Night in Tunisia," we get to the end and Brownie'd go all the way up and hit that high "F" and that's the only thing Max heard. And that's the reason Donald Byrd left the group cause Donald Byrd was scared Max was going to hurt him.

> Max wanted to hear that high "F" and say, "Give me that high F," and Donald Byrd say "I can't," "Give me that high F," "I get a headache," "Get you some aspirins then, but I want that high F" (laughter). We were on the stand in Philadelphia and he left, Kenny Dorham joined us the next night. It cracked us up—"Give me that high F."[41]

In addition to being humorous, Morrow's comments indicate the technical void (not that Byrd was in any way lacking as a trumpeter) that Brown left behind and what Dorham was capable of measuring up to.

In a similar vein, bassist Art Davis recalls meeting Dorham for the first time and Dorham helping him get work with Roach:

> Now, I happened to have met Kenny Dorham; that was sort of the big thing. He came through Harrisburg with an all-star group. He was instrumental in telling . . . I mean, I had met Max, but he had not heard of me in that sense as much. So Kenny raved about me. I was in Philadelphia. I used to go to Philadelphia to hear all of the greats because there was nothing in Harrisburg. The bass player, George Morrow, was late. So they were waiting, and the clubowner was getting nervous. There was a circular bar and the band was in the middle. So they were looking; Kenny Dorham spotted me and asked me to sit in. The first thing he did was put "Cherokee" [a famously fast standard] on me at just a breakneck tempo. Then he did another one real fast, and sort of looked then. He said, "Oh, yeah. Hmmm. This guy is not so bad, then." So George came in and he asked me to stay for the set, and he offered me the job then.[42]

Davis's experience indicates Dorham's impulse to support other musicians while never lowering standards. Dorham's song choice, a staple of jam session "cutting," forced Davis to show off his technical ability or else wilt on the bandstand. The experience paid off; Davis would perform with Roach and develop a close bond with Booker Little, the next trumpet star that followed Brown and Dorham.

Recorded in September 1956 and March 1957 in both New York and Hollywood, respectively, Dorham's second album with Roach, *Jazz in 3/4 Time*, is largely a more easygoing session than its predecessor, featuring mostly mid-tempo waltzes, over which the soloists stretch out. Roach, joined by Dorham, then followed these efforts with a Charlie Parker tribute album. It is something of a comedown from the previous two releases. Lacking a piano but staying in the mold of *Max Roach + 4*, the album often feels like it's missing an essential rhythmic engine or, at the very least, one more variable of rhythm for Roach to play off of. Recorded on January 14, 1957, *MAX*, the group's next album, is a finely swinging date on which piano makes a welcome return to the group. On this album, Dorham's finesse is particularly evident on "Speculation," one of his originals, where he floats over the fast changes in fantastic synchronicity with a peak-form Roach.

Dorham also toured as part of Roach's quintet during this period, while maintaining some side spots. He performed in the band on December 10, 1956, at Café Bohemia, and subsequently played three more dates at that club in February 1957, all Fridays, from midnight to 2 and 3 a.m.[43] Dorham also took part in Roach's two-week stint at the Jazz Room in Chicago early in the year.[44] In May, Dorham appeared at The Continental, a Brooklyn club located near Nostrand Avenue that held regular sessions on Tuesdays and Thursdays, and more formal jazz nights from Friday to Sunday.[45] On June 25, Dorham performed with Roach and Rollins at the Club Tijuana in Baltimore.[46] On August 23, he played in Don Friedman's Randall's Island Jazz Festival as part of Roach's quintet, and the group played "Daahoud," "Delilah," and "Minor's Holiday." A contemporary review from *DownBeat* notes that Dorham played ferociously: "Kenny Dorham, wild and driving on *Mahoud* [*sic*], built a monumental solo on *Delilah*."[47] In September, Dorham played with Roach again, alongside Morrow and pianist Billy Wallace in Baltimore, as part of a concert series put on by the Interracial Jazz Society, a precursor to the Left Bank Jazz Society.[48] In October, Dorham was scheduled to play in a concert at the University of Chicago as part of a slate of shows organized by promoter Don DuFois and sponsored by the *Chicago Review*. A lack of subsequent announcements makes it unclear if this date ever materialized.[49]

A bootleg recording of the December 10 Café Bohemia performance gives a listener a sense of the fire Dorham brought to the group. It features some of the fastest, cleanest playing of Dorham's career. On the group's rendition of "I Get a Kick Out of You," Dorham bursts right out of the gate, taking a short solo that manages to keep pace with an absolutely combustible Roach. Dorham's lines do not falter, and he does not rely either on screeching high notes or on repetitive ideas, while still managing to navigate the chords and play with a strong melodic concept at a remarkable speed. The tempo (roughly 360 beats per minute) is similar to that of their Paris recording of "Maximum," but both Roach's and Dorham's growth as musicians is plainly evident in the greater variation and authority of their playing. Elsewhere, Dorham shows off his technical virtuosity on "I Feel a Song Comin' On," as well as his gift for solo architecture on "Daahoud." The latter track is particularly notable, given the direct comparisons it invites to Brown, who wrote the song and recorded it with Roach, and on which he played one of his most famous (and most studied) solos. What Dorham manages to do on the song is fairly remarkable, as he retains his own sound with its darker tone, more space, and a lateral approach to chords, all the while swinging hard in lockstep with Roach. This recording, perhaps more than any of the studio efforts, makes clear that Dorham was not a lacking replacement for Brown, but rather a star of comparable ability with his own unique style and flair. Once again, Dorham pulled off the same turn he managed in his tenure with Parker, replacing a celebrated predecessor without losing his own musical identity.

The following year, 1958, was no less busy. In February, Dorham made a guest appearance at the Tuesday night sessions at the Swingland Lounge in Chicago,[50] and in March he filled in for Donald Byrd at the Cafe Bohemia, with an assist from fellow trumpeter Idrees Sulieman.[51] Also in March, Dorham joined Roach for a European tour.[52] The band performed in Germany, Sweden, and Belgium, playing at the Brussels Exhibition on April 20.[53] Shortly before the tour, Roach complimented Dorham's musicality in an interview with *DownBeat*, recalling how playing with him brought back feelings from his early days with Charlie Parker and Dizzy Gillespie: "'I get that feeling when I play with Kenny Dorham or Sonny Rollins now,' he says. 'Kenny is another trumpeter who is wonderful to work with. And people aren't aware of his ability as a composer. Miles says the only people he can hear on the horn today are Dizzy and Kenny. And I know what he means. When he wants to hear an inspired horn he listens to them. He doesn't hear emulation in them.'"[54] Roach shows not only the esteem in which he held Dorham, but also Davis's similar estimation of him, which is surprising given Davis's reputedly harsh public persona.

In early June, Dorham played with Thelonious Monk at the Village Vanguard as part of a group with Hank Mobley on tenor saxophone, Wilbur Ware on bass, and Shadow Wilson on drums.[55] On December 5, he performed at the Max ballroom, also known as Club 65, on Broadway and Eighth Street, as part of a series of Friday night jazz dance concerts organized by disc jockey, musician, and five-week Tonight Show host Al "Jazzbo" Collins. Dorham played alongside pianist George Wallington, bassist Addison Farmer, drummer Roy Haynes, and saxophonist Joe Holiday.[56]

Given the prestige of the Brown-Roach organization, it occurred to some observers at the time that Dorham's stint in that group might have been the high point of his career. Looking back in an interview a decade later, however, Dorham made it clear that that was not the case:

> Well no, I wouldn't say that was the high point of my career. That was just the average type of stuff that I was doing. I did that every day; I played at least that well, and a lot of times you have a good day, maybe once a week you have a good day when you play beyond what you've expected. [With] Max I was just doing my regular playing, and with the Jazz Messengers just my regular playing. That's the level, but sometimes when you're feeling right and everything is just right you can reach or really pull something out of up there somewhere.[57]

Once again, when faced with a spotlight moment, one that might have dazzled or intimidated someone else, Dorham took it in stride. And like the musicians who praised him, Dorham himself knew that he had been at the top of his form even before the Max Roach + 4 stint, and that he would be afterwards as well.

Dorham also made a significant appearance in print that year. In the May 15, 1958, issue of *DownBeat*, he participated in a blindfold test. He was played several selections by the interviewer, without being told the names of the recorded personnel. Dorham's takes on each recording are balanced but do not shy away from critique. About "The Duke," a cut from *Miles Ahead*, Davis's first collaboration with legendary composer Gil Evans, Dorham says, "This is a good setting maybe for a jazz piece, but it isn't the type of thing that gives the soloists a push off into really blowing . . . It's not a diving-board kind of piece that encases the soloists, and the arrangement stands out more than the soloists . . . It doesn't have very much soul, though . . . I'll give it three-and-a-half stars."[58] About Johnny Richards's "Stockholm Sweetenin'," Dorham is more brutal: "Well, I don't get anything distinctive about the band . . . I'd rate this very low because I can't tell anything about it. One-and-a-half stars."[59] He gives the biggest compliment to a Chet Baker–Art Pepper recording of "For Minors Only," a tune penned by Dorham's compatriot Jimmy Heath: "It's a nice little vehicle for blowing. The changes sound comfortable. I like it better than anything I've heard so far, because it's progressive, and because it's leaning in that direction. I'll give it a higher rating than anything else. Four-and-a-half-stars."[60]

This blindfold test demonstrates Dorham's willingness, for all of his personal warmth toward other musicians, to be critical of what did not suit his taste. These comments clearly prefigure his later reviews for *DownBeat*, in which he was unafraid to take surprising shots at a number of musicians.

There is some inherent dissonance to this period of Dorham's life (i.e., the 1950s). It is markedly strange to imagine him playing at clubs with Roach,

Rollins, and Blakey while simultaneously working in sugar refineries and bomb factories.[61] It is in no way difficult to surmise that Dorham, after years of refining his trumpet technique, solo concept, and compositional style, was frustrated to require a regular paycheck from dangerous and physically exhausting day jobs. The economic demands of his home life thus placed a perpetual weight on his artistic output. This is not to say he was unable to create—the music of this period is crystalline proof of that fact. It is instead to point out the constant duress he had to perform under. He did not enjoy the relative comforts of some of his contemporaries. The recording dates and live appearances noted here indicate long stretches when he was working steadily, but in between those remunerative periods he had to earn a living, and it was not always possible to do that exclusively through music.

Nonetheless, Dorham also maintained a presence as a leader in this period. In May 1956, he signed a deal with ABC-Paramount, making the recording debut of the Prophets (a clear offshoot of the Jazz Messenger name).[62] The group included Dick Katz on piano, J. R. Montrose on tenor saxophone, Arthur Edgehill on drums, and Sam Jones on bass. Dorham handled most of the writing with some support from Katz, constructing a songbook that mixed several standards with a number of original compositions. Dorham quickly put the band to work, securing a May 21 engagement at Basin Street,[63] and a June return performance at the Syrian Mosque in Pittsburgh.[64]

The group received good press. Reviewing the Basin Street show, critic Nat Hentoff, who was not an early Dorham fan, writes positively of Dorham's growth as a musician, saying he had "matured into a major trumpeter of taste, wonderful time, good and even tone, and even more technical ease than before."[65] He adds that the ensemble works well together ("The unit is as effective on ballads as on faster wailers") and concludes that "These Prophets also tell a story when they blow. There are no notes-for-the-sake-of-notes or hybridized posturing. These are honest, swinging self-revealers."[66]

Earlier, in March of that year, the band played at Café Bohemia and was listed in *DownBeat* as having signed with RCA Victor. While the motivation behind Dorham's pivot from one record company to another is not included in either announcement, it is safe to assume that money played a prominent role in the end result.[67] The band's first recorded outing was the eponymous *Kenny Dorham and The Jazz Prophets Vol. 1.* Dorham's turnarounds shine on the uptempo number "DX." Overall, it is a flowing date, but it lacks some of the fire of their live record. The band later appeared at Café Bohemia again in May and at an informal concert in which pianist Phineas Newborn impressed a small crowd by "picking up J. R. Montrose's tenor and Kenny

Dorham's trumpet successively and blowing them quite well."[68] The group would reassemble for Dorham's live record, *'Round About Midnight at the Cafe Bohemia*, with Bobby Timmons replacing Katz at the piano and guitarist Kenny Burrell joining the ensemble. Given the way that Dorham refers to the group as an "organization" on the Café Bohemia record, the group's structure was likely a cooperative one, building on the Messengers' guiding principle.[69]

The Café Bohemia live record is the essential work of this period. Tracking consecutive nights of Dorham's band, it showcases Dorham's playing in a club setting, successive melodic ideas sprouting upward and outward. It allows for a deeper understanding of the nuance of his time feel, the laid-back ease of his eighth notes. Dorham's playing here has a luxurious quality. His solos are never overlong, but they do afford the opportunity for a greater looseness. Dorham summarized this feeling in an interview with Art Taylor:

> In a studio I try to concentrate more on finesse, to play flawlessly, I might not be as inventive as I would be in a club, because there I can try to straighten it out while I'm doing it. It takes a lot of nerve to do that when you know you're going to hear it played back. It's not as loose when you're playing in a studio as when you're playing in a club. In a recording you really want to turn it on. You lean in wherever your position is from the microphone and try to take care of it from there. Whereas in a club anything goes![70]

This is precisely where the excitement of the recording is generated, in a chance to hear Dorham play on the fly, testing out variations on different versions of songs within the span of consecutive nights, to hear the real interaction of the band and, above all else, to clearly picture the atmosphere surrounding the performance. The recording itself has a full texture, warm and rich with detail. The album's title (borrowed from the name of Thelonious Monk's famous ballad) is an appropriate one. It feels simultaneously like a special moment and a snapshot of any other night where Dorham's group happened to be on the bill. In July, the group headlined at Jack Downie's in Philadelphia,[71] and in August, Sam Jones departed Dorham's band for legendary alto saxophonist Cannonball Adderley's.[72]

In his autobiography, Miles Davis shares a story about a time during this period when Dorham sat in at the Café Bohemia. It is a scene unlike almost any other in the book; Davis praises almost no one. He talks about the innovations of Charlie Parker and, later, Tony Williams, but is extremely withholding of compliments about fellow trumpet players. Yet, in this particular instance, on a note of admiration, Davis acknowledged being outplayed:

> During the final two weeks at the Cafe Bohemia, before I fired Trane and Philly Joe, something happened that I still remember clearly. Kenny Dorham, the trumpet player, came in one night and asked me if he could sit in with the band. Kenny was a hell of a trumpet player—great style, all his own. I liked his tone and voice. And he was really creative, imaginative, an artist on that horn. He never got all the credit he deserved. Now, I don't let just anybody sit in with my band. You've got to know how to play, and Kenny could play his ass off. Plus, I had known him a long time. Anyway, the place was packed that night like it always was back in those days. After I got through playing, I introduced Kenny, who came up and played just like a motherfucker. Just kicked whatever I had played right out of everyone's head. So I was mad as hell, because nobody likes for someone to come on their gig and show them up. Jackie McLean was out in the audience and so I went up to him and asked him, "Jackie, what did I sound like?"
>
> I know Jackie loves me, and he loves the way I play, so he ain't going to pull my leg. He looked me straight in the eye and said, "Miles, tonight Kenny is playing so beautiful you sound like an imitation of yourself."[73]

It is a story that is surprising not just for its tone (and also for Davis's honest depiction of his own faltering) but also for the respect that Davis clearly had for Dorham and his style. Davis saw Dorham not only as technically adept, but as an artistic equal, a distinctive voice, a luminary.

Dorham followed *'Round About Midnight* with a string of slightly more conceptual albums. The first of these was *Jazz Contrasts*, recorded in May 1957, which alternated a standard jazz quintet featuring Roach and Rollins with one augmented by the addition of harpist Betty Glamann. Glamann adds an elegant third stream quality to the slower numbers, as her strummed chords glimmer in the background.[74] Her playing lends a Ravel- or Debussyesque touch to the proceedings. The album is primarily standards, with one Clifford Brown original and one Dorham composition. It highlights some of Dorham's most finely wrought playing, a tight ensemble, and one of the fastest versions of "I'll Remember April" put on record.

On July 7 and August 15, 1958, Dorham tracked *This Is the Moment!*, a surprising release on the Riverside record label—an album featuring Dorham's performance as a vocalist. While the record never had the crossover success of Chet Baker's releases, and while Dorham is not displaying the sort of technical discipline of a full-time singer like Johnny Hartman, it is still fascinating to hear his vocal phrasing alongside his trumpet playing. He viewed these two things as essentially linked parts of his musicality, and the listener can hear it in the way he gestures through the tunes, choosing the articulation of words to emphasize particular phrase endings. This is particularly evident on the album's title track, where his singing of the melody and his trumpet solo over the form follow a markedly similar shape. His voice has a velour softness and warmth, remaining mostly understated. It also features a very heartfelt tribute to Clifford Brown, as Dorham sings a rendition of "I'll Remember Clifford," a ballad by saxophonist Benny Golson dedicated to Brown. The session also marked the recording debut of pianist Cedar Walton, a fellow Texan. Walton would go onto hold the piano chair in Art Blakey's Jazz Messengers during the group's second golden period, alongside jazz giants Freddie Hubbard, Wayne Shorter, Curtis Fuller, and Jymie Merritt.

Kenny Dorham worked with other vocalists in the 1950s, and among them Abbey Lincoln stands out because of their mutual affinity and similarities in musical conception. Both Lincoln's singing voice and Dorham's trumpet style are expressive and emotionally powerful, and they each make use of sliding and bending of notes, dark and brooding lyricism, and blues figures. Dorham joined Lincoln from 1957 to 1959 for a series of recordings on the Riverside label in familiar musical company: Cedar Walton and Wynton Kelly on piano, Paul Chambers on bass, Max Roach on drums, and Sonny Rollins playing tenor saxophone. Among these musicians, Dorham sounds at home and is able to reach expressive heights on a number of the selections. Though the album features all vocal material, the tunes are diverse, with blues and up-tempo numbers alongside ballads like "Don't Explain." According to Joel Dorham, singer Billie Holiday could not bear to hear Kenny play ballads because it made her too sad. Had she been alive to hear his accompaniment of Abbey Lincoln on that tune, which Holiday herself had famously recorded, it would likely have broken her heart. Dorham and Rollins solo in a pianoless format and Dorham also plays obbligato alongside Lincoln's vocals, offering descending intervallic jumps with a muted trumpet. His accompanying lines are by turns sweet and mournful, complementing Lincoln's rueful vocals that range emotionally from tender to snarling.

On this and other tracks, Dorham's and Rollins's solos flow seamlessly into one another, with one continuing the other's lyrical motif. Their musical and personal closeness is evident. On "Softly as in a Morning Sunrise," Dorham's solo is remarkably brief—half a chorus—but he packs in sensitive and understated lines, with his trumpet unmuted. Some tracks, like "Lost in the Stars," do not feature a trumpet solo, as Dorham is content instead to set up Lincoln's melody statement with a few carefully chosen sustained notes that have a celestial quality to them as they swell and fade. "Strong Man," by contrast, is earthy and upbeat, with Rollins and Dorham once again anticipating each other almost telepathically. On "I Must Have That Man," Dorham tears off a solo that reveals his running trumpet style: long, flowing lines of notes perfectly chosen, placed, and articulated, always swinging hard. One gets the sense on these recordings that he is not so much accompanying Abbey Lincoln as building a musical dialogue with her as they develop and complete each other's ideas.

Between his attunement with Lincoln and his comfort with the other supporting musicians, Dorham is poised on these Riverside sessions to deliver some of the most expressive moments of all his recorded material. His warm trumpet sound invites the listener to sit back and luxuriate in extraordinary music produced in an ideal setting. Discussing the date as a whole in an interview with *Metronome Magazine*, Lincoln commented, "It was a thrill to work with musicians like these. I sang things I had never even thought of before, and they were right there with me. Almost like they were reading my mind."[75] And in a later interview, Lincoln emphasized what that experience meant for her in terms of the arc of her life as an artist. "When I recorded the first album I made with Max and Kenny Dorham and Sonny Rollins and Wynton Kelly and Paul Chambers," she said, "I knew I was never going back to doing what I had been doing. I was going to work with these kind of musicians."[76]

Another somewhat unusual session for Dorham was his date with alto saxophonist Ernie Henry, *Two Horns / Two Rhythm*, recorded on November 13th and December 2nd, 1957. Dorham had previously worked with Henry on his 1956 debut, *Presenting Ernie Henry*, but this date was unique for its lack of a chordal instrument. On *Two Horns / Two Rhythm*, the soloists sound freer to follow the arc of their ideas, using the additional space to explore melodic development. The current of rhythm generates enough momentum to keep the lines flowing easily. "Soon" offers a rare glimpse of Dorham at the piano. On the whole, the recording hints at the playful digressiveness of Ornette Coleman's chordless quartets that would follow two years later. It is also, sadly, Henry's last recording before his sudden death at thirty-one from a heroin overdose. Dorham takes an ironic turn in the session by choosing to include "Is It True What They Say About Dixie?" a song recorded by Jimmy Dorsey and by Al Jolson individually that would have suggested multiple meanings for a person who grew up in Jim Crow Texas and who was now living in the time of the Civil Rights Movement. Dorham and Henry are passionate and lyrical as they first take the changes at a fast clip in individual solos and then exchange ideas in a pianoless musical dialogue before the out-chorus. The musicians' brilliant exuberance in working through the song form stands in contrast to staid representations of "Dixie" that appear in various forms in popular culture. Highlighting that contrast is a powerful statement.

Dorham made several other notable contributions as a sideman in the latter half of the decade. On July 19 and August 22, 1956, he played on the final three tracks of *Matthew Gee's Jazz by Gee*, a collection of well-executed, if boilerplate, bebop cuts by an undersung trombonist. The horn melody arrangements are reminiscent of early Clifford Brown and Art Pepper record dates. Dorham's solos are crisp and clean, showcasing the style he perfected through his study of—and alongside—Parker. On March 14, 1957, several days before his LA sessions with Roach, Dorham recorded with West Coast saxophonist Herb Geller on his cool jazz–inflected *Fire in the West*. Finally, in February 1958, Dorham played on the first six tracks of vocalist Betty Carter's lovely record *Out There*, performing as part of the backing ensemble and taking one short solo, an uncharacteristically flashy eight bars on "Babe's Blues."

Dorham closed out the fifties with two of his most polished recordings: *Blue Spring* and *Quiet Kenny*. Recorded on January 20 and February 18, 1959, *Blue Spring* shows off Dorham's writing talents not only as a composer but also as an arranger. Cannonball Adderley, Cecil Payne, and French horn player David Amram all fill out chordal pads, elegant countermelodies, and well-placed hits. The album's overall mood is a gentle one, prizing subtle blend and melodicism over technical showmanship. This is perhaps not such a surprise, given that all the song titles contain the word *spring*. Adderley is in particularly strong form, floating easily over chord changes. Without a doubt, his solos here are instances of what Dorham heard as Adderley "yodeling" on his horn, like a Southwestern cowboy.

Recorded on November 13 of the same year, *Quiet Kenny* is commonly elevated as Dorham's greatest work. But its distinction is somewhat ironic. Labeled by the Penguin Jazz Guide as "minor masterpiece,"[77] it has become Dorham's most well-known album. On a song-by-song basis, this is in part because of the often-played Dorham original "Lotus Blossom,"[78] with its famously tricky transition between a Latin 6/8 and a swung 4/4 time signature, and a wistful rendition of "My Ideal." Dorham's solo on "Lotus Blossom" shows other trademarks of his sound. His intervals stay fairly close together during his more complex lines, primarily employing seconds and thirds to weave in and out of the chord changes, with the occasional fourths, fifths, and octaves appearing for effect on short ideas or concluding phrases. The song itself, recorded many times by artists other than Dorham, features several of his hallmarks as a composer, such as a transition between straight eighth notes and swing, the use of a more open A section followed by a sequence of closely knit chords on the B section, and rhythm section hits built into the harmony and melody. The song is surprising in its small choices, the heightened tension between the E dominant seventh with a sharp ninth and the A dominant seventh with a sharp ninth on the first section of the bridge, or the bass pattern, made up of fifths and fourths, in the modal section that moves stepwise from D down to B-flat and back again. In these moments, Dorham reveals the care he put into making these songs both elegant and intriguing, providing the listener with a balance of surprise and familiarity.

Dorham is backed by a rhythm section featuring Tommy Flanagan on piano, Paul Chambers on bass, and Art Taylor on drums once again. The album is made up primarily of American songbook standards, with three original compositions from Dorham, and the tempos rarely rise above medium-slow. What the album captures is the vulnerability and warmth that animated Dorham's playing and shaded his tone. The ballads in particular reveal a tender side of his sound.

In *Thinking in Jazz*, a landmark survey of the art of improvisation, Paul Berliner includes Dorham in a lineage of masterful improvisers and includes quotes and observations from various musicians about Dorham's harmonic and tonal trademarks.[79] It is telling that unlike other books of jazz criticism, Berliner's text has significant input from musicians and does not solely rely on his own critical assessments. For example, in this book, trumpeter Lonnie Hillyer describes Dorham's playing on "Alone Together" as gently sublime:

> Lonnie Hillyer once commented on the combined effect of these practices after hearing a recorded rendition of the ballad "Alone Together" by his late friend, trumpeter Kenny Dorham. Rendering the piece with his warm, intimate tone, Dorham embellished the melody with spare grace notes and varied its phrasing with subtle anticipations and delays. He articulated sustained pitches with soft unaccented attacks before bending them down and drawing them quickly back again, allowing them to sing with an increasingly wide vibrato. Only once did he interject into the performance a phrase of his own by filling a rest with melodic motion. Seated beside the speakers, Hillyer responded immediately to Dorham. He leaned forward, covered his eyes with his hands, and remained perfectly still under the performance's close. Then sighing, he shook his head, as if waking from a dream, and softly marveled, "K.D.! To think he could say *all that*, just by playing the melody."[80]

Hillyer's admiring commentary about Dorham's playing on "Alone Together" reveals the technical ability that supported Dorham's lyricism, focusing on the quiet complexity of his articulation. As a trumpeter, Hillyer shows a unique admiration of Dorham's chops while underscoring that they were not employed solely in the service of flashy showmanship.

An estimation of *Quiet Kenny* as Dorham's masterpiece folds too neatly into a summary of his story as short and small, the hidden gem of a minor master. While the album deserves its accolades, to hear it offers only an incomplete portrait of Dorham as both trumpeter and composer. While his playing here is markedly sensitive, it is nothing especially new for Dorham. Both *'Round About Midnight* and *Jazz Contrasts* demonstrate his mastery of gracefully slow tempos and lyrical soloing. To end Dorham's story with *Quiet Kenny* is to miss an entirely separate chapter of his later development, excluding as it does the innovations he adopted on his later recordings with saxophonist Joe Henderson and pianist Andrew Hill. It would also critically erase the cool abstraction he incorporated into his albums of the mid-1960s, *Una Mas* and *Trumpet Toccata*. *Quiet Kenny* is a testament to the understated poise of Dorham's sound but, as he would show with time, he still had so much more to share with his listeners.

The late 1950s also marked some of Dorham's earliest forays into music education. Dorham taught at the Lenox School of Jazz in 1958 and returned in 1959. The Lenox School was a music education organization that existed between 1957 and 1960. The school was owned and operated by Stephanie and Philip Barber, a wealthy white couple who purchased a large tract of pastoral farmland in the Berkshires and converted it into a performance space. The Barbers initially founded the Music Inn in 1950, creating a venue for musicians and scholars to perform, discuss, educate, and debate. With the assistance of pianist John Lewis (famed member of the Modern Jazz Quartet who had also played with Charlie Parker), the Music Inn programming branched out into the formally constructed (and more outwardly prestigious) Lenox School of Jazz. Lewis recruited jazz elite to teach there and envisioned endowed chairs for each instrument as a way of retaining top faculty. His proposal, advanced at a time when the program was losing money, went unheeded.

In his history of the school, *The Lenox School of Jazz*, author Jeremy Yudkin writes that the school opened in 1957 with a "small, carefully selected body of students," and it was established as a chartered nonprofit organization.[81] A faculty concert held early on was a catalyst for formalizing the association. In the liner notes to *Historic Jazz Concert at Music Inn*, Nat Hentoff writes that at the concert the "mutual affection and warmth [were] exhilaratingly contagious, and it was this experience that led directly to the decision by the Barbers and John Lewis to form the School of Jazz at Music

Inn, where for the first time . . . young players could learn directly from the men who helped to form the jazz language."[82]

Dorham taught trumpet and composition at the school alongside several other jazz notables, while also running a student ensemble. His tenure on the 1958 faculty was a reportedly happy one.[83] He led an ensemble consisting of alto saxophonist Dale Hillary, baritone saxophonist Dom Turkowski, pianist Peter Loeb, drummer Bernard Wilkinson, and bassist (and fellow instructor) Percy Heath. According to *Metronome*, the group performed well: "This group abounded with swinging soloists and Kenny had rehearsed it to the point where up-tempos were indicated. Actually the group played better during rehearsal than it did at the concert but that is a natural enough occurrence and both Hillary and Turkowski are to be looked forward to."[84] Dorham was also singled out by the writer as being "a very special standout among the excellence" during a faculty performance of a piece called "Faculty Meeting" which brought several of the groups together, including faculty members in The Modern Jazz Quartet and The Jimmy Giuffre Three.

However, by the time Dorham returned in 1959, things had begun to unravel: "It was in the year 1959 that the School of Jazz reached its apogee while in that same year certain events began to foreshadow the change in the atmosphere of the times that would soon lead to the School's demise."[85] Yudkin goes on to describe how several cancelled concerts, one from Miles Davis (who arrived around 2 a.m. and, without apology, performed for a few straggling audience members in the nearby fields), one from Louis Armstrong (who had suffered a heart attack in Italy and was in recovery), and one from Sonny Rollins (who had begun his sudden and mysterious break from live performance), along with ongoing financial struggles made the school's problems readily apparent.

Finally, Yudkin notes, the big issue of that summer was the inclusion of saxophonist Ornette Coleman as a student in the program, which seemed to upset the pedagogical balance of the school.[86] Coleman was a well-known (if controversial) fixture in New York and had released four albums, including the now-seminal *The Shape of Jazz to Come* (1959). Some of the other instructors and students were trying to study what Coleman was doing (some even seeking out his guidance) while others were upset by his very presence at the school. Lewis viewed Coleman's inclusion as a calculated move to draw more attention to the school, but this plan went slightly sideways when not all of the attention was positive. For an educational institution that was still in the midst of defining itself and its ethos, these moments of major media coverage were detrimental. In the Lenox School, Dorham had walked into what appeared to be both a foundationally important moment in jazz education and also a tumultuous one.

Still, Dorham managed to make his mark as an instructor. Trumpeter John Eckert studied at Lenox, and shortly after took a lesson with Dorham in New York. Eckert recalls him being a uniquely supportive teacher: "I wasn't in his group [at the school] but he gave me lessons. And then I went to his house in Brooklyn at one time for another lesson. He was very helpful. I mean, he is the master of bebop chord changes. And how to make them melodies, bring them out. And he's a super sweet person. Very friendly, very helpful, very nice. I didn't appreciate it when I was that age. I had some kind of authority problem with anybody that was older than me. But he was just so friendly and unassuming."[87] Eckert remarks that Dorham maintained this personal warmth even given his stature in the community. Contrasting Dorham's style to Miles Davis's more free playing concept and imaginative approach to changing his groups and genres, Eckert comments on Dorham's undeniable authority as a player: "Kenny Dorham was totally different. He was a classicist. He studied Charlie Parker. And mastered that kind of going through and playing chord changes. He was the master of that, as far as I'm concerned."[88]

As a mentor, Dorham would focus on the essentials of that language, favoring method over mimicry. Eckert says: "He would play a lick for me and tell me to play it and, when I'm practicing, figure out how to play it in all keys. He was very methodical in his approach to playing bebop. He encouraged and respected any young player learning the techniques of the older players like that. What scales to play on what chord and things like that. But he didn't like for younger players to mimic his personal expression."[89] Eckert concludes that he cherishes his time with Dorham, stating, "I'll never forget him and I think about him all the time." Even now, he still hopes he "can get closer in my playing to what he did."[90]

Another student of Dorham's at Lenox, third stream pianist Ran Blake, described Dorham as being very encouraging about his idiosyncratic style of improvisation, in contrast to Cecil Taylor's comments (detailed later in this chapter) about Dorham's disavowal of anything avant-garde or "free." Blake discussed his time at the school in an interview with *Cadence*:

CAD: At Lenox did you find many sympathetic with your approach to music?

RB: Some people. Not Dizzy, Ray Brown did not like me. Believe it or not, Kenny Dorham, whose ensemble I worked with. Kenny encouraged me to play solo in a concert and really did an awful lot

> to lauch [*sic*] me. Also Dr. Willis Lawrence James who I studied the field cry with.[91]

This teaching job also gave Dorham the opportunity to provide his students with the kind of concrete musical instruction that had eluded him when he arrived in New York. In describing his time at the school, Dorham said: "When I came to New York as a young boy to play, those fellows wouldn't tell me anything—even Bird, with whom I worked for a year. If I'd had this kind of chance then, I'd have been poundin' at the gates to get in. I hope these kids realize what they're getting."[92]

There is optimism here, but it also tinged with sadness. Dorham wanted to give his students a level of access to the music that he himself lacked in his early career, but he couldn't help noticing that no one had offered him the same courtesy. He was left to decode the hermetic scripture of bebop on his own, likely through careful dissection of lines from records and live shows. As he says, even sharing the bandstand with Parker never fully elucidated the mysteries of Parker's genius. One thing is clear, though: Whatever rueful memories Dorham might have awakened in himself while teaching at the Lenox School, he leaned into the teaching and gave all he had, holding nothing back. And in addition to his teaching commitment at the school, Dorham played benefits for Lenox, to help keep it afloat.

As the decade drew to a close, Dorham continued to perform in public as well as in the recording studio. 1959 saw him appearing frequently in Philadelphia: at the Club Cavalier in March[93] and again that month at Venango Gardens,[94] guesting with drummer Ellis Tollin. On April 26, Dorham played with his quintet at the Village Gate, featuring Mal Waldron on piano.[95] In July, he played the Diamond Horseshoe Club with his friend Jimmy Heath[96] (who Dorham had helped secure work with the Gil Evans Band during their run at the Apollo Theater earlier that same year).[97] In between those engagements, something happened that once again illustrated both the racial dynamics of the jazz scene in America and also some of Dorham's personal frustrations. He was booked at Soulville for two shows in September along with trumpeter Donald Byrd.[98] The Philadelphia police intervened, canceled the show, and ordered the doors to the club locked as hundreds of patrons gathered outside. The show's promoters, who were leaders of the African American Modern Jazz Club, were taken to the place station, strip-searched, and examined with a magnifying glass for needle marks. Dorham was also searched for narcotics; none were found. The stated justification for the police action was that the club needed $10,000 in renovations immediately.

The *Philadelphia Tribune* account of this incident suggested it was a case of police harassment and racial profiling.[99]

Though Dorham seemed to be everywhere all at once in the 1950s, it was inevitable that some tension would arise with someone somewhere, given Dorham's own strong personality and keen intelligence. In 1958, Dorham made a single recording with free jazz pianist Cecil Taylor and saxophone titan John Coltrane.[100] Initially released as *Hard Driving Jazz*, the album was subsequently packaged under Coltrane's name, retitled as *Coltrane Time*. The session was famously fraught with tension, Dorham and Taylor apparently holding little regard for each other's respective approaches.

In A. B. Spellman's *Four Lives in the Bebop Business*, Taylor cuts right to his complaints about the session: "I wanted to use Ted Curson, who's a much more contemporary trumpet player than the trumpet player I ended up with, Kenny Dorham. Wilson said that the company had this contract with Kenny Dorham and that they wanted to use him, that a big name might sell more records. So as a leader I had to accept some musicians that I didn't want."[101]

Taylor claimed that he expected trouble from Dorham, depicting the ensuing scene with cartoonish acrimony: "He started glaring the minute I walked into the room. He made some subtle and not so subtle statements about the 'way-out music' as opposed to the 'real thing.'" According to Taylor, things deteriorated from there: "By the second tune, 'Caravan,' Kenny started attacking my playing, and this of course killed any excitement that may have been possible in the date, and the first date is the most important on a recording."[102]

Curson was apparently not the only player missing from Taylor's musician wish list. According to bassist Buell Neidlinger, Neidlinger had been Taylor's first choice for the session: "I was told by Cecil to come to the sessions and I did come with my bass and the other guy (Chuck Israels) was there and he had written a tune and like that. He hadn't the faintest idea how to play Cecil's music."[103] Neidlinger's words have the tinge of sour-grapes score settling, but it is interesting to note another source of possible contention for Taylor.

Louis Hayes (the drummer on the record) also remembers the session positively, calling it a "magnificent recording date" with "very unique personnel."[104] He notes that his acquaintance with Dorham came about early in his time in New York: "I came to New York in '56 from Detroit and had the opportunity to join the Horace Silver Quintet. So I was appearing with Horace Silver at that time. I could have only been about twenty. I was brand new in the New York scene."[105] He notes that he played with Dorham a few times in this period, but never became especially close with him: "I did some other things with Mr. Kenny Dorham. I played with him several times on different occasions. But I feel that he was one of the magnificent, outstanding players of his time, playing this art form. His sound, his feeling, and he knew this music [and] interpreted things at a very high level. So I'm glad I had the opportunity to make that history."[106] Hayes adds that they were great colleagues but not personal friends: "I didn't get to know him so much as a person. We weren't buddies hanging out, but our relationship was very comfortable. At one point in my life, I lived in Brooklyn. And he lived in Brooklyn. So I saw him on several occasions and we were around each other during that period of time, but other people were always around, so we were never one on one, just speaking about life."[107]

Regarding Dorham's renown, Hayes said that Dorham already had accumulated respect in the community: "Well, at my young age, he was already here and established himself, as a person, as a musician. I was just getting started. As an artist, he was someone that when you heard him play the trumpet, you knew it was him, if you knew about this music. You could tell that was him playing real fast because he had a distinct way of playing and a sound and a feeling, the whole thing, the whole package. When you heard him in person or on recordings, you knew who it was real quick."[108]

He concludes that the "artists on that date" all had a "distinctive sound" and that he is grateful to have had the chance to have that record be a chapter in his still-continuing story:[109] "I was just about twenty years old, and I was developing, and I'm glad I had the opportunity to be in that company. My life just continued from there, and I'm still involved in this music. I'm happy that life is going on and I'm turning to the person that I am now."[110]

Bassist Chuck Israels offers the most comprehensive account of the session, which he recounted in his 2023 memoir, *Bass Notes*. Hired by the producer of the session, Tom Wilson, Israels's college friend from Boston who would go on to produce Bob Dylan and Frank Zappa's *Mothers of Invention*, Israels was thrilled about the prospect of playing with such heavyweight musicians. He describes the date vividly:

> We got to the studio, on an upper floor of a building on Broadway near 47th Street, around the corner from the High School of Performing Arts on 46th, where I'd been a student four years earlier. Kenny was sweet-natured. Louis was quiet, and John didn't say much that I remember. The mood was friendly, and no one made anything of the fact that I was the youngest in the room and looked different.[111] We played a couple of standards that everyone knew, and it became apparent that four people were doing one thing, while Cecil was intent

> on doing something else. We went our way, he went his, and the two rhythmic conceptions never gelled.
>
> Most musicians I knew had learned to reach toward a smooth meshing of pulsation that helped to center rhythmic nuances and minor discrepancies that were inevitable in each player's personal time signature. Cecil cared not a whit for that. His playing bumped and lurched, landing askew of everyone else's placement. It was never far away, just erratic enough that you couldn't adjust to it. We could only ignore it and find a center for the four of us. That meant we didn't listen to him much. Since we had to shut that part out, Cecil's jagged melodies and purposefully clashing harmonies didn't have much effect on us either. We played the harmonies we knew and let the resulting juxtaposition create what it would. Some people find the results interesting, even intriguing. To me, it sounded like four against one. It's always boiled down to form, tempo, and unity of rhythmic accent for me. Without agreement, it just feels too separate to qualify as an ensemble experience.[112]

Israels also notes his happiness about Coltrane's and Dorham's appreciation of his tune, "Double Clutching": "Kenny and John liked it, and that felt like real acceptance."[113] Contrary to Neidlinger's comments quoted above, Israels was no stranger to abstraction in the music: He would go on to play with avant-garde giant Eric Dolphy and pianist Bill Evans at the latter's impressionist peak.

Given Israels's and Hayes's accounts, Taylor appears to be the one on the outs, as the other musicians had no trouble getting along or clicking with one another musically. Additionally, given Dorham's more lenient comments about experimental music (and his respect for Andrew Hill, a pianist within relative proximity to Taylor's style) and general descriptions of Dorham's personality, Taylor's recollection appears slanted by his intense dislike of Dorham's sensibility. Still, his comments frame the tensions inherent to the session. Taylor's jagged solos and brutalist accompaniment feel unmoored in relation to the steady time of bassist Chuck Israels and drummer Louis Hayes. Dorham seems to ignore Taylor entirely, playing solidly within his standard form, while Coltrane somewhat bridges the gaps in his own solos, moving in and out of the form in accordance with the variables around him. Israels's playing ultimately feels the most spacious, sprinkling dissonance into loose blues lines, undisturbed by the surrounding argument.

For all the music he made in this period, Dorham was attuned to the role of optics in the business. His assessment of himself always seemed to be informed by concerns that included an awareness of his abilities as an artist, pressured by an equally clear understanding of the financial, social, and critical duress he was continually under. Many of the *DownBeat* reviews of Dorham's albums in this period hovered in the three- to four-star range, meaning they were deemed good but not great, the writers often reiterating Dorham's talent as a trumpeter but noting some fault of the record (low-energy solos, a too-large ensemble, bad recording quality) that negated its positives. Revisiting Dorham's take on the scene of the aforementioned mosque concert demonstrates his eye for these things:

> Not having been a regular daily participant in musical employment, I didn't feel that I should allow myself to be put up for appraisal under these conditions—people never forget these occasions.
>
> I could see it there in the headlines of the big music magazine. Something like: "Super Star Fades" or "Out of Orbit," with the first few lines of the review probably reading something like: "Once out of orbit, a falling star becomes a flying saucer which is earthbound."[114]

Dorham's prescient critique of music magazine purple prose aside, the fear he describes was acutely real. Keenly aware of the unreliable nature of popularity, he was afraid of historical erasure. However, at the concert at the Syrian mosque, his story's end was a happy one. He decided to play, regardless of the spectators: "I did go out there after all, and gave them the old one, two, and out, receiving some of the most exhilarating, enthusiastic applause of the afternoon."[115]

Sonny Rollins emphasized that Dorham wasn't just well-liked, but eminently respected in the jazz community as something of an elder, even by people who might have appeared to be his contemporaries:

> Musically we were close. He would understand what I did and I would understand what he did. It's hard for me to put myself in his category. Although we were together and playing a lot together, I always felt that I was learning from him. People see a record that we made together and all that, and it's hard for them to realize it was any other kind of relationship. It's a little bit different than one would imagine. You see a record with he and I together and all this stuff, but you know, I actually looked up to Kenny's musicality. More than it would seem, you'd think we were of equal status. Well, in some ways, but to me he was somebody [where] I looked up to him musically.[116]

Dorham may not have seen himself in this light, but others certainly could not have failed to notice. Dorham's acclaim within the musicians' inner circle is perhaps put best in Art Blakey's introduction of him on the Jazz Messengers live record: "And on the trumpet we have a perennial favorite. He was with the prophet of modern jazz, Charlie Parker, he is our arranger, now, and our trumpeter. The uncrowned king, ladies and gentleman, Kenny Dorham."[117]

CHAPTER 7

CALIFORNIA

Kenny Dorham's family dispersed in the 1940s, giving life to Langston Hughes's poem about escaping the Jim Crow South, "One-Way Ticket":

> I pick up my life and take it away
> On a one-way ticket—
> Gone up North,
> Gone out West,
> Gone![1]

After spending a few years in Austin, Dorham's parents traveled west with Joel and Cloteal by train in 1944 to California, where McKinley Sr. had a lead on work from a friend in Oakland—one of the destination cities named in Hughes's poem. McKinley Sr. secured a carpenter position at the newly opened Naval Supply Depot on the waterfront (later renamed the Naval Supply Center).[2] Kenny did not go with them: He had already enrolled at Wiley College in Marshall, Texas, and then completed a year of military service. Kenny would remain closely connected to his family throughout his life, visiting them in California and Texas when his touring schedule provided the opportunity. The arc of his life touched theirs at multiple points, from the musical pursuits he shared with his parents and siblings to the same attraction Joel and Eva Lois felt toward education as Kenny did. Perhaps most importantly, the reverberation of events in African American history from mid-century on would influence his family just as they did Dorham himself, even when those reverberations made themselves felt in different corners of the country. As shared touchstones, they provide a compelling reason to recount the journeys and key moments in the Dorham family as we reconstruct Kenny Dorham's life and times.

By the time the Dorham family reached California, though, Kenny Dorham was pursuing his musical ambitions through connections made at Wiley. He had acquired impeccable big band credentials by his early twenties, already having played in bands led by Lionel Hampton, Illinois Jacquet, and Dizzy Gillespie. But he was a frequent visitor at his parents' Oakland home as he toured the West Coast with various bands. His brother Joel remembered Dorham bringing famous guests to the house, like Lionel Hampton and Miles Davis, though at eight or ten years old Joel was too young to know that he was among jazz royalty.[3] He would come to that realization later, after his own musical career as a percussionist had begun, by which time many of those jazz greats had become his friends as well. Joel remembered one occasion in 1950 when Kenny was playing in San Francisco and drove with teenage Joel to the club. But he wouldn't let Joel follow him inside; he had his younger brother stay in the car. Miles Davis came outside, Joel recalled, and greeted him enthusiastically as "Little K. D." Miles Davis was not known to the general public as a warm or friendly person, but that was only Miles's public side, Joel said. To those close to him, he was a very different person. They met several times over the years and Davis was always ready with a kind word, including the sad occasion when Joel called to tell him that Kenny had passed. "I guess I'll see him when I get there," Miles replied, grief-stricken, as Joel remembered.[4]

Joel Dorham's eldest sister, Eva Lois, or "Sister Lois," as Joel and Kenny called her, did not move with the family to California either. She had married James Milford McIlveen years before and remained in Freestone County.[5] A lifelong scholar and educator, Eva Lois took a master's degree at Texas Southern, writing her thesis on the poetry of John Milton.[6] Her academic prose is elegantly crafted and impeccably precise, and her critique of gender in *Paradise Lost* is prescient. Eva Lois taught in several Fairfield schools: the Dogan School (a small, formerly segregated school for Black students), as well as Lincoln High School, and later at the integrated Fairfield High School. She was so revered as a teacher, her daughter Dr. Carolyn Yarbro Smith remembered, that school administrators asked specifically for her to join their faculty.[7] Kenny Dorham's uncle on his mother's side was principal of Lincoln High for many years. Kenny would write later on that his mother's family was "not musical, but scholarly."[8] Eva Lois, in fact, was musical *and* scholarly, as she played piano and sang professionally for radio commercials.[9] In any case, Eva Lois's career path went through education and through

Freestone County, where she would remain until her death in 1986, at the age of seventy.[10]

Eva Lois and James Milford McIlveen lived in Fairfield, in town rather than in the country. They raised two children there, James and Carolyn. Eva Lois's aunt, uncle, and cousins on the Manning side lived outside of town. "It was a joy for us to go into the country, so much fun," Carolyn remembers. Her mother's uncle Alfred Manning was a warm man who loved to joke and "talk nonsense." He wanted a baseball team, he used to say, so he had a lot of children. Even though Fairfield was (and is) a small town, it has a main street, businesses, parks, and a highway passing through. The space, the silence, the birds and animals, and the rhythms of rural life in outlying areas such as the Manning land offered a marked contrast with the town environment. Carolyn enjoyed that different world and especially looked forward to seeing her uncle's large family. They were close enough to Fairfield to visit frequently, and Eva Lois and her husband took the children there often. On at least one occasion there was a big family reunion where widely dispersed units of the Dorhams and Mannings from all over came back to the countryside where the family's Texas history had begun.[11]

Eva Lois McIlveen had a powerful impact on Freestone County students through her dual commitments to music and education. She served as choir instructor at Fairfield High School, where she mentored many young people over the years, including multi-instrumentalist gospel musician Bobby Cooper.[12] Eva Lois also taught English. In the classroom she was exacting and held her students to very high standards. Don Awalt, whom Eva Lois taught in the 1970s, remembers that "whatever class she was teaching, you always got a lesson in grammar."[13] When Texas schools were ordered to desegregate during the 1960s and 1970s following the *Brown v. Board of Education* ruling, Eva Lois was in the forefront of the efforts to overcome segregation in Freestone County, guiding Black and white students through the process. The Fairfield High class of 1977 was the first cohort to go through all twelve grades together. When they graduated in 1977, Eva Lois chose "You'll Never Walk Alone" as the graduation song for that momentous ceremony. Her presence in the community and the guiding hand she offered to students in and outside of the classroom are remembered fondly by Fairfield residents today.[14]

Things in the McIlveen household revolved around education. Children Carolyn and James used their college educations to forge different career paths, Carolyn as an educator and James as an entrepreneur working in restaurant management. After a tour in Vietnam, James traveled widely using a private plane, running and developing his businesses.[15] Dr. Carolyn Yarbro Smith studied and then taught at Texas Southern University in Houston and settled in that city. The McIlveens' Fairfield next-door neighbors growing up, close enough to be considered family, were a couple without children, a school principal in a nearby district and his wife who also taught there. Carolyn remembered spending a lot time with the neighbors, who doted on her and her brother James. The families were so close, in fact, that Carolyn was invited in 1955 to drive with her neighbors from Fairfield to New York to see the World Series between the Brooklyn Dodgers and the New York Yankees. It was a momentous series that the Dodgers eventually won. Jackie Robinson had integrated Major League Baseball eight years earlier, and by 1955 the team had a number of talented Black players in addition to Robinson: pitcher Don Newcombe, catcher Roy Campanella, infielder Jim Gilliam, and outfielder Sandy Amoros. Carolyn was less interested in baseball and much more keen to spend time with her cousins, Kenny and Rubina's children. The visit stood out in her mind nearly seventy years later.

This early version of a subway series brought the Dorhams' lives together once again at an important historical juncture. Brooklyn was home to Kenny Dorham and his family at that time, and Carolyn remembered riding bicycles around their President Street neighborhood with the cousins. One day she rode to the corner store at the same time Kenny happened to be passing by. As she parked her bike, Uncle Mac Junior, as Carolyn called Kenny, said, "Oh, baby, you can't go in there." Puzzled, Carolyn asked her uncle why not. "Because that bike won't be here when you come out," Dorham replied matter of factly. It was a long way from Fairfield.[16]

OAKLAND

In Oakland, Kenny Dorham's parents settled first in an apartment near the police station and then in a building on Clay Street, not far from the waterfront and Jack London Square, a future performance venue for Joel and his Latin Jazz Octet. After about a decade in Oakland, McKinley Sr. and Minnie would move back to the east side of Austin, to the East Twelfth Street house, where they would spend the rest of their lives. Joel married, bought a house in Berkeley, and stayed in the Bay Area to raise a family.[17]

Joel got most of his schooling in Oakland. He attended Lincoln Elementary, Westlake Junior High, Oakland Technical High School, and then Merritt College. In school and in the neighborhood, he met and became friends with a remarkable number of people who would go on to national and international prominence in the coming years. At Oakland Tech, Joel met Curt Flood, the star center fielder who in 1970 challenged Major League

Baseball's labor policies. Baseball Hall of Fame inductee Frank Robinson, who would become the first African American manager in the major leagues, and all-star outfielder Vada Pinson were also among Joel's friends growing up. He knew Basketball Hall of Famer Bill Russell, too, though not as well as the others.[18]

Oakland and Berkeley in the 1960s were the scenes of various kinds of ferment and change. The Free Speech Movement on the university campus, the birth of the Black Panthers, and civil rights and antiwar activism were all happening there. Joel Dorham's link to those events was his close friendships with Bobby Seale and Huey Newton. In fact, Newton's sister babysat Joel when he was younger. Both of their families lived in the same Clay Street building, and it was there that Joel met Huey and his older brother, Melvin. Like the Dorhams, the Floods, Robinsons, and Seales came to Oakland from Texas; Russell's and Newton's families came there from Louisiana, and Pinson's from Tennessee. Work opportunities led them north and west and allowed them to settle in states where Jim Crow practices were less prevalent, though they experienced bias in those places as well, to be sure. Joel's friends Huey Newton and Bobby Seale founded the Black Panther party in 1966 while they were students at Merritt College in Oakland, where Joel also studied. Joel Dorham remained friends with Bobby Seale and Huey Newton from the 1940s on, and his friend Ron Dellums spoke in support of the Panthers and appeared at events with them. Joel did not join the Panthers or participate in their activities, but maintained close ties with Bobby Seale throughout his life and with Huey Newton until Newton's death in 1989. In 1967 Newton was incarcerated and then tried for homicide in the death of a police officer, but after his conviction was overturned on appeal, he was freed in 1970. Newton's family asked Joel Dorham, his longtime friend, to accompany Newton home from prison. In a famous photograph, Joel can be seen escorting Newton from the courthouse to a waiting car, surrounded by a crowd of thousands of supporters.[19]

Starting in his preteen years, Joel forged a close, lifetime friendship with future Congressmember Ron Dellums, who served thirteen terms in the US House of Representatives and subsequently was elected mayor of Oakland. Dellums even sought to have Dorham join his congressional staff, but Dorham declined the offer.[20] Still, Joel recruited his friend Herbie Hancock to play at several of Dellums's benefits. Like Dellums, Joel attended junior college in Oakland (Oakland City College, connected organizationally to Merritt College). In his autobiography, Dellums recounts how Joel saved his life when they were younger by defending him against a group of armed assailants in their Oakland neighborhood.[21] Dellums of course had a profound impact on US political history himself during his career in public service. Among many important triumphs, he secured passage, over President Reagan's veto, of the anti-apartheid law that would eventually help to end that system in South Africa. A principled, thoughtful, and avowedly socialist member of Congress, Dellums earned respect from members of both parties in government for his stances and manner of advocacy in such controversial matters as the MX Missile system.

Joel Dorham and Ron Dellums remained close over the years, and in 1988 Dellums read into the Congressional Record a tribute to Joel, a commemoration of the twenty-fifth anniversary of Joel Dorham's Latin Jazz Octet. "Mr. Dorham's band," Dellums said, "plays music which reflects the ethnic richness and variety of American culture through its fusion of Afro American and Latin sounds, figures and rhythms. Joel Dorham, a friend of this member for some 40 years, has carved a historic place for himself in America's cultural history not only as a musicologist, but as one who has been an outspoken advocate of jazz, and one who has campaigned indefatigability and successfully for the inclusion of this significant cultural form in the media of America."[22] When Dellums died in 2018, his friends organized a tribute to him, which featured a live performance by Stevie Wonder.[23]

Joel had discovered the timbales in the early 1960s and formed his Latin Jazz Octet in 1963.[24] For more than fifty years, the group appeared regularly in Bay Area venues, including the Back Room in Berkeley, Armando's in Martinez, and Jack London Square in Oakland. Only the lockdown necessitated by the COVID-19 pandemic ended their remarkably long run. Joel Dorham's Latin Jazz Octet played a diverse repertoire of compositions, from Stevie Wonder to Latin jazz classics, and of course they regularly featured arrangements of Kenny Dorham's music. Although they had on their books a lush, homegrown arrangement of Kenny's famous "Blue Bossa," they concentrated on less well-known Dorham compositions, such as the lovely "La Mesha," written for Kenny's youngest daughter. Joel participated in the Kenny Dorham Project as well, a group that was founded by his arranger, trombonist Jules Rowell, and that is dedicated solely to Kenny Dorham's compositions. The Latin Jazz Octet has garnered a loyal and passionate following over the years.[25]

Joel's musical notoriety surprised even him at times. Years ago, sitting in the audience at Yoshi's, an Oakland jazz club, Joel listened to the great *timbalero* Tito Puente chatting with the crowd about someone he'd like to invite onstage. This musician, Puente said, had a brother who was also a famous jazz musician. "I used to play pool with his brother and Redd Foxx," he continued. "Let's get him up here." Puente called "Oye Como Va" as Joel approached the stage, and a minute later Joel was standing next to Puente in front of a second set of timbales. Joel played well and the audience loved it.[26]

Oakland, sometimes known as the "Harlem of the West," has long been a music hotbed, where important developments in jazz, blues, funk, and R&B have taken place. Slim Jenkins' Club and other Oakland venues hosted major artists through most of the century, and in 2011 the city unveiled a Walk of Fame with stars for great musicians from around the country who had performed there, like Eartha Kitt, Billie Holliday, Dinah Washington, and Aretha Franklin. The Walk of Fame also honors Oakland musicians who have left their mark on music history. There are stars for Earl Hines, John Lee Hooker, Sheila and Pete Escovedo, Sly Stone, David Murray, Carla Bley, the Pointer Sisters—and Joel Dorham.[27]

JOEL DORHAM'S JAZZ ACTIVISM

In contrast to Seale and Newton, Joel Dorham's activism developed around music. In the late 1960s, he became frustrated when his brother was overlooked by critics and concert promoters. When Kenny was not chosen to participate in a trumpet summit at the 1965 Monterey Jazz Festival at which Miles Davis, Dizzy Gillespie, and Clark Terry were booked, Joel contacted the organizers to complain about the snub. Kenny told Joel not to worry about it, but Joel persisted. His loyalty to his brother was strong, and he continued to advocate for greater recognition for Kenny.[28]

After Kenny Dorham's death in December 1972 and the lack of coverage in the press of his life and work, Joel kept fighting to publicize and protect his brother's artistic legacy. By that time, Joel was also developing a musical reputation of his own as a *timbalero.* He was primarily self-taught, having studied *timbaleros* he admired, but he also received guidance from a man named James Levi. Levi showed him some rudimentary exercises and gave him a set of timbales. Joel sat in with Latin vibraphonist and percussionist Cal Tjader and others, and rapidly absorbed musical knowledge and technical command in the Latin jazz genre. After all, he'd been around music all his life, and his parents, sister, and brother were all gifted musically. So it is no surprise that he learned his instrument in far less time than it normally takes and that he was ready to play in public almost immediately. At the same time, he helped Tjader to secure performance opportunities at colleges and universities. Soon Joel had assembled an Afro-Latin eight-piece band under his own name that played to sold-out venues in the Bay Area. On the occasion of their last appearance at The Back Room in Berkeley, the group was billed as "a pivotal force in Latin Jazz."[29] That the Octet has remained intact, with an enthusiastic following, for a half century is remarkable enough; incredibly, Joel kept the band together while working full-time in marketing until his retirement a decade ago. For him, music was a hobby—"like golf," he said.[30] He declined offers to record because he was not interested in traveling to promote new recordings. So he played jazz for the love of it.

Joel's passion for the music, his affection and respect for his brother, and his own musical experiences generated in him a sense of mission to secure greater media attention and support for jazz. What started as advocacy on his brother's behalf eventually grew into a campaign to elevate the music itself. The motivating premise was clear: Here was America's only original art form, its greatest gift to the world, and yet, as Congressmember William Clay put it, "On no commercial network can one find a television series devoted either wholly or primarily to jazz."[31] Joel Dorham's first step in addressing that neglect had been to contact television networks, newspapers, and prominent newscasters, making a case for more jazz programming. He also wrote the Federal Communications Commission.[32] But initial responses were disheartening, and something of a runaround. As Joel put it, "The networks tell you, 'If you don't like what we're doing, file a complaint with the FCC.' The FCC tells you it can't regulate program content, it only grants licenses, and you have to take your complaints to the networks."[33]

Joel was too determined to leave matters there. Next, he contacted the Congressional Black Caucus, joined by musicians Nancy Wilson, Freddie Hubbard, Jackie McLean, and John Handy, and the CBC forwarded their letter once again to the networks. This time, network representatives pointed to "ethnic" programming already on the air, equating jazz content with *any* material featuring or referring to racial or ethnic minorities. At the same time, they questioned the commercial viability of jazz-themed broadcasts, along with "ballet, opera, and even certain styles of rock music."[34] One bright spot was the chartering of a new show called *Jazz Alive*, to be aired on National Public Radio, with an inaugural episode featuring Ella Fitzgerald and Stevie Wonder.[35]

This was 1977. Joel had found an ally in the Honorable William Clay of Missouri, co-chair of the Congressional Black Caucus Subcommittee on Communications within the House Standing Committee on Energy and Commerce. Joel would work with Congressmember Clay for over a decade, and in 1988 Clay would once again read into the Congressional Record a communication from Joel Dorham to network executives regarding jazz programming.[36] 1988 was an auspicious time for jazz in the media. For one thing, as Joel Dorham noted, the film *'Round Midnight*, starring saxophone great Dexter Gordon, had been released two years earlier to critical and public acclaim. The film closes, incidentally, with a performance of Kenny Dorham's beautiful ballad "Fair Weather" by fellow trumpeter and vocalist Chet Baker. A week after Clay's remarks in the Congressional Record, a major studio film about Charlie Parker (*Bird*, directed by Clint Eastwood) was also set to be released. Those well-received works would bear out the accuracy of Joel Dorham's challenge to the networks: "Briefly, you stated that there were no audience for jazz. That was not true then and it is not true now."[37] Additionally, the previous year (1987), Congressmember John Conyers had introduced a resolution (which eventually passed) on John Coltrane's birthday, to recognize jazz as a "national treasure." Decades later, in 2014, Conyers followed up that earlier effort by introducing H.R. 4280, the National Jazz Preservation, Education, and Promulgation Act of 2014. Among other provisions, H.R. 4280 called for the preservation of jazz artifacts in the Smithsonian Institution. Meanwhile, Joel's tireless efforts led to a Pulitzer Prize nomination by California Secretary of State March Fong Eu. Joel was neither the first nor the only musician to advocate for greater public support for jazz; many others have done so. But what is notable about his efforts is that he sustained them over many years while working full-time outside of music, and that he was motivated by his brother Kenny's experience as a musician who gave so much to jazz and yet struggled to make a living.

Looking back over the nearly fifty years since Joel's 1970s efforts at jazz advocacy, it is easy to point to areas of progress. A number of commercially successful films about jazz were made after *Bird* and *'Round Midnight*, including *Sweet and Lowdown*, *The Cotton Club*, *Kansas City*, *The Mambo Kings*, *For Love or Country: The Arturo Sandoval Story*, *Miles Ahead*, *Mo' Better Blues*, *Let's Get Lost*, *Born to Be Blue*, *The United States vs. Billie Holiday*, *Whiplash*, and *Ma Rainey's Black Bottom*, among others. Excellent documentaries about Miles Davis, John Coltrane, Lee Morgan, Nina Simone, and other artists, as well as Ken Burns's *Jazz* series, are available to the public. Jazz instruction at colleges, universities, and conservatories, including through extension programs that are open to the public, draws in new listeners and musicians, who in turn generate a greater demand for jazz coverage in the media. Late-night talk shows give prominent roles to bandleaders who perform a jazz repertoire, including Branford Marsalis, Jon Batiste, and Kevin Eubanks.[38] Dizzy Gillespie, Norah Jones, Wynton Marsalis, Herbie Hancock, and others have appeared on the children's show *Sesame Street*, imparting jazz education to primary-school-age children. College and public radio stations feature jazz programming, and some stations, like WBGO FM in Newark, New Jersey, and KCSM in San Mateo, California, play only jazz.

All of these developments are encouraging. The world looks different because of initiatives by Joel Dorham and many others to educate the public and to press for coverage. Efforts build on each other. Jazz education in primary and secondary schools and children's concerts generate interest and help to change what the public demands and supports. Kenny Dorham once said that older musicians did not share their knowledge and experience with him; he had to figure all of it out for himself, even when learning on the job with Charlie Parker.[39] Today, there are many opportunities to learn about jazz as a musician or as an appreciative listener, from summer jazz institutes to YouTube instructional and historical videos. Technology has generated some of this expansion of opportunities, as it is easier now to transcribe and post a famous solo or to deliver a lecture to thousands of people via podcast.

In an economic system of private enterprise, though, profitability drives decisions about what products and services to offer, and firms search perpetually for new markets. As a result, the decisions about where to allocate private, commercial support for music endeavors is less about the quality of the music and more about where investors can make money. This calculus was tacitly acknowledged in network replies to Joel Dorham's missives in the 1970s and 1980s. Tellingly, the one counterpoint back then to the corporate media's reluctance to support jazz programming were the incipient jazz features on publicly owned and funded NPR. And so the predicament for artists (not only jazz artists, but many others as well) has been and continues to be to prove commercial viability or else be forced to rely on nonprofit or government support. Those supports do exist, of course, to a significantly greater extent than they did in the 1970s. Institutions like the Lincoln Center Jazz Orchestra endure and thrive on charitable support. And major philanthropic entities such as the Doris Duke Charitable Foundation have prioritized grants for jazz education and performance. But the landscape is complex. For example, when music streaming began in the early 2000s, jazz artists suddenly found it much more difficult to make money by releasing albums. Some musicians resorted to selling albums themselves without the marketing assistance of major record labels, and their sales dropped to the point of unprofitability. To make a living, it became necessary for them to travel constantly to play clubs and festivals. And to string together enough of those opportunities, one had to become and remain well-known and in demand among the many jazz bands and individual artists out there. Meanwhile, pop music has continued to draw more media attention and music sales than jazz. In short, some of the same economic challenges that musicians like Kenny Dorham faced in the past remain for jazz musicians today, even though so many things have changed.

Near the end of Kenny Dorham's life, his own observations about the economics of jazz dovetailed with Joel's early comments to government bodies. As noted above, Joel complained that Kenny was snubbed from the star billing at festivals that other trumpeters received. Kenny himself mentioned in a 1962 interview that he left the music scene for a time and took the job at Manny's Music Store because he was not getting enough work as a musician.[40] Later, in an interview with onetime bandmate Arthur Taylor, Kenny elaborated on that criticism:

> If you're not managed by someone who is on the inside, you can float around out here for a lifetime, and nothing ever happens. You see people come up who are less qualified, and everything is all rosy for them. Musicians will probably have to be more political in the future. They will certainly have to be businessmen, because they mustn't leave it up to the guy in the booking agency. He's their real enemy. . . . Instead of the booking agent working for the musician, the musician works for the booking agent. That's all wrong! The musician now has to call the booking agent to find out when he can work. In the meantime the booking agent is double dealing, taking money under the table and on top of the table and looking out for his own interest, not the musician's. That's political![41]

One could ask whether Dorham's handling of the business end of his career had anything to do with his predicament. He had some eighty copyrighted compositions registered to him (not counting the arrangements he wrote for others), but it was more difficult to secure performance, recording, and broadcast royalties without forming one's own publishing company.[42] Dorham initially had one, but he later received an advance on it and sold it.[43] Musical colleagues noted, too, that Kenny often paid too little attention to getting proper remuneration for his creative work, for example when he allowed his most famous composition, "Blue Bossa," to be released on an album where he was only a sideman for saxophonist Joe Henderson, rather than debuting it on an album under his own name.

Whether or not he was sufficiently business-minded, though, Kenny Dorham certainly had a clear view of the ways in which power in the larger society impacted the financial interests of jazz musicians: "Maybe one can't afford to be all musical today, because politics have a lot to do with the economic situation musicians find themselves in. . . . Musicians usually never benefit from anything. They can't borrow money or get any kind of economic satisfaction. Recently there have been some endowment grants and humanities, and a few musicians have gotten a little money. The amount of money you get is kind of insulting."[44] Kenny was blunt about the exploitation he had seen and lived through. At that time, suffering from a debilitating kidney illness he lacked the funds to treat properly, Kenny was rightfully frustrated. "Politics could be useful in music," he told Taylor.[45]

Guthrie Ramsey corroborates the essential (and often detrimental) role that ownership of the rights played in jazz for all musicians, even major stars:

> Performers may have ruled the landscape in some ways, but in others they did not. [Dizzy] Gillespie's attitude toward the financial end of bebop composition counters the prevailing view that bebop musicians cared little about commercial rewards: "All the big money," he writes, "went to the guys who owned the music, not to the guys who played it. . . . Our protests against being cheated and ripped off never meant we stood against making money." On the contrary, Gillespie claims that "being politically inclined against commercialism or trying to take over anything never figured too prominently with me." It's worth mentioning here that owning the rights to bebop compositions was a priority to record company owners such as Henry Lubinsky of the Savoy label.[46]

Quoted in the same section of Ramsey's book, Max Roach puts a finer point on this idea: "The only reason that the music of the Gershwins and all these people lived during that period was because all the black people, the Billie Holidays, Ella Fitzgeralds, Dizzy Gillespies, Charlie Parkers, the Monks, the Coleman Hawkinses projected this music, used this music and kept it alive."[47] Where other musicians had the savvy (and sometimes cutthroat) instinct for quickly copyrighting as much of their music as possible, Dorham was known to give away compositions and arrangements to his friends. While money was being made from his own records and the records where he had appeared as a sideman, he was seeing very few dividends—a fact that demonstrably did not escape his notice.

Kenny Dorham's keen understanding of power and privilege in the music business, drawn from bitter personal experience, could be described in the language of political theory as a wider understanding of what constitutes the political. Dorham rightly saw that power is in play all throughout modern society, not just in the workings of government. A wider notion of the political would include every setting, every human relationship where access to resources was at issue, where life chances could be affected, where competition occurred. Dorham's own life furnished countless examples of the ways that power operates in a racialized society that ostensibly held opportunity for all, but in fact reinforced long-entrenched inequalities and rewarded already powerful individuals and groups by preserving and strengthening their positions.

Dorham's comments in his interview with Arthur Taylor address the politics of race as well as economic exploitation.[48] It is not that he is saying something unknown; rather, he is stating things that often go unacknowledged. One of Taylor's goals in interviewing Dorham and other jazz musicians was to get them to speak freely and openly about the complexities, paradoxes, and difficulties they faced while living their pathbreaking lives in music. Nobody could tell this tale better than Kenny Dorham.

Joel Dorham's activism intensified after his brother's passing, but fortunately his music career began while Kenny was still alive, so that his brother got the chance to hear him. He recalls Kenny paying him a visit in Oakland in the late 1960s on the way back from a trip to Mexico. Joel was anxious for his brother to hear his developing percussion style. "Joel, your drumming is good, but your rap is better," Kenny teased him.[49] He must have been pleased to see the life Joel had built for himself in California. Oakland was Joel's home base for everything in his life; he rarely had the need or inclination to leave. Kenny, by contrast, was traveling constantly, both within and outside the United States. On that visit to Oakland, word spread that he was in town, and a groundswell of support developed for him to play at one of the area clubs. Joel recalls arranging a set of dates at a club on San Francisco's Divisadero Street. Reluctant at first to perform, Kenny eventually agreed and then quickly recruited California contacts, including bassist Leroy Vinnegar, and put together a group that played sold-out shows for the weekend.[50]

For much of Joel's adult life, he worked to preserve his brother's legacy in two ways: through music and through activism. In 2018, Joel sat for an interview with KCSM, the Bay Area jazz station, and reminisced about his brother's life and work, as well as his own. The interview featured a "desert island" selection of his favorite Kenny Dorham recordings, and a cut of Joel's own band playing "Blue Bossa." In a sense, the KCSM segment brings things full circle, with Joel recapping his message via a jazz station that works to curate and preserve the music through dedicated and knowledgeable radio personalities, including Clifford Brown Jr., the son of Dorham's friend and fellow trumpeter, now a communications specialist and jazz educator at the station who has taken up Joel's challenge to ensure that the art form receives the attention, support, and appreciation it is due.

The Henry and Patsy Manning land near Butler, Texas. Photo by Robert Pallitto.

Eva "Minnie" Dorham. Courtesy of Dana Dorham and Michele Barrows Dorham.

McKinley Howard Dorham Sr. Courtesy of Dana Dorham and Michele Barrows Dorham.

Post Oak, Texas, where Kenny Dorham was born. Photo by Robert Pallitto

Ward Prairie, where Dorham worked as a cowboy. Photo by Robert Pallitto.

Kenny Dorham at Wiley College. Courtesy of Texas Music Museum.

Dorham playing at the Metropole Hotel, Toronto. Photo by AlWebster007. CC BY 2.0.

Dorham with Max Roach and Sonny Rollins at the University of Wisconsin-Milwaukee, 1957. Wisconsin Historical Society, WHI-142270.

Ad for Gretsch instruments featuring Dorham. Public domain, via Wikimedia Commons.

The Dorhams' daughters (Keturah, Leslie, Evette, LeJuine, LaMesha). Courtesy of Keturah Dorham Holley.

The Dorham home at 1499 President Street, Brooklyn, today. Photo by Robert Pallitto.

Dorham in a recording studio, 1970. Michael Ochs Archive via Getty Images.

Keturah Dorham Holley, Rubina Dorham Robinson, and Evette Dorham (l to r) at the Freestone County Historical Museum plaque dedication event, 2012. Courtesy of Freestone County Times.

Joel Dorham. Courtesy of Dana Dorham and Michele Barrows Dorham.

Joel Dorham outside a Bay Area club. Courtesy of Dana Dorham and Michele Barrows Dorham.

CHAPTER 8

ONE MORE TIME

The 1960s were a complicated time for Kenny Dorham. He made a number of watershed albums as both a leader and a sideman, firmly cementing his place in the legacy of Blue Note records and the hard bop and post-bop eras. Still, the later years would prove increasingly difficult both personally and financially. After 1964, Dorham's appearances on stage and in the studio declined. That year would prove to be both a high-water mark and a falling-off point. As a leader, some of Dorham's most well-known songwriting happened in this period. Simultaneously, his playing shifted, becoming more varied as he seemed unafraid to push into new territory.

Some of the recollections about Dorham from this period—the end of the 1950s and beginning of the 1960s—come from Dorham's friend Bernard Drayton, who knew Dorham in Brooklyn and was just out of high school at that time. Drayton would go on to become a pioneer in sound engineering, music production, and advertising at a time when only a few advertising firms focused on African American audiences. Drayton considered Dorham a mentor and close friend. Even though Drayton came from a musical family—his father, Charlie Drayton, was a bassist who played with Billie Holiday and Louis Armstrong, and Bernard's son Charley is now Bob Dylan's drummer—his own career arc moved him away from music performance and into production. But with Dorham, Drayton would talk, more often than not, about topics outside of music, from people they knew in common to current events. And of course, fashion. Drayton recalls seeing a sharp-looking pair of eyeglasses at a high-fashion shop on Nostrand Avenue and, knowing Dorham would spot them, Drayton bought them himself before Dorham could get there.[1] He would seek out Dorham for conversation and guidance, and they sat on the front steps of the President Street house, with

Dorham frequently appearing in his bathrobe. Always, though, Drayton would come away from those conversations with something "beyond what you went there for."[2] Seeing his mentor on the street was always exciting, and Dorham would show up in all kinds of places, even working the counter at their friend Larry's grocery store at Utica and Pacific streets. As Drayton's career progressed, he approached Dorham about a recording project featuring the trumpeter's band live at a local club, Blue Morocco. Dorham agreed, Drayton recorded the shows, and they planned to market the project. "Maybe Blue Note will take it. I'll call Alfred [Lion] and find out," Dorham promised.[3] While the recording was not issued back then, it was scheduled for release on Resonance Records early in 2025, under Dorham's name and with the title *Blue Bossa in the Bronx: Live from the Blue Morocco*. It took more than sixty years, but people will finally be able to hear the Blue Morocco performance (described in greater detail below in chapter 9). Drayton views the record as a tribute to his friend, a "brother worthy of much praise."[4]

Dorham recorded a great deal in the early 1960s. On February 11 and 12, 1960, he recorded his album *Jazz Contemporary* for the Time label. His band included baritone saxophonist Charles Davis, pianist Steve Kuhn, bassists Butch Warren and Jimmy Garrison, and drummer Buddy Enlow.[5] The album is not Dorham's most spirited outing, but his soft touch on "Monk's Mood" and "Tonica" is remarkable, as is the haunting sentiment he is able to convey with his articulations of the melodies and his choices in spacing and accents. Likewise, it is a treat to hear him on record with Davis, his friend and longtime bandmate, familiarity evident in their harmonizing and Davis's countermelodies, and Garrison's firmly rooted basslines here preview the fulcrum he would provide for the vaunted John Coltrane Quartet. The date is also notable for being Kuhn's recording debut.

In an interview with *Cadence*, Kuhn described first meeting Dorham at Lenox and then going on to working with him regularly: "I was chosen and got this scholarship for three weeks in Lenox, Massachusetts (summer 1959). So during this three weeks I got to meet a lot of well-known people in Jazz, the MJQ, Kenny Dorham, Gunther Schuller. Two weeks after I got to New York, Kenny Dorham was looking for a pianist and I started to work with him in his quintet."[6] Kuhn's subsequent comments were bracingly honest, but offer a rounded picture of Dorham as a person and boss:

CAD: Then you did the *Jazz Contemporary* date on Time with Kenny Dorham.

S.K.: He was a sweet man, great player, very lyrical, warm, who cared nothing about the business and therefore really didn't get the recognition. He was somewhat bitter about Miles' success and Dizzy, he felt he belonged up there. Verbally he used to say this. He loved to play and he loved women and he got into trouble lots of time with women. At one point I was sort of like the treasurer of the band, he used to call me "Blumberg" because I was Jewish and the only White guy in the band. He'd give me the money and say "You take care of it."

CAD: Make it grow.

S.K.: (laughter) . . . he was a sweet man, especially his ballad playing. Many nights he'd be playing and tears would come to my eyes. And he really knew what he wanted (musically) and he could play the keyboard quite well.[7]

While it is uncomfortable and disappointing to imagine these scenes and comments from Dorham, one can easily see that Kuhn's words also reiterate what Dorham's other bandmates said about him: He was a generous boss, an incredible musician, and an essentially kind person frustrated with the fact that recognition was eluding him, even at the height of his career.

On January 15, 1961, Dorham recorded his most personal album, *Whistle Stop*. It encapsulated vivid impressions of his childhood and offered a portrait of a Texas jazz pioneer who synthesized themes and sounds of country life with the hip sophistication of modern jazz. By most measures, the album should be in the canonical list of Blue Note releases. It features rhythm section dynamos Philly Joe Jones and Paul Chambers, as well as label stalwarts Hank Mobley and Kenny Drew. The tunes sparkle, situated firmly in the hard bop mode, each solo crackling with ensemble electricity and the strong push of a propulsive rhythm section. Jones's crisp snare accents practically drive the entire band. The tunes serve as pristine examples of the kind of hard-swinging material that the label built its image around. "Philly Twist" is a simple blues head, with carefully placed melody stops. "Buffalo" is another blues tune that simmers in a heavy shuffle as the soloists turn riffs. "Sunset" sounds like material from *Una Mas* or *Afro-Cuban*, both in its elegant Latin melody and steady transitions in and out of straight eighth notes back into swing. It also features Dorham playing with a mute, a somewhat rare occurrence. "Whistle Stop" and "Windmill" are, as their titles imply, burners that feature Dorham, Mobley, and Drew navigating the changes with playful ease. The panoramic "Sunrise in Mexico" relies on precise hits and interwoven bass and piano patterns. Dorham's solo is brash, building on repetitions of the melody, on bends, and on stung staccato notes. Jones is a standout here as well, for his careful use of dramatic dynamics. The morbidly named

"Dorham's Epitaph" is a stunning ballad, making surprising leaps and demonstrating Dorham's high register capabilities. Each song reveals the level of detail Dorham put into his compositions. As many musicians can attest, the songs on *Whistle Stop* cannot simply be played off of lead sheets and out of fake books. Each song features its own unique elements, like band accents, unison lines, unusual section lengths that deviate from typical four-bar structures, and shifts in feel.

Notwithstanding the stellar musical performances on this record, *Whistle Stop* is also notable for its evocation of Dorham's childhood. Almost all of the songs make some reference to elements of his early life in the Southwest. The listener finds him trying to translate these images into music, evoking shifting moods of the desert and the plains. In Dorham's own view, "Buffalo" tries to capture the heavy galloping of a buffalo in motion (it is also the name of an unincorporated community near his childhood home), just as "Whistle Stop" attempts to paint a sonic picture of the locomotion of a train in the manner of so many blues songs before it. "Sunrise in Mexico" largely speaks for itself. Dorham commented that "the skies down there are low and everything looks different."[8] This may explain the piece's tessellating sections, as it moves from a rubato opening to a Latin melody to swinging solos. It is easy to imagine any of these songs appearing in the sun-scorched backdrop of a John Ford film, scoring the widescreen expanse of the American West.

However, this is not to say that the music is strictly programmatic. Instead, this album, more than any of Dorham's previous work, provides a sideways look at his Texas roots. Brent Hayes Edwards offers a critical structure to better understand the meaning of the particular choices of song names. In his book *Epistrophies*, an innovative critical study of the intersection between jazz and literature, Edwards writes about saxophonist and composer Henry Threadgill's unorthodox song titles. Edwards explores the idea of the title itself and presses on the definition to imagine its greater potential meanings:

> To take the "word" of *any* title as a "very small aperture" or "keyhole" into the work, then, is not to take that language as programmatic—the definitive "anchorage" of the work of art to a restricted set of meanings—but instead allow the inevitable failure of language to allow the singularity of the work to emerge precisely as a product of its unnameability. The title allows us to experience the work not because it is the "right identifier" but because when we enter the work through it, we can "keep reaching outside that moment of the word to the next." This stunning passage begins to suggest what it would mean to recalibrate the relation between title and work entirely, and

> in that sense may be a useful way to clear the ground of expectation for a consideration of Henry Threadgill's song titles.[9]

Edwards imagines Threadgill's titles as "points of entry, "hints about the contours of a composition, frames or windows," and "associative clues."[10]

Edwards goes on to explain that Threadgill circumvents the typical signification of most jazz song titles—namely, direct evocation of a personage or mood. His comments give a lens through which Dorham's own title choices might be viewed. While Dorham may not be quite so elusive with his song names, *Whistle Stop* offers a kind of panorama of his Texas childhood, inflected with the mixture of driving blues rhythms and more Southwestern straight eighth note numbers. The tunes are not strictly narrative, but their titles reveal Dorham's literary preoccupations, offering the listener small musical windows or keyholes into those childhood memories alluded to in Dorham's "Fragments of an Autobiography."[11]

The tunes are carefully constructed with surprising turns that never inhibit the flow of the swing or the looseness of the improvisation. It's also interesting to hear Dorham play with a kind of mirror image of various incarnations of the Miles Davis Quintet (Mobley would record with Davis for the *In Person Friday and Saturday Nights at the Blackhawk* album in the same year) and soar to higher reaches. When one considers what Dorham was able to achieve with the same group of musicians Davis used, it becomes clear why Miles Davis admired and respected him so much. In fact, Davis's longtime drummer, Jimmy Cobb, once opined that Dorham was "the better trumpet player" of the two.[12] Their creative output was dramatically different, having in common only a strong sense of swing and roots in blues and bebop. Kenny Dorham was uniquely and completely himself, veering toward the understated and romantic, whereas Davis preferred edginess and abstraction. *Whistle Stop* also showcases Dorham's ability to utilize a bluesy growl, markedly contrasting the careful shape of his snaking chord substitution runs and slick turnarounds. In a way, *Whistle Stop* is a premature summation of a lifetime artistic quest. Dorham spoke often about his aspiration to present an homage to his childhood. Freestone County had left such an imprint on him, and he strove to pin down the ideas he was chasing as his playing and compositional style matured and evolved. He could play Western-sounding or rural melodies right from the start, but in 1961 he was ready to share a completed vision of his childhood, coherent and unified around the theme of rural Texas. This is not to suggest, of course, that his subsequent performances were anticlimactic. They weren't. Rather, Dorham sought to say, in a single musical statement, who he was and where he came from, and it is a success.

The productive phase that Dorham was in as the 1960s dawned can also be seen in his performance schedule as well as in the release of the *Whistle Stop* album. He guested with saxophonist John Handy (a Charles Mingus alum) in Jim and Paul Eller's Showplace in Greenwich Village in July 1960, where he was introduced as "the cool, no-coast man."[13] It is striking to think that at the same time as Dorham and Handy played groundbreaking jazz in the Village, Bob Dylan was making his own impression on New York concertgoers just down the block, playing a very different style of music but one that shared colors with Dorham's palette. In August, Dorham had a residency with the Jazz Artists Guild;[14] from there he was off to Chicago to play the Counterpoint supper club in November.[15] A Black jazz musician (or their agent) cobbled together a group's performance schedule from white-owned clubs, Black-owned clubs, publicly sponsored events, and guest appearances. Musicians complained bitterly that the restricted opportunities for Black artists to play required them to travel vast distances; this predicament has been offered as a reason for Clifford Brown's and Richie Powell's deaths by auto accident en route to Chicago from Philly.

Other performance dates for Dorham in 1960 included a stint at the famed Five Spot Café in March for an engagement that ran through the middle of the month, splitting the bill with John Coltrane.[16] Dorham appeared at the club with his quintet again in April,[17] June, and October.[18] Billed as the Jazz Prophets, Dorham's group, including Charles Davis on baritone saxophone, Butch Warren on bass, Buddy Enlow on drums, and Steve Kuhn on piano, received a positive review in a June issue of *DownBeat*: "The recently formed Dorham quintet had a highly successful run at New York's Five Spot. It plays a set of ballads with a nice blending of modern sounds and recognizable melodies."[19]

Dorham also played a date at Small's Paradise in May, which was written up in a brief but warm review for the Tavern Topics column in the *New York Amsterdam News*: "Kenny Dorham who has been successfully blowing his wonderful music in the Village for the past several months, is playing at Small's Paradise this week with his wonderful Quintet. The group is a modern but not too far out swinging jazz group."[20] Dorham played with alto saxophonist Jackie McLean for a relatively prestigious single-night engagement at Town Hall on April 16 of the same year.[21] This collaboration would lay the foundation of their later collaboration on a live album. That spring, his quintet also played at the Jazz Gallery.[22]

In August, a glowing write-up of Dorham's career up to that point appeared in *The Jazz Review*. In the article's conclusion, critic H. A. Woodfin made the plain case for Dorham's entry into the jazz canon: "Whatever the public image of Dorham, a serious examination of the body of his work shows incontestably that he is, along with Davis and Farmer, one of the modern masters of his instrument and the originator of a style which is both new and impressive."[23] In September, Dorham brought his quartet to the newly opened Jazz City, U.S.A., a Greenwich Village jazz club that boasted a soda bar and record counter on its ground floor, along with upstairs seating.[24] Dorham also kept steady work as a sideman. On July 5 and 8, he played on *Eastward Ho! Harold Land in New York*, a hidden gem from tenor man Land, featuring a comfortable group working within the bebop idiom over mostly medium tempos. The trotting "Slowly" is the highlight.

1961 was a similarly busy year for performing and touring. Dorham was back at the Jazz Gallery for a week in May,[25] followed by an Albemarle Towers, Brooklyn, gig with Max Roach and his Big Beat Band.[26] Dorham traveled to Brazil in July, a trip that would prove instrumental in his introduction to bossa nova and later inspire one of his most famous compositions. His time in Brazil is partially documented on the poorly repackaged—and egregiously titled—posthumous 1988 release *Hot Stuff From Brazil*.[27] Although recorded under Dorham's name, he plays on only three tracks: "Wee Dot," "Night in Tunisia," and "Autumn Leaves." Dorham's performance is standard on the first two songs, but really shines on the third number, on which he extends comfortably, moving between triplets and eighth notes with elasticity and drawing out the melody with decorative addenda. The concert took place at the Teatro Municipal in Rio de Janeiro as part of the American Jazz Festival in Latin America on July 16, 1961. Dorham performed alongside alto saxophonist Zoot Sims, tenor saxophonist Al Cohn, flutist Herbie Mann, trombonist Curtis Fuller, pianist Ronnie Ball, bassist Benny Tucker, drummer Dave Bailey, and percussionist Ray Mantilla, in various configurations.

In an interview with *Cadence* magazine, Fuller complained about Columbia's handling of the recording's release, highlighting the company's manipulation of Black artists in the interest of profit, echoing Dorham's comments on the same subject:

> I'm speaking of economics. I was with Columbia for awhile, but Columbia didn't do right by me. As a matter of fact I went to South America with a group. They were just telling us about the Bossa Nova then and I came back and we recorded Kenny Dorham, Tommy Flanagan, myself and a bunch of us. We recorded the Bossa Nova, told them this was the new music in South America. "Yeah, all right," they recorded it, boom and sit it on the shelf. Stan Getz comes back and boom our record is still sitting on the shelf. Madison Avenue style,

> they pick one guy, they get something good and they cram it down your throat. They dictate it, it has nothing to do with the style or tone. If Jay Johnson had been white, he would have been a master—we know that. He won a Downbeat poll, a little placque [*sic*] on the wall, that means nothing. But he couldn't get a job working in any studio at that time. Whereas they'll take a Bill Watrous and he'll make a million dollars and he's not new on the scene, been around as long as J.J.—got to be 50 years old.[28]

Like Dorham, Fuller was all too aware of the role that optics and marketing played in the music business, how musicianship and technique mattered little in the face of slick packaging.

In August, Dorham returned to New York and played an outdoor show in Riverside Park.[29] Later in the month, he went out to Los Angeles for an engagement at Club Town Hill,[30] where he presented his new Southwestern suite, with Clifford Jordan sharing the horn duties. On November 21, Dorham played at the Black Orchid, also in Los Angeles, with a band composed of Jackie McLean, Walter Bishop Jr., bassist Leroy Vinnegar, and Art Taylor.[31] Formerly the Hillcrest Club, where Ornette Coleman made a famous live recording with pianist Paul Bley, the Black Orchid was a new venue that would fold a few months later, in February 1962.[32] A verbose review in *DownBeat* notes that the piano was egregiously out of tune for the show: "The plain fact is that the keyboard instrument (it cannot be called a pianoforte) confronted by Bishop and his colleagues on this job was an instrument of torture worthy of Torquemada."[33] The writer goes on to compliment Dorham and "his fine, fat tone and electrifying flights," as well as the rest of the band, before complaining in the final paragraph about the crowd: "On opening night this rather depressing saloon was full of hippies who didn't seem to mind the supreme insult to music and men embodied in the cursed keyboard."[34]

Dorham had brought this same band to the Jazz Workshop in San Francisco on November 13, 1961, a performance that would be taped and released in March 1962 as a live recording.[35] Titled *Inta Somethin'*, the album showcases Dorham playing gracefully over standards like "It Could Happen to You" and "Lover Man."[36] McLean provides counterpoint to Dorham's more traditionally "inside" playing, as he demonstrates an exploratory approach to harmony in his solos.

Capitalizing on this chemistry, Dorham recorded again with McLean on April 15, 1962, at Sound Makers in New York for his album, *Matador*. The highlights of this session are "Melanie," a three-part composition by McLean, and "Prelude," Dorham's arrangement of an eerie piece by Brazilian classical composer Heitor Villalobos. "Melanie" features some surprising modal soloing from Dorham, while "Prelude" shows his way with an open phrase, as he plays in duet with pianist Bobby Timmons. "Prelude," like "Dorham's Epitaph," reveals a darker shade of Dorham's sound, one tinged with melancholy and rumination. Dorham recorded with McLean once more on June 14 at Rudy Van Gelder's studio in Englewood Cliffs, though the tracks would not see the light of day until Blue Note released them in 1978 as the first half of the album *Hipnosis* and, later, as the second half of the album *Vertigo* in 2000.[37]

That summer, Dorham reunited with McLean to play in an aptly titled, lightly attended all-star concert at The Town Hall. Dorham was joined by McLean on alto saxophone, Dexter Gordon on tenor saxophone, Walter Bishop Jr. on piano, Reggie Workman on bass, Roy Haynes on drums, and newcomer Kelvin Knowles. After an introductory trio set from pianist and emcee Billy Taylor, Dorham and Gordon opened the second set with "Wee Dot," then played "The End of a Love Affair" (a Gordon feature) and "Solar" (a Dorham feature). McLean joined for his feature on "Let's Face the Music and Dance," and Knowles came in for a version of "Just Friends." Finally, the whole band played "Jackie's Blues" and closed with a rousing version of "A Night in Tunisia." Critic Ira Gitler wrote that the concert was strong and that Dorham played well despite some technical issues: "Dorham was having lip trouble that occasionally led to ragged articulation, but even this could not offset the intricate beauty of his lines or the insistence of his swing."[38]

That same June, Dorham was scheduled to play with the Contemporary String Quartet at The Square East, another defunct Greenwich Village club.[39] He also participated that month in another blindfold test for *DownBeat*, this time speaking more enthusiastically about the records. He offers unabashed praise for Lee Morgan, saying in reference to Morgan's recording of saxophonist Wayne Shorter's "Suspended Sentence" that "Morgan is one of my favorites among the young trumpet players."[40] Likewise, Dorham speaks fondly of Miles Davis's "Oleo" from *At the Blackhawk*: "Miles is everything that everyone thinks he is—one of my favorite trumpet players. . . . Always unique and personal, though, always with something of his own to say."[41] Dorham concludes the piece with an optimistic look at the landscape of up-and-coming players: "As I said, there are so many fine new trumpet players coming up: Lee Morgan, who plays very well for his age; Freddie Hubbard, who is very very flighty—it's hard to make a comparison between him and Lee."[42] On June 25, Dorham closed out the month by taking part in the annual Gretsch Drum Night at Birdland, joining his regular band with performances from four featured drummers.[43] In August, Dorham, along with pianist and composer George Russell, was part of a panel that awarded scholarships to young musicians through the Jazz Arts Society,[44] and in November he "played a pre-Thanksgiving dance at the Dawn Casino."[45]

In 1963, Dorham appeared in the pages of *DownBeat* once again, with a letter published in the March 14 issue. This letter, titled "Kenny's Lament," decries the loss of two radio broadcasts: "I am writing to express my lament that radio stations WWRL and WRFM have discontinued their live broadcasts to the New York audience. Allen Grant was emcee (and indeed a very fine one). I'm sure that many others join me in regretting that the shows did not remain in the New York area."[46] In February, Dorham performed in a benefit concert for pianist Sonny Clark's family, held and recorded by Blue Note, following Clark's death earlier that year, on January 13.[47] In May, Dorham started making regular appearances at the Sunday night Jazzline sessions at the Cinderella Club in the Village,[48] often playing alongside drummer Roy Haynes.[49] The following month, Dorham joined a committee with Dizzy Gillespie, Sonny Rollins, and Jackie McLean and helped set up the Charlie Parker Memorial Fund, a scholarship aimed at bolstering Parker's public legacy while providing financial support to a musician or composer and extending the reach of the New York School of Jazz (an offshoot of the previously mentioned Jazz Arts Society).[50] Dorham brought in his quintet, featuring Joe Henderson on tenor sax, for a fundraising concert at the Carnegie International Endowment Center on June 3, splitting the bill with the Sonny Red Quintet and the Ted Curson Quartet. That same month, *DownBeat* gave a shout-out to Dorham's brother, Joel: "Trumpeter Kenny Dorham's brother, Joel, a timbales player, who lives in Berkeley, heads a Latin quintet that is playing casuals in this area."[51]

Michael Cuscuna, a record producer who founded Mosaic Records and who has reissued troves of classic Blue Note material by Kenny Dorham and others, got to know Dorham in the mid-1960s, when Cuscuna was still in high school.[52] After meeting Dorham in clubs and speaking with Jane French, who managed Dorham at the time, Cuscuna got the idea to ask Dorham to play his high school prom. To his surprise, the answer was yes. In fact, Dorham saw the date as a way to escape for a night from the club scene and play for a different audience. So in June 1966, Cuscuna and his fellow dance organizers met Dorham and his band at the train and drove them in family station wagons to the high school. Cuscuna found the musicians, Dorham in particular, in good spirits. The quintet was probably the most illustrious ever to play a student prom: Dorham's trumpet plus Sonny Red on alto sax, Albert Dailey on piano, Cecil McBee on bass, and Frank Gant on drums.

Cuscuna worried about how a student audience steeped in the incipient rock-and-roll of the time would react to a jazz quintet made up of musicians in their thirties and forties, but evidently his enthusiasm for the music outweighed his concerns, and he asked the school to hire them. He needn't have worried. Dorham and company played their Blue Note repertoire of Latin, funk, jazz standards, and ballads to a very receptive audience. Though bebop and hard bop jazz are not known as dance music, everyone danced throughout the performance.[53]

Taking a longer view of Dorham's musical lineage, the compatibility of his music with the setting is not surprising. The early blues and jazz imprinted on him as a boy in rural Texas grew out of country dances, barrelhouse saloons, and Deep Ellum street music. As Dorham translated those sounds into the modern jazz idiom in over four decades as a performing musician, one could pick up any one of his recordings and relate to the emotional immediacy, the soulfulness, and the constant swing of his playing. The blues are always there. Cuscuna himself recalled that what impressed him most about "Una Mas" when he first heard it was the trumpeter's ability to sustain a groove over the extended length of this title track without flagging. Dorham's contribution to the Blue Note catalog of the mid-1960s made it "one of the great periods of jazz," and Cuscuna considered "Una Mas" itself to be "among the most moving stuff I've been exposed to."[54] Dorham remained friends with Cuscuna from then on, nicknaming him "The Little Red Schoolhouse" in reference to their first association.

Dorham certainly had his highs and lows in musicianship during the 1960s. At times, listeners noted that his playing was "ragged," that his "chops were shot."[55] Even at recording sessions there were times when his playing was not clean or precise. At least two Blue Note sessions went unreleased for that reason.[56] Trumpet players are plagued with such problems. Too much playing, a bruise on the lip, or any number of causes can affect the horn sound over the short or long term. For Dorham, those common issues were compounded in the 1960s by failing health (ultimately, renal failure) and the intrusion of day jobs such as a stint with the Postal Service and a job in the reeds section of Manny's Music Store in midtown Manhattan.

In the mid-1960s, Dorham demonstrated a clear willingness to branch out musically, with a string of some of his strongest albums. On March 21, 1964, he recorded on pianist Andrew Hill's *Point of Departure*. While it is difficult to fully summarize the impact of the recording in total, its influence still looms large in the playing and writing of young jazz musicians today. It is easy to see why Hill selected Dorham for the session and what his contribution to it was. With songs too prickly and angular to be part of the mainstream, but too through-composed to be grouped under the free jazz umbrella, *Point of Departure* is an underrated masterpiece, considered by many musicians to be Hill's crowning achievement. From drummer Tony Williams's oceanic changes in pulse to reed player Eric Dolphy's birdsong multiphonics, the players flourish on each track, turning the forms inside out, before returning to their assigned roles.[57] In addition to Hill, Dolphy, and Williams, Dorham played alongside tenor saxophonist Joe Henderson and bassist Richard Davis on the session.

In contrast to Dolphy, whose name was becoming synonymous with a certain kind of wildly adventurous—though not quite free—approach to style, Dorham is an interesting choice. His solos show him operating in a context different from his previous bebop and hard bop outings. He is free to lean into a more chromatic approach to harmony, playing ideas that hew more closely to the interaction of the ensemble and less to the stricture of standard chord changes. It is the closest a listener can get to hearing him play free jazz. Dorham fleetly navigates the knotted forms of each tune, but really shines on "Dedication," a dark and meditative ballad. The musicians present that day claimed to have seen Dorham shed a tear during the recording, as he was so moved by the song's elegiac mood.[58] Similarly, on "Spectrum," his lines dance around in shadowy dissonance with Hill's accompaniment. In a contemporary review, music journalist Phyl Garland wrote that Dorham showed "surprising affinity for the avant garde" on these tracks.[59]

Henderson, Dorham's close friend with whom he was recording other groundbreaking material for Blue Note, had to convince Dorham to participate in the *Point of Departure* session. As Henderson recalled,

> I can remember doing *Point of Departure* with Kenny, trying to convince him that he could do that date. He just thought it was not really his scene. If you check his history you will find that he'd been recording much more in the mainstream, kind of in the center, with a lot of breadth and depth. Andrew was out on the far left at that time. So I worked with Kenny on some of the tunes figuring out something for him to do. It was like, let's try this scale here on this chord progression. . . . I'd give him three or four scales and he would immediately know what to do with them. The fact that I had to convince him to do this session really made me feel good, because I could give him something. He'd given me so much, and to watch him do it, well that made me so happy.[60]

In the album's liner notes, Hill said of Dorham: "Kenny I consider the most underrated player in the business. His problem is that he's so nice, and people seem to associate greatness with meanness or bitterness. In this business, you have to create some kind of angry or tough image of yourself to be accepted. He told me he liked this date so much because it made him think and play in new directions and in the process he proved again how musical and flexible a trumpet player he is."[61] While Hill's words are kind, they also emphasize something echoed in other comments about Dorham: his aversion to self-image. Dorham's friendly and open demeanor, coupled with his lack of self-promotion (in sharp contrast to a figure like Miles Davis, who was often known for his aggressive assertions about being credited on songs, albums, and even band names) did not allow Dorham to build a public image. Likewise, Dorham never went the route of flashy showmanship. His live albums feature minimal stage banter. He seemed to prefer to let the music stand without lengthy prefaces and addenda. Hill recognized Dorham's occupation of a role like this: recognized but not known so widely outside their circle of contemporaries.

In this period, Dorham developed a close kinship with Henderson. Henderson would make his recording debut on Dorham's *Una Mas* and would include Dorham on a triptych of his own records: *Page One*, *Our Thing*, and *In 'n Out*.[62] Recorded on June 3, 1963, at Van Gelder's studio, *Page One* was Henderson's debut album. It is commonly known for premiering one of Dorham's most played compositions, "Blue Bossa," a Latin number inspired by his Brazil trip. The song is commonly played in jam sessions and favored by beginner jazz musicians, as it allows for simple modal playing over its brief sixteen bars, which also makes it a suitable choice for rock musicians used to improvising with particular scales for long stretches. But viewing it as a jam session workhorse fails to capture the scope of what Dorham was trying to do, as he successfully wove together multiple strains of influence into this shadowy gem. In the preface to his 2015 poetry collection, *Blue Fasa*, writer Nathaniel Mackey unspools the cultural intersections of the piece as he explains his homage to it in the title of his book:

> Blue Fasa's title samples two distantly related black musical traditions, the West African griot epic the Dausi, which includes the story of Gassire's lute and the lost city of Wagadu, and trumpeter Kenny Dorham's hard bop classic "Blue Bossa," influenced by the emergence of Brazilian bossa nova and introduced on tenor saxophonist Joe Henderson's album *Page One* in 1963. . . . Both have to do with

> disruption and displacement, the latter in particular valorizing while evincing an absorption and a creative digestion of dislocation, the tradition of durability underscored by the hard in hard bop, an ability to roll with, or swing with, the unexpected and the new that we hear in the buoyancy of Dorham's "Blue Bossa." Said to have been influenced by Dorham's trip to the Rio de Janeiro Jazz Festival in 1961, the tune takes in the "new trend" or the "new wave" or the "new appeal" that was bossa nova, making what was a softening of samba more like samba, bluesier, more propulsive, more boisterous touching it, especially during solos, with the memory of harder diasporic time (a direction tenor saxophonist Archie Shepp takes even farther in his version of "The Girl from Ipanema"). That memory telescopes a history of creative incorporation of what was typically much more disruptive or even catastrophic, a digestion both rhythmic and "ythmic" (the anagrammatic versioning of the mythic and the clipped, syncopated form of the former coined in the course of these two series).[63]

In his smoothly discursive style, Mackey manages to elucidate an essential quality of the piece, one that speaks to its endurance as a stalwart of many set lists—namely, that it draws on several musical traditions, fusing the feel and spaciousness of bossa nova with the chord hinges of hard bop. Where Dorham's piece is unique is that it is subdued and dark, in contrast to the breeziness of Stan Getz's famous rendition of the Jobim bossa nova songbook, suggesting, as Mackey underscores, a more "catastrophic" history. In line with Fuller's earlier comments, it is sadly fitting that this piece did not receive the same acclaim given to Getz's Grammy-winning hit: here, and on later compositions, Dorham's bossa is not suitable for poolside lounging or as dinner party background music.

The album highlights the high degree of comfort between Dorham's and Henderson's sounds, both in the blend of their tones and in the integration of two horn harmonies on melodies and vamps. The rhythm section features McCoy Tyner at the piano, Butch Warren on bass, and Pete La Roca on the drums. The session itself has a kind of restrained feeling to it, smoothly assured throughout. Both Tyner and the horn players do not burn much in their solos, even on the faster numbers. They seem more concerned with the outgrowth of melodic ideas.

For all of the fanfare surrounding "Blue Bossa," the album's real shining moment is Dorham's ballad, "La Mesha," named after and dedicated to one of his daughters. Featuring a lovely shuffling of nonfunctional chord changes and a yearningly lyrical melody, it is a haunting song full of shading and subtlety.

Dorham takes a solo that is fittingly similar to his mode on *Quiet Kenny*. He plays the melody, taking certain moments to provide ornamentation.

The remaining four tracks are Henderson compositions, the most notable among them the jam session favorite "Recorda Me" and the lovely "Jinshirika," which reveals Henderson's fondness for major seventh with sharp eleventh chords. "Homestretch" is the only particularly fast song on the album, and even there Dorham sounds like he's holding back, acting as more of a sideman rather than indulging in the running flights of notes that had become his trademark.

Henderson and Dorham returned to Van Gelder's studio on September 9 to record *Our Thing*, the second Henderson album that Dorham played on. It maintains a distinctively off-kilter sound. More driven than *Page One* but not as heated as its successor *In 'n Out*, the sound of *Our Thing* seems attributable to the discursive and crabbed style of pianist Andrew Hill. The aptly named opening number, "Teeter Totter," features a Monkish intro from Hill followed by a charging horn melody. Hill's comping follows a similar schematic, landing as sharply as Pete La Roca's decorative snare hits. Bassist Eddie Khan provides steady time, occasionally dropping into open-string strumming towards the end of the form. Henderson takes a long cooker of a solo. Here, in comparison to *Page One*, Dorham sounds willing to experiment in longer, more open improvisation. An alternate take of "Teeter Totter" is shorter in run time but feels a bit looser, and Henderson takes the first solo instead of Dorham. The gentle "Pedro's Time," a Dorham composition, is another Latin-to-swing piece. Dorham is lyrical, leaning on held notes in the A section and blues turnarounds in the B. Hill's solo (as is the case for most of the tunes) is always in the pocket of the feel, but grows increasingly thorny and abstract as it develops.

The title track, "Our Thing," is a quick one with an odd-meter bridge. "Back Road" is a minor, bluesy song with stops that Dorham utilizes in an earthy solo filled with emphatic, accented playing. Hill, too, digs into these embedded hits and builds his melodic ideas out of and around them, weaving between dissonance and gospel chords. The final number is another of Dorham's more famous works, "Escapade." Its main section turns in bright chords before a moody bridge featuring a modal figure which Khan and Hill play in unison. The medium tempo gives everyone room to stretch out. Dorham takes a strong solo, confidently using a wide range of his register and keeping his ideas unrushed. Hill navigates the twists in the chord changes with some harmonic crunch. The head out feels appropriately relaxed, culminating in a rising horn line that closes out the record. The song itself is another wonder of Dorham's construction. His use of the D-flat ninth with sharp eleventh chord as a passing point between an A-flat major ninth and a G-major seventh allows for a logical but subtle surprise in the A section, while the floating B-flat pedal on the G-flat major seventh and G-flat major seventh with sharp fifth chords shrouds the first four bars of the bridge in modal mystery. Once again, Dorham's use of detail mirrors that of a master painter: He understands the subtle differences of shading and the impact made on the piece as a whole by slight changes in bass motion and altered tones. The songs on this album yield great solos but are much more than just vehicles for blowing.

Dorham returned once more to Van Gelder's on April 10, 1964, to record the final studio collaboration that he completed under Henderson's name. This album is a great look at a different side of Dorham's style, brought out by the heat of a volcanic rhythm section. Once again featuring McCoy Tyner on piano, the album *In 'n Out* pairs Tyner with a musician who likely is his most recognizable counterpart, Elvin Jones, on the drums. These two juggernauts are supported by the fulcrum of bassist Richard Davis's expansive time. The album features two Dorham compositions, "Short Story" and "Brown's Town," which find the musicians in more of a hard bop mode. "Short Story" features a nice "Elvin Latin" A section which slides easily into a swinging bridge. Dorham's solo unfolds carefully as the players float on the medium tempo. Henderson cycles through some shapes and patterns but develops his solo primarily in the framework of the form. While some modal moments do creep in, it's a song that largely wouldn't sound out of place on either *Page One* or *Our Thing*. Tyner's solo is nimble, gliding around Jones's bass drum and ride cymbal. Jones trades with the horns briefly in a controlled detonation.

"Brown's Town" is a minor tune studded with stop-time and yet another sly piano-bass figure. Dorham plays confidently, while the bass gets abstract against the tectonics of the drums and piano. Dorham's solo is blues-inflected, with stinging repeated notes, but also digs into moments of chromaticism. The title track, "In 'n Out," is a Coltrane-esque chord workout. After Henderson and Tyner burn through the changes, Dorham opens with long tones before diving into rapidly shifting melodic ideas that twist and turn with the unstable harmony. It is thrilling to hear him in this context, the shape of his lines bent—and occasionally overwhelmed—by the fiery foundation beneath him. "Serenity" and "Punjab" also went on to be notable items in Henderson's song catalog, featuring his challenging harmonies and careful melodic construction. The album makes its case as a very clear predecessor of what would become Henderson's most notable record date, *Inner Urge*, which would find him with Tyner and Jones once again, exploring modal boundaries without losing his ghostly lyricism.

The electricity of Dorham's collaboration with Henderson was presaged by their work together on club dates. This is captured on *Live at the Flamboyan* (2009), a live recording made at the now-defunct club in Astoria, Queens, on January 15, 1963.[64] Joined by Henderson, Dorham plays a few tunes that would shortly be included on *Una Mas* (an album to be discussed below), including "Straight Ahead" and "Una Mas," as well as standards like "Summertime" and "I Can't Get Started." The band is crisp, giving Dorham a springboard to playing lithely. He sounds comfortable, his full tone intact as he floats through ballads and drives hard through Latin vamps. In some places, Dorham clearly is working through solo material that he later incorporated into the new record. Like the earlier Café Bohemia record, *Live at the Flamboyan* on the whole is a glimpse at Dorham's playing in the moment, without the filtering influence of the studio, and it is remarkable for catching the spark that went into what was likely just another gig for Dorham.

In the winter of 1963, Dorham spent time in Scandinavia, recording and performing with local musicians in Denmark, Sweden, and Norway. From this period there are two albums as well as a television performance (one of the only easily accessible video recordings of Dorham in circulation) and a bootleg recording.[65] *Short Story* is a quintet session, recorded on December 19, featuring Niels-Henning Ørsted Pedersen on bass, Alex Riel on drums, and Tete Montoliu on piano, as well as Allan Botchinsky on flugelhorn, providing a mellowed mix with Dorham on melodies. While Dorham is in consistent form here, the record itself feels more like a blowing session than a fully developed album.[66] Recorded on December 5, *Scandia Skies* features similar personnel.[67] The title track is gentle waltz with an impressionistic solo from Dorham. The album has the same free-wheeling feeling of *Short Story*. Both albums were released on the SteepleChase label, in 1979 and 1980 respectively, and were recorded at Jazzhus Montmartre, a jazz club in Copenhagen.

Similarly, the Metropole Club bootleg, recorded in Oslo in January 1964, showcases Dorham in a quartet format with Tore Sannes on piano, Bjørn Pedersen on bass, and Jon Christensen on drums. It is particularly uncanny to hear Christensen at this early stage in his career, playing in a way that strongly resembles Max Roach and Tony Williams. Christensen would go on to gain acclaim in Keith Jarrett's European Quartet, a group that seemed to avoid swing entirely, preferring broken eighth notes and rocky backbeats, leaving Christensen to fill space with textural, free-form fills, almost never repeating a phrase.

In a video clip from this period, pulled from a live show at the Golden Circle, a club in Stockholm, Sweden, Dorham is poised, standing sharp as he cuts through chord changes with the confidence of his early bebop days.

Listening to these recordings, it feels as though Dorham found a new fire in his playing that winter. His playing in all of these instances is as graceful as it is slick, never faltering in tone or feel.

Also in 1964, Dorham's penultimate record as a leader was released. *Una Mas* had actually been recorded at Van Gelder's in March of the previous year. The album is often dismissed as a secondary record in Dorham's catalog. Many critics say that at this point in his career, his solos sound tired and repetitive. Comments like these reveal a lack of interest in assessing Dorham's evolution as both an improviser and a composer. The band features a young Tony Williams and Herbie Hancock on drums and piano, respectively, with Richard Davis on bass and Joe Henderson once again on tenor. The rhythm section plays comfortably with different grooves, digging into a bossa nova on "Una Mas" and alternating swing and straight eighth notes in an off-kilter style on "Sao Paulo." Williams and Hancock, particularly, shine here, their comping creatively outlining with the rhythmic intricacies of the songwriting. It is once again interesting to hear a rhythm section with Dorham that would shortly go on to be members of a Miles Davis group—his Second Great Quintet—although the artistry of their playing is already evident on these songs.

Dorham here sounds enlivened, stretching out on the first track in a solo that gradually cooks. His playing on this record is somewhat more abstract, leaving more room between ideas, occasionally approaching the development of his ideas in riffs. On the swinging songs, particularly a mid-tempo rendition of "If Ever I Would Leave You," Dorham is softening his tone and playing tenderly, in singable phrases. It is a short record, with only four tracks clocking in at thirty-six minutes, but is undeniably a career best in Dorham's catalogue. The album's arrangements also received regards from fellow musicians. When asked about playing Dorham's "Una Mas" with his band (including arrangements and trumpet playing from Don Sickler), T. S. Monk, a drummer and son of Thelonious Monk, praised Dorham's compositional ability: "Kenny Dorham was no doubt the greatest small ensemble composer and arranger of all times."[68]

Somewhat prophetically, Dorham made the following comment to writer Nat Hentoff in the album's liner notes: "All I can say is that if it's going to happen, it'll happen. But it's going to have to happen within a reasonable time. After all, I'll soon be into my 25th year on the trumpet. Anyway, however it goes, I'll just keep playing. That's where the basic satisfaction is at."[69] Feeling the wear of years of not receiving his due, Dorham offered that comment, revealing the level of resignation he felt about the music business. He suspected that if things did not begin to turn around, he wouldn't be able to continue on for much longer. At the same time, he knew he could never walk away from music entirely, as it was such an essential part of who he was.

On September 14, 1964, Dorham cut his final album as a leader, *Trompeta Toccata*. Recording at Van Gelder's studio, Dorham joined with Henderson one last time, accompanied by Albert "Tootie" Heath (Jimmy's brother) on drums, Richard Davis on bass, and Tommy Flanagan on piano. The album is relatively brief, featuring only four extended tracks: "Trompeta Toccata," "Night Watch," "Mamacita," and "The Fox." The album simmers in grooves, featuring Latin vamps and soul jazz funk. Dorham's solos are both heated and mysterious as he sprawls out over the songs, embracing a freedom largely unheard in his previous records. The whole band keeps the energy up throughout, with Flanagan, Heath, and Davis locked in and pushing hard. The title track opens with an ominous introduction, as Dorham plays a declarative phrase with dramatic vibrato, backed by soft padding from the band. From there it shifts into a deep Afro-Cuban rhythm. "Night Watch" is a strutting number, rooted in a shuffling feel. "Mamacita" is a bossa nova, which was reportedly so magnetic that Blue Note producer Alfred Lion and photographer Francis Wolff began to dance in the studio during the session. "The Fox" is a blazingly fast tune that features some of Dorham's most daring soloing to date, as he wends his way through rapidly changing harmonies. Dorham suggests in the album's liner notes that the tune had three registers of meaning: It references the foxes he trapped for furs during his Texas childhood, that bassist Richard Davis reminds him of a fox, and that it had a "foxy" melodic movement.[70] Dorham's comments to the writers of his liner notes were invariably thoughtful—by turns playful, witty, or enigmatic, but always reflective of his probing mind.

While Dorham would go on to make other recordings, *Trompeta Toccata* stands as his last major statement as an artist. The bittersweetness evoked by listening to it comes from hearing the possibility of what might have come next for him, had opportunity and financial support followed.

Ironically, some of Kenny Dorham's most important moments outside the recording studio came in the mid-sixties, just as his recording career was losing momentum. He and Joe Henderson formed a rehearsal band, or a reading band, that met regularly at a New York club and drew the top talent on the jazz scene. As Joe Henderson told it, "Kenny and I put a big band together somewhere around 1966 right after I left Horace Silver. There was a bunch of musicians that were around in the New York area getting into all kinds of things they shouldn't, just being involved in that dissipating lifestyle only because they had nothing to do. So the big band filled that gap and gave them something to do."[71] It also allowed working musicians to keep their skills sharp and challenged them by putting soloists and ensemble players up against the best of their colleagues. They eventually began recording some of the charts written for the band. It outlasted Kenny Dorham's involvement and continued on well past the end of his life, but the rehearsal band represents another of Dorham's contributions to music beyond his compositions and improvisations on the bandstand and in the studio. The rehearsal band performed in public occasionally—late in 1966 at the Brooklyn Apollo, for example.[72] And Dorham and Henderson's association continued into 1967 when they did a July show at the New Century Auditorium in Philadelphia.[73]

Dorham's wish to teach music to kids came true when he signed on in 1964 as a consultant with Harlem Youth Opportunities Unlimited and Associated Community Teams (HARYOU-ACT), a nonprofit organization that merged two civic groups working to improve life for Harlem residents. Dorham's association with HARYOU-ACT followed the Harlem riots that had shaken the city in the summer of 1964. In a turn of events all too reminiscent of today, a white police officer had shot and killed a Black youth in front of multiple neighborhood witnesses. When the police department and city failed to act against the officer, residents took to the streets, and many people were injured and one died in the ensuing unrest. Dorham got involved with the arts division of the nonprofit and ran a big band and music studio for kids. Among his students was René McLean, stepson of Dorham's musical colleague Jackie McLean. Dorham recorded at least one concert, given at PS 175 in August, along with Barry Harris, Julian Euell, and Albert Heath under the auspices of HARYOU-ACT. The playing on the tape is smooth and demonstrates the high level of polish Dorham brought even to informal settings. Dorham also worked alongside blues pianist and fellow Texan Sammy Price to organize various music events for the organization. HARYOU-ACT featured parades, marching bands, and jazz performances, advertised via flyers around the neighborhoods.[74] Dorham would later express his appreciation for the organization in a letter published in the December 30, 1965, issue of *DownBeat*, writing, "I'd like to thank Dizzy Gillespie and Jim Heath for their assistance in establishing the present HARYOU-ACT band-workshop repertoire."[75]

Along with conductor Rheet Taylor, Dorham assembled a group of Harlem high school students into a jazz orchestra and rehearsed with them for several months for a series of high-profile performances, including one at baseball great Jackie Robinson's home and one at the 1964 New York World's Fair.[76] Dorham's quintet also provided musical accompaniment for the Harlem Youth Dance Group later in the year. The dance ensemble was composed of Harlem students—two of whom were awarded scholarships that year—and directed by Ron Davis, a choreography student at Teachers College of Columbia University.[77] Dorham's involvement with Harlem's young artists continued for several years, and in addition to his knowledge of the trumpet and his improvisational genius, Dorham shared his composing and arranging expertise with the young musicians. In 1967 the HARYOU-ACT student orchestra (once again under Taylor and Dorham) performed the students' compositions at the Countee Cullen Library.[78] The works included "Wet Birds Don't Fly at Night," "Not So Quiet City," and "Roots of Grass in Asphalt."

HARYOU-ACT sought federal money from the Johnson administration and received some. But there was tension between the two component organizations. Dorham found himself amid cross-currents of civil rights history as the two principal leaders at odds with each other were the powerful Harlem minister and congressmember Adam Clayton Powell, on the one hand, and Columbia University research psychologist Kenneth Clark, on the other, whose "Doll Study" had swayed the 1954 Supreme Court toward outlawing racial segregation in *Brown v. Board of Education*. This clash of heavyweights did not seem to dissuade Dorham from participation, though: as noted, he stayed with HARYOU-ACT for several years. This stint was another manifestation of Dorham's passion for teaching, which would become a central part of his legacy.

Dorham had been giving his time and talents to benefits, festivals, and charitable events at least since the early 1960s. In October of 1962, he presented a jazz concert for children at the Brooklyn Museum,[79] and earlier that year he played at the Federation for the Handicapped and at the Leake and Watts Children's Home in Yonkers,[80] which had begun in the 1830s as an orphanage. Dorham brought jazz stars Jackie McLean, Arthur Taylor, and Walter Bishop Jr. with him for the concert, and followed up the music that day with a presentation to the children about the fundamentals of jazz.[81] Dorham also connected with the Jazz Arts Society to raise money for scholarships and teaching opportunities. One Jazz Arts Society function Dorham attended was a May 1962 Penthouse party;[82] another was a program featuring his own compositions.[83] Other dates included a Brooklyn fashion show with Abbey Lincoln[84] and a concert at the Museum of Modern Art with saxophonist Clifford Jordan, drummer J. C. Moses, and bassist Teddy Smith.[85] In something of a novelty act, Dorham backed boxer Sugar Ray Robinson on Robinson's 1962 vocal album.[86] On August 13, 1963, Dorham played the Benin Arts Summer Festival at Hopkinson Manor in Brooklyn.[87] These charitable gigs show a musician rooted in the community and seeking ways to give back, even if he felt that he hadn't received the fame, remuneration, and respect due him. Dorham was a fixture both in the Brooklyn community and in the wider New York City community.

In 1964, Dorham's friend Jimmy Heath pulled Dorham into a related teaching opportunity with Jazzmobile, a nonprofit music education organization based in Harlem. According to Heath,

> [i]n 1964, I began teaching at Jazzmobile at PS 201 on 127th Street and Madison Avenue. Jazzmobile was a lifesaver from two standpoints: It helped me get a little bit of money every week, and it kept the music in the community. We were teaching people from the community the continuum of our music so that it wouldn't die. We wanted young people to have the option of making a living in different ways—writing, performing, recording, and teaching. We as teachers weren't making the biggest dollar, but we were surviving musically and doing something that we loved, that we thought was worthy of continuing. Some of the early teachers were "Daahoud" Freddie Waits, Tootie [Heath], Richard Davis, Billy Mitchell, Jimmy Owens, Lee Morgan, and Kenny Dorham. We had something valuable that music students would come to Harlem to get, and we could offer it to those who couldn't afford to go to music school.[88]

While Heath states that there were two aspects to the work, sustaining the music and getting some measure of income, this appeared to be very much a labor of love on the part of the teachers, a means of sharing information with the next generation and providing their students with the opportunity for different career paths. For Heath, and likely also for Dorham, this work was deeply rewarding, as it elevated them as mentors, gave back to the community, and kept the lineage alive.

Describing the same period of time, Heath also mentions his involvement with the Left Bank Jazz Society, which

> gave cabaret parties one or two Sundays a month. . . . They would call me and ask, "Jimmy, who can you get for the next concert." I recommended Kenny Dorham, Pepper Adams, and other artists. The audiences were very jazz-oriented, middle-aged people who really liked the music. They would bring their own food and booze, and they had fun eating, drinking, and enjoying the music. They didn't make noise during the performance, but they partied all the same. The cabaret afternoon was held at the Alho Club at first; later, they moved to the Madison, and after that to the Famous Ballroom near the train station, where they were located for many years. The New York cats loved going to the Left Bank Jazz Society because of the

audience. The Left Bank was a different kind of groove; we were going to have some fun.[89]

Dorham appeared at several shows for Left Bank. On February 14, 1965, he performed with Heath, drummer Donald Bailey, pianist and vibraphonist Jimmy Wells, and drummer Teddy Hawke at the Madison Club in Baltimore.[90] On April 25, he played at the Murphy Fine Arts Center at Morgan State College in Baltimore again with Heath, joined by alto saxophonist Sonny Red, baritone saxophonist Pepper Adams, pianist Cedar Walton, bassist Reggie Workman, and drummer Roy Brooks as part of the Left Bank Sunday afternoon concert series.[91] On September 1, he was back at the Madison with Clifford Jordan, bassist Phil Harris, pianist Claude Hubbard, and drummer Purnell Rice.[92] An archival recording of the Morgan State show captures the band playing expansively, stretching out on "Bluesville," a boilerplate hard bop tune.[93] Dorham builds gradually, kicking off short, bluesy ideas before building out his solo with denser lines featuring his trademark substitutions. Brooks takes a particularly dynamic and deconstructive solo at the end of the song.

Heath's comments about Left Bank shed light on a different sort of issue faced by many jazz musicians: the audience. The overwhelming background noise on many live albums, including many of those mentioned here, readily demonstrates that even for the most famous musicians of the period, the listeners at a club often treated them as background noise, an element of ambience for drinking. What Heath and seemingly others such as Dorham appreciated about this particular club's clientele was their focus on the music. These gigs gave musicians the opportunity to play to a crowd that was there for them and also was familiar with the kind of musical sophistication these bands possessed. One suspects that both the Left Bank experience and the Harlem civic work were a mixed bag for Dorham—rewarding, but not without some frustration and wistfulness about where he was in life after all he'd given to music. This also was a personally difficult time; Dorham's relations with his family were strained, and his health was not robust, a sign of things to come.

It is difficult to attribute the tipping point of Dorham's career to a single factor. Likely some of it was financial pressure, coupled with a loss of gigs and recording dates. In a 1962 radio interview, Dorham candidly discussed his struggle to find steady gigs. Despite being booked by the same agency as Miles Davis, Dorham could not get consistent work in music, and decided to "hang up [his] gloves, so to speak."[94] The agency offered him only "five or six jobs" in the shocking span of two years. He blames this state of affairs on the "criminal undercurrent" of the music industry, namely the producers who want to "make all the money."[95] He predicts that until musicians take these means into their own hands (recording, distribution, rights, etc.) this battle will continue indefinitely. At that time, Dorham managed to play occasional gigs, but paid the bills "working six days" a week at Manny's Music Store.[96] He remarked that he spent Sunday, his single day off, "shooting pool or going to the gymnasium, doing calisthenics."[97] He added that he got satisfaction from offering "tips about playing the horn, care of the horn" to young admirers who came to the store. When asked pointedly about his feelings on the state of his career, Dorham said, sadly, "I hope I'm not bitter, but I don't feel good about it. Maybe somewhere, out of some place, something will happen. Something is very enclosed within me that is very hard to express myself."[98]

Despite this interview taking place before the real downturn of his career, Dorham seemed to have a somber prescience about the future. He was aware of the fact that things would not ultimately go his way, and he understood the forces that would shape this outcome. Once again, his talents alone were not enough to stave off harsh economic realities. He expressed a desire to not become bitter, but it is hard to imagine him feeling content with this loss of time and recognition.

As Cuscuna mentions, it is also possible that his playing suffered periodically in the period immediately following 1964. Some of it was also likely social, as the music itself had no shortage of public criticism. In an interview given towards the end of his life, Dorham described the rain cloud of negative perception that hung over the music: "Usually it's upper-middle-class people who put a stigma on musicians. Unfortunately a few of them happen to be black. This stigma has a political angle. When you have a stigma on you, it affects your earning power—you can't make money. Drugs have always been on the scene, and musicians are noticed because they are always in the public eye. Whereas other people who are not in the spotlight can slip and slide around for their whole lifetime. Whatever a musician does is known because people like to talk about musicians."[99] Dorham viewed the weight of public opinion as artistically and financially crippling, creating an environment in which the cards were already stacked against jazz musicians. His growing disillusionment with these conditions seems to have pushed him away from being involved in music full time.

Whether a contributing factor to this disillusionment or as a result of it, a change in Dorham's personal life also took place during this time. At some point in 1964, he began living separately from his wife and daughters. The details are unclear, but the resulting pain is clear from the scant evidence that exists.[100] He remained in contact with them and referred to them in a 1970s interview.[101] Moreover, he spoke at the end of his life about a desire to reunite with them.[102] Since Dorham lived only eight years beyond the separation from his family, he ran out of time to accomplish that wish. While specifics of these internal family events will remain a mystery, it is undeniable that the dropoff in his recording and performing, the decline in his health, and the move away from his family all date from the same period.

Still, Dorham continued to find some outlets to play in the latter part of the decade. He collaborated with Sonny Red again on two occasions shortly after the Morgan State performance. On December 27, 1965, Dorham participated in a benefit concert for WBAI radio station at The Village Gate bringing a quintet that included Red, Walton, bassist John Ore and drummer Hugh Walker.[103] The group played the Johnny Mandel song, "The Shadow of Your Smile," also known as the love theme from the film *The Sandpiper* (1965), as well as "Straight Ahead." Dorham would perform with Red again on February 25, 1966, at the Half Note club with Walton, Ore, and Walker, playing much of the same material as on the Village Gate occasion.[104] A live recording of the concert shows Dorham in top form, particularly in its second half as he performs a glittering rendition of "Shadow," complete with nimble solos from both Dorham and Walton, and Dorham completes a blistering circuit through "Straight Ahead" at the set's close.

Additionally, Dorham rounded out the mid-1960s with two all-star performances and some jam session appearances. On March 25, 1965, Dorham participated in a memorial concert at Carnegie Hall honoring Charlie Parker on the tenth anniversary of his death. Dorham performed alongside fellow luminaries Coleman Hawkins, Roy Haynes, Dizzy Gillespie, and Lee Konitz, playing on the final piece of the night, a medley featuring the tunes "Bird Watcher" and "Disorder at the Border."[105] On July 2, 1966, Dorham performed as part of a trumpet showcase at the Newport Jazz Festival alongside Dizzy Gillespie, Thad Jones, Howard McGhee, Bobby Hackett, and Ruby Braff on cornet, and Clark Terry and Jimmy Owens on flugelhorn. The rhythm section features Billy Taylor on piano, Kenny Burrell on guitar, Gene Taylor on bass, and Vince Schaeffer on drums.[106] A rare video recording shows Dorham playing "Disorder at the Border" once again.[107] While he takes the lead confidently in his solo, the listener can hear his discomfort on the crowded stage, as the overbearing texture of several horns buries many of his lines and the rhythm section's hookup never seems to come together. Still, it is easy to see what other musicians referred to as Dorham's commanding presence on the gig, as he stands imposingly tall, carrying his horn with poise and firing off lines at a steady clip.

Dorham had a history with George Wein's Newport Festival that went back to 1960. Though Wein was outspoken in his advocacy for jazz and jazz artists, the larger dynamics of race and economics could not be extricated from the music world. Musicians often noted the underrepresentation of Black musicians and the predominance of white groups (as well as differences in pay) at festivals and in the industry as a whole. Moreover, like so many other aspects of American culture, profits from jazz performances accrued to white Americans. As author Ashawnta Jackson puts it, "Record labels tried to figure out how to make money from Black music while stripping away its associations with Blackness."[108] In response to those realities and to the restrictive influence of commercial pressures on the artists' creative freedom, Charles Mingus, Max Roach, and others organized a 1960 Newport Counter-festival. Kenny Dorham joined them, performing with his own group and also with musicians associated with other styles of jazz: Coleman Hawkins, Jo Jones, and Ornette Coleman.[109]

The counter-festival was a notable event in Dorham's life. In addition to the rarity of his crossing eras and styles with forays into swing and free jazz, it also represented his energy and activism concerning the economics of the music business. Dan Morgenstern and others who knew Dorham noted his awareness—and frustration—with the way artists were treated, particularly Black artists. Dorham himself spoke of the problem, notably in his lengthy interview with his friend and fellow musician Art Taylor.[110] Predictably, press coverage of the events of the 1960 Newport Festival focused more on the unrest caused by drunken festival-goers at the main event rather than the smaller, peaceful performances organized by Mingus and Roach.[111] In a stroke of foresight later that year, writer and activist Nat Hentoff convened the Newport Rebels, Dorham included, to attempt a recording of the numbers that had gone unrecorded at the counter-festival itself.

The story of the 1960 Newport Rebels has another layer, though. While Mingus, Roach, and other "rebels" were victimized by an economic system designed to benefit whites, they attained greater notoriety as compared to Dorham. For Dorham, it was the same old story: Musicians showed him a world of respect, but the nonmusician public, and critics especially, listened more closely to Miles Davis and Dizzy Gillespie, as well as to Mingus and Roach. To put it another way, Dorham made the sacrifice that protest requires, but missed out on the rewards enjoyed by his fellow protesters. In future years, Dorham was a presence at Newport, if more often than not a participant in jam sessions such as the one described above featuring Dizzy Gillespie, Thad Jones, and others.

The year 1966 also saw Dorham returning to Austin for the Longhorn Jazz Festival, another George Wein–organized production designed to tap into the rich jazz history of the state.[112] Dorham was an obvious choice for the bill, and the event was something of a homecoming for him. He reconnected and posed for photos with two other notable Texans, fellow Anderson High alum Alvin Patterson and swing-era piano master Teddy Wilson, who also was an Anderson graduate. Dorham and Wilson visited a reception with Anderson students, and the moment was captured in a photo and included in the school's yearbook for that year. The seventy-five-piece Yellowjacket Band were made honorary ushers for the festival.[113] Dorham remarked that he never would have dreamed of a festival like this happening in Austin back when he was a student at Anderson. "These are grandiose times here," he said.[114]

Stretching out at informal sessions and get-togethers was common at jazz festivals in those days, and musicians in town for this one gathered after hours to continue playing their music. One journalist recalled a particular late-night scene, more of a musicians-only event, at which Dorham showed up. A few members of the public found their way in, though, and one of them asked Dorham to perform "I Can't Get Started" "the way Bix Beiderbecke played it."[115] He caught Dorham in a generous mood, as the session was not a proper occasion for requesting tunes or even one at which the public was welcome. And there was a cultural significance in white audiences' frequently expressed preference for white jazz musicians like Beiderbecke that could quite reasonably provoke offense. Of course, in a segregated nation, white musicians profited more from jazz than did the Black musicians who created it. Dorham registered none of these valid objections, however. Instead, he simply said with a smile, "Man, I wish I could play it like Bix did. If I could do that, I'd be doing alright." And then, of course, he proceeded to play it his way, reprising the performance of that ballad on the 1963 Flamboyan live recording mentioned above. Someone in the crowd asked whether he would come back to Austin. "Sure baby, next time around. Oh I'll be back, I'll be back."[116] He would in fact return to the festival in 1967, both as a performer and as a journalist covering the event for *DownBeat*.[117]

Performances had decreased for Dorham by the midpoint of the decade. He played a benefit concert for promoter Peter Lang (sharing the stage with comedian Flip Wilson) in February of 1965,[118] and two engagements at Slugs' in Brooklyn (where fellow trumpeter Lee Morgan would be shot to death a few years later), one in August[119] and another in December with James Spaulding.[120] The following year, Dorham played the Club Ruby in Jamaica, Queens, in February[121] and filled in for Freddie Hubbard at Slugs' for a week.[122] As noted, Dorham did participate in the 1966 Newport Festival, but as part of a trumpet workshop with a number of other trumpeters.

In 1966, Ronald Shannon Jackson, known for his associations with free jazz pioneers Albert Ayler, Ornette Coleman, and Cecil Taylor, moved to

New York after receiving a scholarship to New York University's music program, a result of Dorham's direct advocacy.[123] Jackson vividly recalls accompanying Dorham at several shows:

> Playing with Kenny Dorham was more like the essence of a dream-type thing. It was more esoteric, ethereal feeling, and I always felt like I was floating after each set. He was very warm and lyrical. It was like playing with a jazz vocalist. Because of the way he played and the way his tone was, you had to listen a lot to him when you played. Or, more to the point, in order to enhance anything, you had to be right where he was, which would allow him to open the whole thing up, to get the flow going. You couldn't be overbearing in volume. You had to be very, very supportive. He was the type of person who would allow you to lay the foundation first and then would say, "I'll play on top of that," rather than the type of person who says, "I'll lay the foundation and you play around this." Playing with Kenny was more like backing a Nancy Wilson-type jazz singer.[124]

Jackson captures Dorham's warm, lyrical sensibilities but also points to something deeper about his sound. The dance that Jackson alludes to—"you couldn't be overbearing in volume" negotiating with "I'll play on top of that"—showed that Dorham was not concerned with leading the charge on the bandstand, but rather with cultivating a moment in which he could "flow" with the song and "open the whole thing up." Jackson also identifies something that is often missing from descriptions of Dorham's playing: an "ethereal feeling," the sense of mystery surrounding his deliberate choices. Dorham's more reticent solos read differently in this light, shadowy instead of tired, delicate instead of weak. His playing, as Jackson describes it, was contingent on the moment in which it was happening: the night, the band, the venue. He was not interested in simply playing on top of his peers.

CODA: A VIEW OF THE FUTURE FROM THE MID-1960S

What lay ahead for Dorham at mid-decade was foreshadowed by some of his comments and by the observations of friends and peers that have been recounted in this chapter. The first half of the 1960s featured both exploration of new ground and also productive output. Dorham made several of his most personal and influential recordings and found fulfillment in music education. He was active on the music scene in New York and elsewhere. But he had not attained financial security after two decades as a professional musician, and he knew that the odds of a change in fortunes were slim. Naturally, he would speculate about what he might have done differently, not in terms of creative vision, but in choices made. During the *Notes and Tones* interview with Art Taylor a few years later, Dorham remarked about the economic outlook for most musicians:

> I've always had a feeling that it may not be a good thing to only want to be in the music, but that was the thinking of the musicians who came up in the Louis Armstrong era. Pops wasn't political, he was all music. . . . Maybe putting politics into music is okay if it's advantageous to the musician. . . . Musicians like myself and a few others I know get such meager amounts. You figure, well, what was it all for? Maybe I could have just made bombs and belonged to the destructive side of society. That may be why people mess with drugs; they feel it's a way out, at least as long as they're high.[125]

In an oblique way, Dorham was both questioning his own avoidance of the political and noting that Pops (Louis Armstrong) had navigated the same choice previously. *Political* has different connotations depending on context. It could mean speaking out about rights, justice, and privilege, or it could suggest a willingness to make compromises in order to protect one's own interests. Other musicians and activists, both then and now, have phrased this criticism in terms of what Armstrong was willing to talk about and what he wasn't. Brent Hayes Edwards has discussed Armstrong's reticence about speaking publicly on race and politics, in contrast to his private comments and correspondence, where he was less guarded.[126] Armstrong's choices of what to say publicly may have resulted from a careful calculation. Like many public figures, he was mindful of what would affect his standing and opportunities. To note this navigation of the public realm is not to find fault (or to excuse), but simply to point out the choices and consequences involved. Viewed in this light, Dorham's contrast of Armstrong's stance with his own appears more complex.

The complexity of Armstrong's position notwithstanding, Dorham's broader statement here is a plain one. Why should a Black artist who put in that level of time and concentrated effort in studying the intricacies of harmony, rhythm, and composition not be compensated as though jazz were art music? The realities of this pressure would eventually lead to Dorham largely disappearing from the scene. *Trompeta Toccata* was his last release as a bandleader, and he would mostly appear as a sideman on a handful of releases in the late sixties and early seventies.

CHAPTER 9

IF EVER I WOULD LEAVE YOU

LOST YEARS

Dorham's output after *Una Mas* was relatively limited. He performed as a sideman on a handful of albums but appeared less consistently on the jazz scene. This disappearance can be attributed to a number of different factors. Artistically, the music began to move in opposing directions and to differing levels of commercial success toward free jazz and fusion jazz, two genres Dorham demonstrated a lack of interest in. Personally, he was beset with a number of health problems that made it difficult for him to continue the same gigging and touring lifestyle. Most severe among his health issues was chronic kidney disease, for which he eventually required regular dialysis treatments. Even before that condition developed, he had been diagnosed with high blood pressure. He had separated from his family. Many musicians characterize this period as an extraordinarily difficult one for Dorham, as he seemed to slowly lose the will to keep fighting for his life.

In 1966, Dorham had the solemn duty of acting as pallbearer at the funeral of pianist Bud Powell, another bebop star in the Parker-Gillespie constellation. A contemporary news account depicted the scene as crowded and somber: "Between the corps and the limousines were friends and admirers, though more people were on the sidewalks or just outside the lines. Next to the cars were the pallbearers: James Weaver, Freddie 'Freeloader' Tolbert, Tony Scott, Willie Jones, Kenny Dorham, Eddie Bonnemere, all names in the music world."[1] Powell's death seemed to mark the end of an era. Dorham was not only burying a friend—he was watching a changing of the guard, as the next decade of jazz would be dominated by the fusion and free subgenres. During this time, many students of the bebop school, Dorham among them, would be forced to either adjust to the new styles or to have their careers left out in the cold.

One of the strongest appearances Dorham made in this period was on Cedar Walton's 1967 debut album, *Cedar!*, recorded on July 10 of that year. On the handful of tracks he plays on, Dorham sounds composed and poised, with solos that showcase his careful crafting of lines. The album is a relatively textbook study of sturdy, late-style hard bop, with some prime examples of Walton's refined songwriting.

Also in 1967, Dorham played a club date at the Blue Morocco in the Bronx, at the intersection of 168th Street and Boston Road, fronting a band with Cedar Walton on piano, Paul Chambers on bass, and Denis Charles on drums. The version of "Blue Bossa" from this performance cooks; the rhythm section offers a hot setup for the simmering choruses of his solo.

This is the live recording mentioned in the preceding chapter that Bernard Drayton made and that was finally released by Resonance Records in April 2025. Drayton described its importance in revealing Dorham's enduring stature and ability, even in the later stages of his career: "When this show was recorded, Kenny was so highly regarded among musicians that even though he didn't have a regular band, he was always able to get the best musicians available to play with him. The performances that night were right there. The vibe was just one of those KD vibes. For a guy who wasn't able to play on a regular basis owing to his health issues, he was on fire and so was the band."[2]

In 1968, Dorham recorded a live album with pianist Toshiko Akiyoshi, with Lew Tabackin, Akiyoshi's husband, on tenor sax, Ron Carter on bass, and Mickey Roker on drums. Carter had played with Dorham previously. They had first recorded together on little-known saxophonist Rocky Boyd's *Ease It*, at a session at Bell Sounds in New York on March 13, 1961.[3] The album was later reissued by the Black Lion label as *West 42nd Street*, under Dorham's name, in 1989. Carter and Dorham went on to work together once more on Milt Jackson's *Invitation*, recorded on August 30, October 31, and November 7, 1962, at Plaza Sound Studios.

Carter recalls Dorham fondly, remembering how he would elevate other people's sessions: "We liked to call Kenny the sideman-leader. He had the best horn. He walked into the gig with an air. He brought integrity." Carter also notes that Dorham wrote "arrangements the way they were supposed to be," his charts featuring "some really great bass parts." Echoing Bernard Drayton's comments, Carter adds that Dorham's elegance was not just musical but also sartorial, as he "had great suits—he and Max Roach were the only ones at that time that had tailor-made suits."[4]

The Village Gate concert yielded crystalline results, with Tabackin and Dorham blending beautifully over Akiyoshi's fluttering melodies. Tabackin recalls meeting Dorham a few times before the session, in the different nodes of the New York music network. Tabackin states that every instance held something meaningful for him: "All these little encounters were always beautiful."[5] He fondly describes their first run-in, as well as the circumstances that led to the album:

> The first time I met him was when I was sixteen. I had just started playing the tenor, and I came out from Philly. I came to New York with a friend, and I went to Manny's Music Store . . . a famous music shop on Forty-Eighth Street. I wanted to try some mouthpieces, so I'm trying some mouthpieces and some guy comes over and says, "You sound good, you have a nice sound." And I looked at his shirt and he had initials on his shirt, K. D., and I recognized him from PR stuff and photos. . . . He was very nice. In those days, he did some work at Manny's to supplement his income. . . . That was really inspiring, you know, "Hey, Kenny Dorham likes my sound."[6]

They met again when Dorham heard him play at his first New York jam session:

> Years later, I moved to New York in 1965, and my first night in New York I went to this club called The Dom in St. Mark's Place, and I was told I could sit in there, and I figured I'd better force myself to go out and be assertive, which wasn't my personality, but I figured I had to do it. I show up at this place, and Tony Scott was running a jam session, and I went over to him and said, "Can I sit in?" and I got up on the stand, and I'm looking at the front row and there's like some guys sitting there with their arms folded, like judges, you know? One of them, I recognized, is Kenny. So I played and I could actually hear them talking. . . . "Sounds like he practices a lot." So that was the second kind of meeting with K. D.[7]

Dorham's comments indicated to Tabackin that he was working on the right material, but hadn't synthesized it into something that sounded comfortable. Tabackin delves into the session he recorded with Dorham, organized by his wife, pianist Toshiko Akiyoshi:

> Two years later, Toshiko put together this quintet recording up at The Gate. And she engaged K. D., and so we rehearsed and we started talking and he remembered me, you know, from the Dom's situation, and he said, "You got your shit together, man." He was complimentary about my progress, which I appreciated. We had a long discussion about things. Trumpet players and stuff. He was a little bit down on Dizzy's tone. He loved Clifford and all that. He was really beautiful. He was a real gentleman, warm guy, you know, supporting. . . . He played a solo on one piece; on that date, I think it was the first night and, you know, it was perfect. It was really quite poignant. That was his thing. He was special.[8]

The tune Tabackin is referring to likely is "My Elegy," which Dorham floats through, never dropping an idea or falling off a line. Tabackin summarizes this quality in Dorham's playing as elegant brevity: "His playing was never bombastic or . . . extroverted like Freddie [Hubbard]."[9]

Tabackin's remembrance of Dorham is shaped by the sense that Dorham was always on the scene, a presence whose opinion was both moving and motivating. The small arc of their time together suggests the development of Tabackin's playing: Dorham observing some core talent, then perceiving Tabackin's growth and finally acknowledging his development into a mature musician. Once again, Dorham was shepherding new young musicians into the music. The record itself is a testament to this, as sax and trumpet blend smoothly on Akiyoshi's songs, recalling Dorham's earlier pairings with Hank Mobley and Joe Henderson.

It was no coincidence that Dorham played a mentoring/encouraging/assessing role in Tabackin's musical career. Picturing Dorham standing, arms crossed, alongside the stage in something of a musical jury, one thinks of the higher levels of formal music education and how student performances are evaluated. Dorham took on a teaching role at numerous points between the late 1950s and the very end of his life. His generosity and supportiveness even extended, at one point, to lending his trumpet to then-fifteen-year-old Jimmy Owens so that Owens could sit in with Dorham's band for the first time.[10] While teaching at the Lenox School in Massachusetts in the late 1950s, as mentioned above, Dorham noted how fortunate his students were to have a structured experience, or even any sort of help at all with the advanced study of jazz.[11]

Nowadays, students are even more fortunate, with jazz camps, lab bands, and structured programs headed by leading musicians proliferating at the high school, college, and graduate levels. Phil Schaap characterized Dorham's pedagogical role even more emphatically, arguing that Dorham created the "blueprint for the educational aspect of jazz" and ran a "system of training younger musicians."[12] This system reached back into Dorham's time teaching younger musicians in Harlem through HARYOU-ACT, as mentioned in the preceding chapter. In fact, Dorham explained his late-1960s decision to move away from recording in part as being motivated by a desire to focus on his teaching work with HARYOU-ACT.[13]

Dorham was not entirely finished with recording, however. On June 4, 1968, Dorham recorded on pianist Barry Harris's *Bull's Eye!*[14] Harris was viewed largely as an acolyte of bebop traditionalism, playing in a way that did not incorporate the modal innovations of 1960s revolutionaries like McCoy Tyner and Herbie Hancock. Instead, Harris hewed close to the pristine linear construction of Bud Powell and Charlie Parker. This album features Dorham on trumpet, Charles McPherson on tenor saxophone, Pepper Adams on baritone saxophone, Paul Chambers on bass, and Billy Higgins on drums. Dorham plays fleetly, recalling his days with Parker and demonstrating no discernible decline in his chops. The title track opens the record and kicks off at a blazing tempo, as the players race through the rhythm changes. Another highlight is "Barengo," a slick Latin number that almost cinematically intimates a desert landscape in its subdued groove. Dorham plays in a cooler mode on this song, opening with spacious ideas before delving into more woven lines in the bridge. While the album does not push genre boundaries, the musicians sound assured as they work through familiar material, showing a care for motivic development that became increasingly rare in the aftermath of fusion and free jazz. Harris's plight in this period was not so dissimilar from Dorham's. To an audience beginning to look for the newest thing, adherents to older forms were being pushed to the side.

On December 16 of that same year, Dorham recorded on Cecil Payne's *Zodiac*, a conceptually expansive work from the veteran baritone saxophonist. The album, recorded for the Strata-East label, would not be released until 1973.[15] Payne opens up on this date in a way his instrument's traditional role rarely allowed him to on other recordings. For such a late period in his life, Dorham's tone is remarkably intact, rich, and warm, particularly on the elegiac opening track, "Martin Luther King, Jr." Elsewhere on the album, Dorham sounds consistent, if lacking some of the urgency and sharpness of his earlier playing. The album is a minor gem, featuring Wynton Kelly on piano and also in a surprising turn on organ, with Wilbur Ware on bass, and Albert Heath on drums. This album also provides a glimpse into the protofunk that was developing in the cracks between hard bop and fusion, as

Heath lays into some boogaloo grooves. Before the Harris and Payne record dates, back in spring of 1968, Dorham had also played at the Sterington House in Montclair, New Jersey.[16]

In the spring of 1969, in Town Sound Studios in Englewood, New Jersey, Dorham played on Clifford Jordan's *In the World*, another adventurous item on the Strata-East catalog, later released in 1972.[17] The album consists of four fairly open tunes that rest on long modal stretches. Like *In 'n Out* and *Point of Departure*, this album offers an interesting glimpse at Dorham playing outside of his usual circumstances, as he still trades in his usual substitution-heavy vocabulary and keeps his lyricism in the slower moments. Some of the ornaments Dorham plays on the final tune, "856," are as close as a listener is likely to get to hearing him play free jazz. August of that same year saw Dorham playing at the Both/And Club in San Francisco, in advance of which he sat for the KCSM interview with Jim Toman cited above.[18]

Dorham also managed to book some live dates in this lean period. On May 8, 1967, he performed at the Blue Morocco with saxophonist David "Fathead" Newman, alongside Ronnie Matthews, Paul Chambers, and drummer Candy Finch.[19] A bootleg recording from the show features some fine playing from Dorham.[20] While his tone is darker, his execution remains nuanced and crisp.

Pianist Frank Strazzeri worked with Dorham in the late 1960s, and described the consistently high level of playing he brought to the stage:

> That [playing in Dorham's band] was in the later '60s, basically in the Los Angeles area for a couple of months. Clifford Jordan, George Morrow, and myself, and Donald Dean (drums). That was the best jazz job. What a great player, nice, I liked him. One night I went in the club and I heard him playing and I said, "Geez, they're playing without me." And he was in there with just the drummer playing fast like Clifford Brown. And one by one we got on the bandstand and we exploded from the first thing. Man what a hip band that was, what he made us sound like in six weeks, we were burnin'. We were playing like Max Roach tempos and it felt like a ballad.[21]

A live album from this period gives credence to Strazzeri's observation. On May 26, 1968, Dorham performed at the Club Ruby in Jamaica, Queens, as part of tribute concert for Fats Navarro, Clifford Brown, and Booker Little (an interesting place for Dorham to be in terms of lineage, given that these men were his professional contemporaries, not his predecessors).[22] Dorham appeared beside fellow trumpeters Woody Shaw, Bill Hardman,

Blue Mitchell, Richard Williams, and Walter Kelly, with a rhythm section that included pianist Lonnie Smith, bassist Peck Morrison, and drummer Walter Perkins. This set, one of several summits organized by jazz promoter Jim Harrison, was released by Trip Records, a label specializing in low budget reissues, and was titled *A Trumpet Tribute.* A retrospective review from *JazzTimes* accurately describes the special encounter between Shaw and Dorham: "Shaw-23 at the time-dazzles with explosive pentatonics. His work on an uptempo version of 'What's New' answers the song's title with a conception that would eventually solidify his place as an innovator. Dorham, on 'Bags Groove' and 'Confirmation,' shows off his mastery of bop's harmonic language. You can hear how he had influenced Shaw at the time."[23]

Despite some tepid playing from the rhythm section (Morrison and Perkins never seem to find a comfortable pocket, and Perkins often seems to wander away from Smith's comping altogether), the set is a fascinating document. Dorham brings some of his late-career best playing to the date, demonstrating the muscular bebop language he helped to pioneer, while a young Shaw points the way to the next big innovation on the instrument with his shocking command of fourth and fifth interval leaps, while evidencing Dorham's clear influence on him in both tone and harmonic conception. The other trumpeters, particularly Hardman and Mitchell, play well but fall in line behind Shaw and Dorham. Strangely, it is Walter Kelly who draws the most crowd attention with his screeching high notes, despite a fairly obvious technical gap between him and Dorham. On the final tune of the night, Clifford Brown's "Sweet Clifford," both Shaw and Dorham are in top form, revealing their expert control of fast tempos.

Dorham closed the 1960s with another Left Bank concert on March 23, 1969, in a band with Jimmy Heath, Cedar Walton, bassist Walter Booker, and Albert "Tootie" Heath,[24] and kicked off the 1970s playing a few nights at the East Village club Port of Call East at the end of February.[25] Poet and novelist Ishmael Reed recalls spending time talking with Dorham and listening to him play at Port of Call. "Kenny was a delight to be around," Reed said. "I was always glad to see him. For one thing, he had a fascinating mind and his interests went well beyond the music scene. He was a ladies' man, a gentleman and a creative observer of the scene. I always bought him a drink—he liked rum—because I enjoyed his company and knew he was great."[26]

Dorham's final recording was a short spot in a Charlie Parker memorial concert at the North Park Hotel in Chicago on August 16, 1970.[27] He played "Just Friends" and "Summertime" with a sextet consisting of Ray Nance on trumpet and violin, Joe Daley on tenor sax, Muhal Richard Abrams on piano,

Rufus Reid on bass, and Wilbur Campbell on drums. Dorham still sounds polished, but his weariness shows.

On May 26, Dorham played a gig at a Jazz Adventures session in New York with tenor saxophonist Bobby Jones's "swinging quintet," alongside pianist Cedar Walton, bassist Herbie Lewis, and drummer Harold White. The announcement in *DownBeat* said that Dorham had reportedly "been taking it easy lately due to high blood pressure" but "felt well enough to play," adding that "[h]e is presently concentrating on teaching, composing and completing his autobiography."[28] At this point, Dorham's health issues were apparently well-known in the community. A caring note from the Collective Black Artists in the May 10, 1971, issue of *Expansions* magazine expressed well-wishes for Dorham during a hospital stay: "Brothers Kenny Dorham and Thelinous [*sic*] Monk are both ill. Kenny Dorham is in Flowers Fifth Ave. Hospital, NYC. . . . If you would like to send cards to Brother Kenny Dorham, please do, as for Brother Monk let us all hope for his speedy recovery. We must begin to show the concern that we have for 'OUR' talented Brothers, so they can continue to bring their vital, artistic messages to the people. CBA and Expansions extend their warmest feelings to K.D. and T.M. as many of our colleagues do."[29]

In one of his last public performances, Dorham played in the Collective Black Artists Orchestra on June 13, 1971, as part of the Left Bank Jazz Society's concert series at the Famous Ballroom in Baltimore. Dorham appeared with trumpeters Joe Gardner, Johnny Coles, and Jimmy Owens; trombonists Kiane Zawadi, Charles Greenlee, and Vincent Holmes; saxophonists James Spaulding, Sonny Fortune, Jimmy Heath, Roland Alexander, and Kenny Rogers (no relation to the singer-songwriter); pianist George Cables, bassist Reggie Workman, drummer Rudy Collins and vocalists Dee Dee Bridgewater and Don Jay.[30]

In the 1990s, the Schomburg Center conducted a series of interviews by bassist Larry Ridley with various jazz luminaries, in an effort to preserve the oral history of the music from an inside perspective. Among those recorded were pianists Walter Bishop Jr. and Ronnie Matthews, as well as saxophonist Charles Davis.

Walter "Bish" Bishop Jr. met Dorham while playing with Charlie Parker and went on to record with him on multiple occasions, on two of Dorham's post-Parker dates, in addition to Hank Mobley's *Mobley's 2nd Message*.[31] Bishop recalled Dorham's focus, averring that "Kenny was very much into the music," adding that for a long time he assumed players, composers, and arrangers stayed in their corners for the most part, but then noted that

"Kenny Dorham came along. . . . [H]e could play, compose, arrange, which put a hole in my theory." Bishop admired the depth of Dorham's knowledge and practice: "He was a complete musician, he could play piano, he could run lines not just chords, like many horn players can. And he could play tenor saxophone. A little Dexter flavor."[32]

This last observation about Dorham's playing the saxophone is an interesting one picked up later by other musicians. Trumpeter Bobby Shew, a devoted Dorham fan, said that Dorham himself referred to a strong connection to the saxophone in his music: "I think, with the exception of Lester Young, Kenny Dorham was probably one of the most brilliant harmonic geniuses of all time. This cat knew the ins and outs of chord changes. A friend of mine used to speak to Kenny all the time and has taped interviews and conversations with him. He said he asked Kenny where he got all his information and Kenny said he got it from Lester Young. Like Lester had it all down."[33]

In addition to Dorham's aforementioned harmonic brilliance, Bishop also appreciated his assistance in landing good work. Bishop commented that Dorham had likely pushed for him to be picked for the piano chair in Parker's band: "Kenny was a dear friend of mine and I think he had something to do with getting me in Bird's band."[34] Bishop also described the experience of watching Dorham work through his trumpet playing when he first arrived in New York: "Kenny was always an inspiration because I watched him grow, he used to come around Minton's and play and like half the notes would get hung up in his throat, some of the stuff was like scrambled eggs, that I heard eventually clear up and he got his sound and he was one of the most underrated of the trumpet players. He had a way of playing that was really uniquely his. The way he used to play those, what you would call cadenzas, inside out, outside in, the turnarounds. I really loved him."[35]

Dorham also gave verbal support directly to Bishop. "Kenny was really inspirational to me because he loved my playing [he said] 'yeah Bish, you about a mile behind Bud.' That made me feel so good."[36]

This wellspring of knowledge was further highlighted in a story Bishop told about playing with Dorham at the Five Spot, as part of Clifford Jordan's group. He said that on the bandstand there was "this piano [music], and I wasn't into reading that much, and these chords that were all . . . oh man, what do I do with this stuff. . . . [S]o he starts it off and I start scuffling and he says 'Bish what's happening, what's a matter man?' and he said 'Oh Bish this is your stuff, this is what you play.' And he sat down and played my voicings, he wrote this stuff tailored [to me] but I couldn't read it. . . . That taught me a lesson."[37]

Bishop's compliment showed not only the depth of Dorham's harmonic concept but also an appreciation of his wide view of music as a whole, and his ear that was strong enough to pick up Bishop's nuanced, fourths-and-fifths-centered approach to voicings. At the end of the interview, Bishop restated their closeness, as well as the plight of Dorham's public image: "He was my main man. . . . Very underrated, very underappreciated."[38]

In the same interview, Ridley also offered an anecdote about the late period of Dorham's life, remembering his own final phone call with Dorham: "I spoke with him a few weeks before he died and at that time I was playing with Sonny Rollins at the Village Vanguard and I called him up and I said Hey KD, What's happening? How you feeling man? Just wanted to check him out because I loved him. I was tight with him, fellow Virgo. I told him I was down there with Newk. [He said,] 'Oh yeah? Y'all down there, you two Virgos, I know y'all got some bad shit goin' on down there.' With that Texas accent of his."[39] Ridley and Dorham's palpable connection, clear in the mirthful warmth of Ridley's comments, is felt in Ridley's ending remark: "He was certainly beautiful, he was a very sweet guy."

Noted for lengthy stints with Sun Ra, Archie Shepp, and Elvin Jones, saxophonist Charles Davis played with Dorham several times, both live and in the studio, as previously discussed. Davis considered Dorham to be a profound influence: "A tremendous influence on me, musically he could take melodies and just make things happen, when nothing was happening he would make something happen musically, just the twist of a note, using a different chord. . . . I asked him one day to show me something and he said, 'you'll get it.' And I've been trying to get it ever since."[40] At which point, he laughs.

Pianist Ronnie Matthews was a friend of Dorham's who lived in the same neighborhood in Crown Heights. From a very young age, Matthews shared the stage with Roy Haynes, Freddie Hubbard, and Art Blakey. He played with Dorham on the *Flamboyan* live recording, demonstrating a powerhouse style evenly inflected by different schools, echoing Bud Powell, Wynton Kelly, and McCoy Tyner.

Matthews recalls that Dorham was always generous with his time and mentorship: "He, for me, was very special. . . . [H]e was another one of the people who was in Brooklyn . . . who would say 'stop by the house' and you would go and get a lesson in musical life."[41] As a pianist, Matthews was, like Bishop, impressed by Dorham's facility on piano, recognizing its impact on his compositional chops:

> Oh boy . . . Kenny Dorham was like hanging out with a dictionary. He had all of the definitions of whatever, I mean it amazed me, [that he]

> as a trumpeter, that he could sit down at the piano, you know not with super fantastic technique but his knowledge of harmony and how to move from here to there was very unique and he had enough facility on the piano so that he could just sit down and create something, I mean it was like magic, watching him create some of the things that he did, "Una Mas" for instance, which is actually something that preceded "Sidewinder," which was a big hit of Lee Morgan's that whole rhythm . . . just that sort of Charleston beat, it didn't become a big hit like "Sidewinder" did but [he] had written that rhythm on that song, which was a fantastic tune and made a great recording with Joe Henderson on Blue Note.[42]

Matthews ends by restating the impact Dorham had on his journey in the music: "And I had the opportunity to work with him quite a bit, another really important person in my life."[43]

While these three interviews explore different directions and periods, Dorham appears in all three as a somewhat consistent figure: as a mentor, friend, and joker, a complete musician who never took himself too seriously, and a tremendous talent who did not receive the public recognition owed to him.

In 1965, Dorham secured a position writing record reviews for *DownBeat* magazine—a "dangerous thing for a musician to do," according to then-editor Dan Morgenstern.[44] In fact, Morgenstern advised Dorham against doing it, suggesting that he was really "sticking his neck out."[45] Dorham persisted, though, publishing reviews as well as other commentary on the future of the music. This move was well-received by a number of readers and musicians. Having the inside perspective of a respected musician was draw enough, but Dorham's clarity and verve as a writer added significantly to his appeal as a critic.

Dorham was welcomed to the magazine in the issue for June 3, 1965. A brief note appeared alongside of his middlingly positive review of vibraphonist Gary Burton's *The Groovy Sound of Music*:

> **K.D.—Famous Initials**
>
> Kenny Dorham, trumpeter and composer of renown, turns to critical writing with this issue. He is the first major jazz musician to join DownBeat's staff of record reviews.
>
> Dorham's career is distinguished: he has worked with the big bands of Dizzy Gillespie, Billy Eckstine, and Lionel Hampton, but it is his small-band trumpeting that has gained him the accolades of musicians and critics. Dorham is perhaps best known for his work with Parker

> from 1948 to 1950, but he was also the original trumpeter with the Jazz Messengers (1955) and replaced Clifford Brown with the Max Roach Quintet after Brown was killed in June, 1956. Since '58 he has led his own groups.[46]

In total, Dorham wrote about twenty-eight pieces for the magazine, constituting a solid body of work with a variety of viewpoints. Some of his judgments are fairly surprising. He gives Freddie Hubbard's simmering *The Night of the Cookers, Vol. II* three stars ("Hubbard is excellent, but the album is tired")[47] but bestows four on Maynard Ferguson's *The Maynard Ferguson Sextet* ("Fine programming and an improved Maynard, who was last seen [heard] on the final chord passing the sonic barrier");[48] which feels wrong by several metrics. Ferguson, though technically gifted, was never a trumpeter mentioned by musicians or critics in the same breath as Hubbard and Dorham.

Anyone expecting Dorham to play nice in print would have been almost immediately disappointed, as he made his harsher opinions plainly known. The Dorham piece that drew the most reader attention (and some ire—the magazine published two unhappy responses in subsequent issues) was his "Two Views of Three Outer Views," a triple review of Albert Ayler's *Spiritual Unity*, Byron Allen's *Byron Allen Trio*, and Giuseppi Logan's *Giuseppi Logan Quartet*, all released by the ESP-Disk label. The article is unabashedly brutal; Dorham awards Ayler and Logan no stars and Allen a single star. Dorham wholeheartedly rips on Ayler's playing: "After the first chorus, Ayler does something—I don't know quite what he is trying to do—but it sounds kind of like a baby crying for candy with a whining ball in its mouth—wanting to play music and not wanting to, while holding a musical instrument."[49] He continues on his tirade, describing the playing on a later track: "A baby can do this if it can produce the air for the sound. A baby is free. Ayler is free. Free as a bird. Ayler is free of everything except melody and Father Time (the march of time itself—clock and cadence). He sounds like a very frustrated person. He is also playing a very controversial music. At this point it's not worth the paper it takes to review. Too far out. He passed the moon and the stars."[50] He writes with similar harshness about Logan: "I suppose this is an alto being blown into or blown around. A good grip on the instrument might have enhanced the aim. . . . For some unknown reason I could take Logan under specific conditions. But he better get out of that smoke-filled room, walk out on Bleecker St., and catch some air."[51] He is more lukewarm on Allen, but levels the same critiques about aimless playing: "The Allen record is a little better. . . . Allen enters, playing a horizontal line that has nothing to do with chords or anything being played by the others except an occasional cadence."[52] This review shows that Dorham was capable of being divisive and sharp but also evidences his gifts as a stylist. His writing is witty and imagistic but notably direct, in contrast to other critics contributing to the publication.

Dorham's relationship to the free jazz scene more broadly was complicated. He could be dismissive, but he also sought to understand the concepts and forms they were trying to apply to their music. Dorham may have disliked Ayler, but he played with Andrew Hill and supported Ran Blake when other beboppers would not. For Dorham, the litmus test of something being palatably avant-garde was whether or not, in his estimation, there was a deliberate thought process behind it. Trumpeter Bobby Bradford, a bandmate of free jazz pioneers Ornette Coleman and David Murray, described a conversation he had with Dorham one night after he came off the bandstand:

> I remember Kenny Dorham pulled me aside once, and he's one of my heroes, right? He asked me, "What key was that last tune you guys played?" I said, "Well, I don't know, exactly. It wasn't in any real key." He said, "See there? I knew that was all a buncha bullshit!" But he was tryin' to figure out for himself, was this thing valid. 'Cause he wasn't sure. I think he was disturbed by it. And it wasn't accessible, cause you didn't have any guidelines, like you had in bebop. And I couldn't explain 'cause much of what I was doin' was intuitive, via what Ornette [Coleman] was doin'.[53]

Just as Dorham was capable of being caustic, he was equally capable of being humorous in a more complimentary context. He gives trumpeter Ted Curson's *The New Thing & The Blue Thing* (1966) three and half stars, concluding his review with tongue-in-cheek praise of the longtime Mingus associate: "For the rapid progress made by Curson in the last two or three years and because I'm flattered at his sound more like me than anyone else, I rate him 100 stars. The tracks, though, were a little long for what they had to say. But the originality of the compositions alone is worth 3½ stars."[54] In a 2004 interview with Joe Maita, jazz critic Gary Giddins relates that Curson later asked Dorham about the review, and Dorham offered a similarly comical response: "[Dorham] reviewed Ted's album and went on and on about how great it is, and gave it three and a half stars. Ted asked him, 'Kenny, if you love the record so much, how come you gave it only three and a half stars?' And Kenny told him, 'That's what they gave [Dorham's] *Trompeta Toccata*, and that record's just as good as yours.'"[55]

This anecdote conveys a mischievous side of Dorham that other musical colleagues remarked upon. For example, Benny Golson remembers asking

Dorham, years earlier, about his approach to improvisation and getting an explanation that "was one of the wildest, most aberrational I had ever heard."[56] Dorham told Golson, "When I come to a chord and want to do something different, I come in from the side and jump on it. Sometimes I come in from the front, but quickly back up." Afterward, Golson said, Dorham "seemed proud of his bizarre explanation."[57]

Readers' reactions to these reviews were largely positive, though not unanimously so. A letter titled "Dorham's Delight" praises Dorham's contribution to the magazine:

> I think the idea of having a known jazz musician as one of your critics was a refreshing one, and DownBeat couldn't have made a better choice than Kenny Dorham.
>
> His thoughts are direct and to the point, and the "hip" verbal cliches are out of sight. This should add to some of the long deserved appreciation Dorham has missed.
>
> James Brown,
> New Rochelle, N.Y.[58]

A New England fan writes,

> My congratulations to DownBeat on having Kenny Dorham as a member of the record reviewing staff. I find him an excellent critic. His experiences as a No. 1 trumpet player, as a composer, and as a fine teacher qualify him exceedingly for the job he is doing for DownBeat. I find his ability to discuss and analyze the music a very refreshing and welcome approach to criticism.
>
> Peter R. Farmer
> Boston, Mass.[59]

Another notable review, and one of Dorham's most positive, is his four-and-a-half stars take on Miles Davis's *E.S.P.*, an album that is now firmly part of the jazz school canon. Writing about the album, Dorham is clearly impressed by the discipline and mystery of the record in terms of both the compositions and playing, but he doesn't seem to especially like the direction it points the music in. Initially, Dorham dives into the structure of the music, then praises Shorter's vertical fluidity:

> The theme of *E.S.P.* [the title track] consists of 16 bars of a very mystic, haunting, thriller type of melody that repeats, with Davis and [Wayne]

> Shorter playing parallel, the tenor voiced a ninth above concert, which gets an alto-trumpet unison effect. It's a somewhat fresh approach to the usual unison trumpet and tenor playing.
>
> Speaking of extrasensory perception, one has to be aware of what goes on during the creative act—the technical and psychological things, as well as the emotional, which will automatically be involved after one applies one's Fourth Wall (concentration) to the act/art of improvisation.
>
> In his solo, Shorter seems very familiar with the structure, as if he might have written *E.S.P.* (Miles is listed as co-composer with Shorter), but as is usual with most excellent saxophonists, they can maneuver the vertical structure in such a detailed fashion that they oftentimes sound better than the composer's version—considering the saxophonist in question didn't write it. This is a natural technical asset of the reed family—25 to 30 keys compared with the brass family's customary three.[60]

Dorham then offers a more measured estimation of Davis's contribution, complimenting his concept while questioning its basis:

> Miles, a vertical and horizontal improviser, solos next. Because of the technical deficiency of the trumpet, he is forced into a cat-and-mouse intrigue (arouse interest by baffling) with the horizontal and vertical layout of composition—unless he does it by choice, which I doubt. However, he plays mostly horizontally.
>
> Miles is a master cobbler, softening his leather in the first chorus or so, pounding the leather where he will later stitch it—an astronaut taking his job out for a dry run in preparation for a trip to another planet. (I don't think all Miles' jets were working, but he made a soft landing.) ESP can be—if not properly used—dangerous. If it's avant-garde like this, if it has higher aspiration with basic roots, then it must be built on something far-reaching. A lot of intuition—awareness—was necessary to bring this track off successfully, for it quite easy to get lost in the form, making the title apropos.[61]

Dorham concludes:

> I like to rate albums in the way that they move me emotionally as well as otherwise. Emotionally, as a whole, this one is lacking. It's mostly brain music, Miles is very crafty here and, because he is, so esthetic to the profession and perhaps enlightening to the avant-garde. I'm giving him a rating with reservations. This type of music has that drone

> thing that I don't like but because of the almost flawless presentation, I give five stars but only four stars for writing and effort and no stars for the over-all sound. ESP music in general is monotonous—one long drone. It's not for me.[62]

This review is fascinating on a number of levels. Here, Dorham is reviewing one of his contemporaries at the height of his powers, leading a band that will be remembered as one of his greatest (if not the outright greatest). While Dorham does not take a jealous swipe at Miles, he does observe that Davis seems to lean into minimalism and abstraction, and that he lacks the detailed harmonic sophistication of his bandmate Shorter. It is impossible to imagine Dorham not feeling a certain degree of frustration about the gap between them, as Davis was entering a renaissance at the same time that Dorham himself was struggling with a downturn.

Equally interesting is the note the review ends on. Dorham reiterates how technically and artistically strong the album is, but says that he remained unmoved by the "drone thing" that dominates its sound. What he is likely referring to here are the sort of nonfunctional harmonies that Shorter and pianist Herbie Hancock were using in their compositions for this band in this period. Whereas bebop was founded on the basic harmonic logic of standards, with dominant seventh chords acting as connective tissue between major and minor seventh chords, these new compositions explored the sound of more isolated chords that have no direct pathway to each other, allowing improvisers to focus more on modes than on the smooth navigation of standard changes and the use of substitution turnarounds.

This iteration of Davis's band, which included Shorter and Hancock alongside Ron Carter and Tony Williams, did not pioneer this sound. John Coltrane's quartet and Bill Evans's trio both had already mined this field heavily, but Davis's quintet brought this style to its logical extreme, with greater ensemble interactivity and graceful abstraction. *E.S.P.* was the beginning of a new period of musical revolution and, seeming to perceive this coming change, Dorham appears frustrated by what he knows it will bring—a wave of lesser "brain music" imitators and a likely rejection of the beautiful intricacy of bebop. The review is all the more valuable for this perception, as Dorham knows what he is hearing and tells the reader so outright. What Dorham also seems acutely aware of is that this innovation did not belong to Davis—or at least not solely to Davis—despite his name appearing on the record cover.

Dorham could also dole out generous praise in his reviews. He awards five stars to a student tribute to Oliver Nelson, *A Tribute to Oliver Nelson—Jazz in*

The Classroom, Vol. IX, writing, "The time, effort (trumpets, brass in general, endurance—chops), dedication make this a five star attempt. My hat's off to all concerned."[63] He likewise praises his one-time bandmate Dorothy Ashby, giving her album *The Fantastic Jazz Harp of Dorothy Ashby* a solid four stars, extolling her "slick" style and "gliding in Wes Montgomery-like style of octave approach."[64] Dorham ends that review brightly, with this reflection: "Comments: Excellent chord maneuvering by Miss Ashby on her instrument. The tracks are short but the performances (solo and accompaniment) are excellent. She's the presiding D.A."[65]

Sometimes, Dorham's issue is not with the musicians but with the date itself, or else with the conditions that are readily apparent in the recording. He writes of Sonny Stitt and Don Patterson's *Soul People*: "It's another quickie date—'Meet me at the studio later.' The choice of personnel is good, but the preparation I can't rate very very high. Musical accomplishment? What Stitt has done already is all well and good, but I would like to see him really become interested in music, life, for he is an excellent innovator—pacesetter. Five stars for Sonny but 3½ for the album."[66] At the same time, Dorham could be equally dismissive of music that he found insufficiently ambitious. He writes critically about Thelonious Monk's *Monk Misterioso*: "This is an easygoing, 1940s 'hard jazz' solo format album in general. The rest is quite fresh in harmonic and linear concept; however in some ways this is like a local on an express track—with the current avant-garde as the express. Which makes this sound like an old record. Loaded freight. Too passive, not enough hustle."[67]

Dorham himself could communicate so much musically that it is not surprising that writing also suited him. According to Morgenstern, Dorham "was a natural writer, he really was a gifted writer" who "needed very little editing."[68] Morgenstern particularly liked a longer piece that Dorham wrote for *DownBeat* titled "Fragments of an Autobiography" (cited at numerous points in this book), the first part of a longer work that Dorham intended to write but never got to finish. "Fragments" came out in the 1970 *DownBeat* Yearbook special issue, which meant that regular subscribers did not get to see it. Once again, Dorham's efforts to get his work in front of a wider audience were thwarted, although "Fragments" has been cited often since its publication. In this article, Dorham's desire to put himself on the record about both his musical history and the working conditions he endured is clear and his motivations obvious.

Dorham is not the only composer to attempt to define himself and his music for the benefit of his audience and also perhaps with an eye to his legacy. Saxophonist Marion Brown also decided to pen a critical text about his album *Afternoon of Georgia Faun*, discussed by Brent Hayes Edwards in *Epistrophies*:

> One answer may be encapsulated in something Brown said in a 1966 panel discussion on the "new jazz." "People try and interpret what the artist is really trying to say in his medium," Brown observed. "I don't think I ever heard anyone say that my lines, my sounds say this. Of course, if he says it in words it means that." So Brown compiles his own book on his record in order to have his say as to what his music "means": to claim the critical prerogative rather than abdicating it. As Eric Porter rightly summarizes it, Brown's book "responded to the critical vacuum by creating a dialogue about the album. In doing so, he not only set forth his avant-garde aesthetic philosophy and artistic agenda but also positioned the artist as the ultimate arbiter of the meaning of his or her music."[69]

While Brown was part of a different stylistic movement than Dorham, the root of his writing was markedly similar: to begin and to define the conversation surrounding his work, to preempt pushback or claims on his own music, particularly because both these musicians were aware that the conversation would begin with or without their own input. Unfortunately Dorham began writing his autobiography as his career was already on the wane.

It was also during this time that Dorham wrote one of his last jazz works, a ballad titled "As I Live and Breathe." Despite worsening health, Dorham continued to write both music and prose, to give interviews, and to teach, perform, and record right up until the very end of his life. Dorham's interview with Arthur Taylor for Taylor's book *Notes and Tones* was given in the last year of Dorham's life, and his 1968 recording with baritone saxophonist Cecil Payne was not released until the year after Dorham's death. And he maintained his community commitments even when his health, personal life, and financial circumstances were not what he wanted them to be. For example, in September of 1970, he organized a benefit for the "crack drum and bugle Carter Cadets Corps" of Bedford-Stuyvesant after their equipment was destroyed in a fire—perhaps recalling his Yellowjacket marching band days back in Austin.[70]

Another factor in Dorham's declining health was his lingering addiction to heroin. Heroin use wears down the body and its systems. Over time it can collapse or clog blood vessels, which can damage the kidneys and other organs. At the end of his life, Dorham suffered from chronic kidney disease and required regular dialysis treatments, which essentially do the work of functional kidneys by removing waste and excess fluid from the blood. Dorham struggled with the dialysis regimen—both its monetary cost and the toll it took on his body and spirit. As his friend and musical collaborator Jimmy Heath recalled it, "[h]e decided not to go. He'd had enough of it, and he said he wasn't going. His lady friend told him, she said, 'Man, if you don't go, K.D., then you can't stay. You're gonna die, man.' He got tired of that dialysis thing, and he split."[71] It is impossible to state exactly the balance in Dorham's mind between the impulse to live and breathe and the impulse to give up fighting the disease that was destroying his body. In fact, it may be more accurate to say that the balance shifted at different moments. People suffering from debilitating illness and experiencing intense physical pain are buoyed one minute and laid low the next as pain ebbs and flows and comforts come and go. For Dorham, of course, one comfort was music, whether playing it, writing about it, listening to it, or teaching it. We know that at times musical experiences rallied his spirits and helped him to fight to stay alive.

Fellow jazz stars Bill Hardman and Charles Davis organized a benefit for Dorham on October 1, 1972, at the Id Club in Brooklyn. The event was attended by a throng of prominent artists including Sonny Red, Barry Harris, Kenny Barron, and Cedar Walton, and raised a thousand dollars. Shortly afterwards, *DownBeat* magazine published an appeal for contributions to help Dorham, noting that he required fifteen hours of dialysis per week.[72]

In December 1972, a group of Boston musicians got together to hold a benefit concert for Dorham. Mark Harvey, a minister as well as a trumpeter himself (and, later, a Massachusetts Institute of Technology faculty member), was associate pastor of Boston's historic Old West Church, and he sought to create in that Methodist church what Reverend John Garcia Gensel had done with St. Peter's Lutheran Church in New York, on Lexington Avenue. St. Peter's was known as the "jazz church," and Rev. Gensel held a regular service called "Jazz Vespers."[73] Rev. Harvey instituted a similar service at Old West, but also participated in musical events himself, along with a jazz orchestra specializing in free jazz. Harvey had never met Kenny Dorham, but like so many musicians—and especially trumpeters—Harvey knew and admired Dorham's music. So Harvey conferred with trumpet colleague Claudio Roditi—just arrived at Boston's Berklee School from Brazil—and produced a benefit concert at the Old West Church. It was to be held on Sunday, December 3 at 8:30 p.m., and the price of admission was $2.50. In the midst of preparations for the benefit, Harvey got a call in the parish office from Kenny Dorham himself, who had gotten word of the concert and wanted to attend. Harvey speculated that his own friendship with bebop trumpeter Howard McGhee might have given him credibility with Dorham.

But he recalls worrying that Dorham might be too weak to make the trip. On the other hand, he asked himself, "How do you say no to Kenny Dorham?"[74]

On the afternoon of the concert, Harvey found himself in the office once again, this time sitting across from Kenny Dorham, who had made the five-hour trip from New York by bus. A photographer captured the moment, as a frail and bespectacled Dorham sat posed almost formally in his chair, his eyes at once revealing pain and serenity. He looked older than forty-eight but was dressed elegantly in a red sweater and plaid dress pants. Harvey was struck by how thoughtful and down-to-earth the great trumpeter was in person as he asked modestly if he could play at the concert. The plan was to open with a performance by two separate groups, and then to play the Dizzy Gillespie classic "A Night in Tunisia" with a ten-horn trumpet choir. Dorham would take the first solo. He'd then return for another solo, and also play the bridge and cadenza before closing the performance of the tune. The second half of the concert would feature Roditi's group. Along with Roditi, trumpeter Herb Pomeroy and drummer Alan Dawson were the most familiar names among the Boston musicians to perform at the concert.[75]

The old landmark church was decorated with stars hung across its balconies in honor of the occasion. Three hundred Bostonians packed the church that early winter night to hear Dorham and the other musicians and to pay their respects. After the opening acts had concluded, Dorham and the other trumpeters took the stage along with a rhythm section with Alan Dawson on drums, Ray Santisi on piano, and Chris Amberger on bass. Dorham stood off to one side until the solo section began, and then he played over the changes to the classic tune as he had done so many times before. This time, he played "to show us that he was still here."[76] Though tired and lacking in strength, he shared with the other trumpeters and the audience the warmth, creativity, and unerring sense of swing that had defined his playing since the 1940s. None of the subsequent soloists could match him, but they came over to stand by his side, one after another, as they finished soloing. The audience responded warmly. "I played one tune and got a standing ovation!" Dorham said afterwards, somewhat ruefully. "It was beautiful, but it makes me sad too; sad that the ovations never happened when I was healthy."[77]

The concert ended, and Dorham boarded the bus to New York that same night. He was scheduled to play at Minton's in Harlem the next night, December 4—Minton's, where so much jazz history had been made; Minton's, where Dorham had absorbed the lessons of early bebop and earned the renown that would send Charlie Parker after him with an invitation to join Parker's immortal quintet. By the next night, though, Dorham was too weak to play. The trip to Boston had taken too much out of him. He made it to the club, but did not take out his horn. He just listened. At the close of the evening, he went home. He would never pick up the trumpet again. He passed away in his sleep and was found the next morning.

An anonymous musician quoted in Berliner's *Thinking in Jazz* describes a similar scene, albeit with a likely mistaken date, Dorham somberly attempting to play until the very end: "'A friend of mine saw Kenny Dorham playing somewhere the night before he died. Kenny was playing on crutches,' he recounts with admiration, 'but he was playing right to the end.'"[78]

The world's response to Dorham's passing mirrored the reception he got as a living musician. *The New York Times* published an obituary of barely thirteen lines, misstating Dorham's brother's name and omitting entirely his sisters and his mother, all of whom were still living at the time. The sum total of the obituary's description of Dorham's trumpet style, gleaned from a recent *Times* review, was "quiet and precise."[79] No mention was made of any of his associations with Parker, Roach, Blakey, Henderson, or any other prominent jazz musicians.

As always, musicians took note. A memorial concert was held at St. Peter's Church, and George Wein organized one in San Francisco as well. Mark Harvey delivered a moving eulogy at the New York memorial. "It doesn't seem fair," he said, "to share an evening with such a beautiful human being who deeply moved the gathered congregation, and then to have him taken from us so quickly. The truth is that in reaching out to help this afflicted soul, we were blessed by his presence and brought more closely together."[80]

Services were held December 8 at St. Peter's in New York, with music. Then Kenny Dorham's body was sent to Austin, where he would be buried in East Austin's Evergreen Cemetery. A funeral service in Austin was held Sunday, December 10, 1972, at the Wesley United Methodist Church, Reverend J. H. Carruthers presiding.[81] Dorham's burial followed, with six of his old Anderson High classmates serving as pallbearers: Willie VanZandt, Larue Mays, Alvin Patterson, O'Quinn Cairo, Jeffrey Jones, and Grady Granberg. Alvin Patterson, the Anderson band director and a close friend of Dorham's, reflected on his friend's passing. He believed that Dorham's "lifelong ambition was to teach," and that "Kenny, despite his fame and popularity, never quite achieved his goal" of a teaching career.[82] At the time of his passing, Dorham was still enrolled in the NYU jazz program, where he was learning, but mostly mentoring other aspiring musicians. And he "had recently contacted Dick Goodwin, director of the U-T Jazz Ensemble, about transferring to U-T to complete his degree and play with the U-T jazz band."[83] There is something absurd about an artist of Dorham's stature asking to play in a college ensemble, but he knew that a secure teaching job required credentials that minimally included a bachelor's degree. So he had a plan, but ran out of time to execute it.

Melody Maker published a lengthy retrospective of Dorham's life written by Richard Williams,[84] and *DownBeat* ran a news piece on Dorham as well.[85] *Expansions* would later include Dorham in an "In Memoriam" piece: "Collective Black Artists note the passing of our dear brothers Louis Armstrong, Cal Massey, Wilbert Odell Bascomb, Kenny Dorham, Lee Morgan and W. C. Handy Jr., and we extend our heartfelt sympathies to their families."[86]

Musical celebrations by fellow artists who fully grasped the gravity of Dorham's passing continued to pay tribute. The Longhorn Jazz Festival in Austin had been started by George Wein in 1966 and had regularly featured Dorham. That event spawned the Annual Southwestern College Jazz Festival, and its 1973 version was dedicated to Dorham. Longhorn Jazz Festival president Rod Kennedy spoke eloquently of Dorham at the 1973 College Festival: "Dorham's great interest in young people led him immediately to visit with the youth of his neighborhood when he came home to the festival in 1966 and '67. . . . We think that Kenny's unselfish interest in jazz education set an example for many of the young people who are still in school because of their pursuit of jazz training through the lab band programs in high schools and colleges all over the country as well as in special programs which Kenny helped organize."[87] But Kenny Dorham could not organize or teach or play any longer. After an all-too-brief, action-filled life, he was at rest.

CHAPTER 10

LEGACY

A DORHAM RENAISSANCE

The Van Gelder recording studio in Englewood Cliffs, New Jersey, sits on a wooded lot off Sylvan Avenue, nestled in evergreens. With its low roof and natural wood siding, it brings to mind a Buddhist temple: modest, unassuming, and private, existing in harmony with its surroundings. Certainly no one passing by on the street would suspect its central role in music history, or even recognize it as a studio. Yet from its founding until the present, Van Gelder's studio, with locations in both Englewood Cliffs and Hackensack, New Jersey, has produced countless jazz masterpieces and remains in demand by producers and record companies. The classic Blue Note studio records of the 1950s and 1960s were made at Van Gelder's, and sessions for Impulse, Prestige, Verve, Muse, Criss-Cross, CTI, Reservoir, and High Note, among others, also used the Van Gelder studio. Kenny Dorham's self-titled debut as a leader was recorded at Van Gelder's Hackensack location, as was *Afro-Cuban*. The recordings *Quiet Kenny* and *Una Mas* were made at Englewood Cliffs, along with the trio of sessions where Dorham played under Joe Henderson's leadership: *Our Thing*, *Page One*, and *In 'n Out*. The interior walls of the studio are lined with photos of jazz immortals like John Coltrane and Billy Strayhorn. The lathe Van Gelder used to cut his insignia for each record is still there today, as is the Steinway piano that Thelonious Monk played.

Rudy Van Gelder was an optometrist with a passion for jazz, and he started his recording operation in his parents' Hackensack home, eventually moving it to the current location in nearby Englewood Cliffs. He was reportedly secretive about his methods for capturing sound and possessive of the recording equipment, preferring to handle it himself. Secret methods or not, the unique acoustics of his recording space drew many musicians and producers to utilize it. It is difficult to describe the way the wood interior both absorbs and reflects the tone of different instruments, particularly trumpet. Playing there, one feels the presence of so many departed jazz greats, and also the way the walls shape the sound. It is not only pure and brassy tones that shine in that room, but more subtle inflections and warm trumpet sounds that do not have a sharp edge to them. Kenny Dorham's understated approach to the horn utilized a softer, rounded tone, and often bent or swelled notes for emotional effect. The Van Gelder space showed off Dorham's trumpet sound in particular by picking up his sometimes burry tone, as well as off-beat accents, double-tonguing, and stop-time. Dorham's horn sound seemed to find a home in the studio's angled ceiling, in its walls, and in its corners.

Van Gelder bequeathed his studio to Don and Maureen Sickler upon his death in 2016. But even before that, the Sicklers were involved with the studio, and Maureen Sickler worked on projects with Van Gelder right up until the end of Van Gelder's life. Don Sickler is a versatile artist from Spokane, Washington, who has spent a long career in music playing trumpet, arranging and transcribing, and producing jazz recordings. As a jazz musician, he has toured and recorded with Ron Carter, Joe Henderson, Jimmy Heath, Philly Joe Jones, and many other jazz greats. One of Don Sickler's long-term projects has been bringing the music of Kenny Dorham to a contemporary audience, both through his own recordings and through arranging and transcribing Dorham's work. Don owns the publishing rights to Dorham's catalog, and he makes the lead charts and solo transcriptions available inexpensively to musicians through his jazz lead sheets project.[1] As Don explains, "I was always attracted to his music, and I didn't really know why until I started transcribing it. I realized the intricacies he put in for the rhythm section." He continues: "With Kenny Dorham's music, you can't just take a lead sheet and hand it out to the bass player, the pianist and the drummer, expecting to get what he did on the records."[2] Don discovered that one of Dorham's secrets as a composer was to write for the entire ensemble, giving them a more polished and cohesive sound collectively. In this, the rhythm section—particularly the drummer—was central. "Dorham always worked with the great drummers: Art Blakey, Kenny Clarke, Max Roach," Sickler notes in a *New York Times* article by Ben Ratliff. "The drummers are the ones that define the music, no matter what anybody says, and Kenny had the ability to know how to write for the drummers, to get the drummers to play their music. You listen to tunes like 'Minor's Holiday' and you know that's written for Blakey."[3]

Don Sickler had the chance to experience Kenny's inclusive and particularized writing first-hand in 1984, when he convened an all-star group of Dorham alumni at Van Gelder's for a recording called *The Music of Kenny Dorham*.[4] The project was part of Sickler's effort to secure greater posthumous recognition for Dorham. He chose music from Dorham's Blue Note recordings of the 1960s, which had been done at Van Gelder's. At that point, Sickler was able to secure a musical supporting cast who had all played with Dorham: Ron Carter on bass, Cedar Walton on piano, Billy Higgins playing drums, and tenor sax legend Jimmy Heath sharing the front line with Sickler The record is a fitting tribute, rendered with careful fidelity to Dorham's original plan by including every bass hit, drum break, and interlude that he wrote in. Selections vary in tempo and structure, from the intense and intricate "The Fox" to the lovely ballad "La Mesha" to "Escapade" with its intriguing twists and turns, intermittent loping, and stop-time.

Sickler explains the challenge of faithfully reproducing Dorham's multifocused attention on all the instruments involved. "Once he started getting involved with Hank Mobley and the Jazz Messengers," Sickler says, "his rhythm-section approach became very unique. Every player has his own little role, and you really have to write out parts for each to make it work. Most guys still try to take Dorham's stuff, make a lead sheet, and hand it out to everybody, and wonder why they can't get it to work."[5] It *does* work on this recording. The group is tight, every accent and tempo shift happens at the right time, and the record swings from start to stop, as if Dorham's passion flows through the arrangements by alchemy. The musicians sustain an enthusiastic groove. Sickler's solos reveal a pure and sometimes sweet trumpet sound as he slides from one chord to another via neighboring tones. He does not emulate Dorham in every respect—his tone, phrasing, and spaces are different—but he is mindful of the musical essence of each of the tunes chosen, and he conveys that. Jimmy Heath's tenor blends with Sickler's horn in a way reminiscent of Hank Mobley playing with Kenny Dorham. Heath and Sickler utilize effectively deployed long chord tones by one horn as the other solos.

It is difficult to choose a favorite or most memorable tune on a record of such consistently high quality, but "La Mesha" stands out for the feeling it creates through every melodic twist in the solos by sax, trumpet, and piano, which are suitable to a tune inspired by Kenny's then-three-year-old daughter, LaMesha. "La Mesha" is harmonically complex and challenging for the soloist, but like all of Dorham's writing, the complex structure is merely a means to the end of conveying powerful and evocative moods. Here, the affection and wistfulness one feels in the presence of one's young child comes through. Incidentally, when Don Sickler met with Dorham's widow and their five daughters to settle financial aspects of the recording, he realized that LaMesha did not know about the song her father had written for her. After all, she was three when he wrote it, and she did not know her father well. Don Sickler played the original Kenny Dorham version of the namesake song for her and she was overwhelmed hearing it and began to cry.[6]

In 1999, around the twenty-five-year anniversary of Dorham's passing and the seventy-fifth anniversary of his birth, Sickler assembled a group of jazz musicians who had played with Dorham to offer a multinight tribute at the Jazz Standard in New York. Ron Carter was there on bass once again, Dorham alum Ronnie Matthews played piano, and the great drummer Kenny Washington represented the next generation of jazz stars. Roy Hargrove appeared alongside Sickler on the front line for one night. Tenor saxophonist Mark Shim completed the group. The ensemble played six nights of Kenny Dorham's music, each night with a specific theme. One night was the music he made with Joe Henderson; another, titled "As I Live and Breathe," paid homage to Dorham's vocal writing and performance, with the singer Roberta Gamborini performing alongside Sickler. The final night was billed as "Blues in Bebop," predictably featuring the blues compositions that were so fundamental to Dorham's musical identity. English tenor player Ralph Moore guested on that last night.[7]

Don Sickler's efforts to secure recognition for the artistry of Kenny Dorham also led to the proper crediting of "Fair Weather," an intricate Dorham ballad that was featured in the 1986 film *'Round Midnight.* Starring Dexter Gordon, the film was based on the life of pianist Bud Powell and chronicled Powell's life in Paris, where he performed for supportive audiences and escaped American racism. "Fair Weather" is sung and played on trumpet by Chet Baker at the end of the film.[8] The composition was said to have been written by Bud Powell, but Sickler established that Dorham had written the both the music and the lyrics. In fact, there is a homemade recording of Dorham at the piano singing and playing the piece, and a handwritten score has also been found.[9] Thanks to Sickler, Dorham's authorship of "Fair Weather" was established, and that fact is now reflected in the BMI catalog.[10] The song's use in the film is yet another episode in the saga of Dorham's creative work attaining notoriety without being associated with him. Most people who saw *'Round Midnight* do not know that he wrote its final song. Dorham would eventually get his due when trumpeter Nicholas Payton recorded the first instrumental rendition of the song on his 1994 debut, *From This Moment*, with the proper accreditation. Payton invests the song, a clear homage, with melancholy and mystery as he plays sparsely, focusing on his full phrasing of long notes.

Dorham's friends attributed these instances when Dorham missed out on the rewards of his creative work at least in part to Dorham himself. As Rollins put it, "Kenny just never seemed to have that promotion, and that could be because he was too sweet a guy."[11] Likewise, as quoted earlier, Andrew Hill said of Dorham, "His problem is that he's so nice, and people seem to associate greatness with meanness or bitterness. In this business, you have to create some angry or tough image of yourself to be accepted, and therefore, too many people take Kenny for granted."[12] Dorham seemed more apt to promote other musicians than to take the limelight for himself. Horace Silver, Ernie Henry, and Joe Henderson were some of the most famous musicians Dorham encouraged early in their careers and helped to establish in the jazz world.

The affection, respect, and esteem Dorham garnered from other musicians has been a recurring theme in uncovering events from his life. In 2012, a series of commemorative events was held in Dorham's original hometown of Fairfield, Texas, by the Freestone County Historical Museum and the Trinity Star Arts Council. A plaque was dedicated in Dorham's honor, his family was invited from around the country, and multiple concerts were held. Dorham's friend and musical colleague Charles Davis (baritone sax) was invited to perform. Even though Davis's wife had just passed away, he made the trip to Texas and played the concert, then returned home immediately afterwards. Despite his own terrible loss, Davis was unwilling to miss the chance to honor his friend. Rubina was there, and her daughters Keturah and Evette came with her. A plaque recognizing Dorham's life and art was dedicated during the ceremony, and it stands on Fairfield's main street, in front of the historical society building.[13]

Depending on how you count it, there have been at least five generations of jazz musicians to encounter Kenny Dorham musically or to incorporate Kenny Dorham's contributions into their own playing. In *The Oxford Companion to Jazz*, author and trumpeter Randy Sandke writes about Dorham's influence trickling down through subsequent generations of Blakey's later horn sections: "The various bands led by drummer Art Blakey established the most significant trumpet dynasty in modern jazz. His first unit featured Kenny Dorham, whose harmonic inventiveness influenced sax and trumpet players alike."[14] Dorham's language was adapted by younger trumpet stars like Lee Morgan and Freddie Hubbard, both of whom would fill his spot in Blakey's all-star band: "A young musician, initially under the impression that the phrases he had copied from Lee Morgan were unique, realized after learning several Kenny Dorham and Dizzy Gillespie solos, that Lee Morgan 'had taken phrases from both of them.'"[15]

Morgan and Hubbard, then, were among the first generation to be influenced: These were Dorham's contemporaries who were his age or a bit younger. We have already noted some of the comments made by others of roughly the same age—Sonny Rollins, Benny Golson, Miles Davis, and Walter Bishop, among others, detailing their first-hand recollections of Dorham as a warm and generous, if sometimes enigmatic colleague. Tenor saxophonist Jimmy Heath was also a member of that first generation. He published an autobiography in 2007 in which he looked back over his long association with Dorham, starting with the trumpeter's first recording on the Debut label:

> The Debut Records date was fascinating because of Kenny's playing and his musical ability and quest. We were very close in our search for new harmonies and new ways of playing, as was Miles. We would regularly discuss the music, and our conversations would deal with reharmonization and modernization of songs, especially standards. These sessions would start at the piano, which reminded me of how I learned from Dizzy when he came to my house in Philadelphia. I learned that I needed the piano to create. Kenny could play the piano. He would say, 'Hey, Shorty. Dig this change here. You can play this here instead of playing that. You can play a half-step up on this instead of the usual change.' These were innovations he thought of or had learned from being around Charlie Parker or Dizzy. We would transfer information, and the information in musical terms would usually be about altered chords, what scales could be played on those chords, and how to enhance a composition by selecting certain notes to play the melody. These concepts were part of reharmonizing melodies. We compared original compositions and got suggestions and opinions from each other.[16]

Heath also recalled learning from Dorham about reharmonization, which "involves working with melody notes. If a composition has a melody note on the third, that might be changed. One of the songs Kenny was working on was 'Be My Love,' a popular tune made famous by Mario Lanza. Kenny changed the chords. Instead of playing G minor to C7 at a certain point, he would put in a passing chord of C-sharp minor 7 to F-sharp 7, a tritone away."[17] Here, Heath explains the way that Dorham sought to develop an expanded harmonic vocabulary, using scales that would momentarily heighten the tension in a changing chord before landing at its resolution. As Heath also notes, this approach expanded on the bebop approach approached by Parker and Gillespie. Outside of the music theory talk, what Heath also reveals is the warmth at the root of his musical relationship with Dorham. Much like Dorham's bond with Rollins, Heath and Dorham's craft talk was informed by a deep sense of camaraderie, readily apparent in Dorham's humorously calling Heath "Shorty."

Their closeness was also evidenced in a recommendation Dorham made to Orrin Keepnews, record producer and founder of the Riverside record label. Keepnews remembered that "Kenny Dorham and a couple of other musicians gave me the impression that Jimmy was a very remarkable player and somebody who clearly had managed to overcome his earlier substance abuse problems."[18] Dorham thus supported Heath's career in a way that went beyond the standard call for a recording session or club date. From what Keepnews suggests, Dorham not only vouched for Heath's musicality, but also his character.

Heath describes himself, Dorham, and Tadd Dameron as "romantics." Heath felt that "Tadd had a romantic quality and a melodic sense that was more lyrical. . . . [He] had a soulful way of writing I really admired."[19] While this comment mostly focuses on Dameron, many of the qualities Heath identifies in Dameron's writing seem synonymous with Dorham's sensibility as a composer: lyrical, soulful, and comfortably suited to words. Without stating it outright, Heath also pinpoints a yearning element that sits just beneath the surface of Dorham pieces like "La Mesha," "Passion Spring," and "Lotus Blossom." Elsewhere, Heath praises Dorham's songwriting talents, describing one of his compositions that appeared on the Milt Jackson's 1962 release, *Invitation*: "On that album, Dorham's 'None Shall Wander' became a favorite of mine, and I used it with my students when I began to teach. Kenny is one of my all-time favorite composers, and that was the second time I was on a record with him."[20] It must be noted that Dorham plays with a phantom-like sound on this particular track, toggling between supporting harmonies behind Jackson and brief spotlight moments.[21]

After Dorham's contemporaries comes the generation made up of musicians like Larry Ridley, Mark Harvey, Don Sickler, Jimmy Owens, and Ronnie Matthews, who heard Dorham or played with him in his later years. The recollections of Ridley, Harvey, and Matthews were shared in the previous chapter. To those reminiscences should be added those of Charles Tolliver, a trumpeter born in 1942. In an interview with Art Farmer, Tolliver describes the profound influence Dorham had on him, particularly how Dorham's harmonic concept seemed to come directly from Parker's harmonic language:

"When I heard how KD articulated things like these solos on 608 and things like that. . . . [H]e was actually playing saxophone stuff."[22]

Tolliver describes his initial arrival in New York as a time in which Dorham was his primary predecessor: "But I was also a lot more into KD then too as my main, I think, trumpet influence. In that period." He goes on to add that he met Dorham at the famous Five Spot club, which Tolliver described as a kind of social conduit for the scene as a whole: "I met everybody at the Five Spot."[23] Tolliver is a kind of mysterious, shape-shifting player. His vocabulary is wide, encompassing the bebopisms of Dorham and Parker with the same ease that he employs Coltrane-shaded modal language. Where Dorham's impact feels the most present is in the darkness and buoyancy of Tolliver's tone. This quality is strongly audible in his playing on *Members Don't Git Weary*, an album recorded with Dorham's former boss and bandmate Max Roach.[24]

Dorham was widely known for making generous gestures of various kinds to younger musicians like Tolliver. In a 1989 interview with *Cadence* magazine, late trumpeter Eddie Gale described his experience studying with Dorham:

> Kenny Dorham was my first trumpet teacher, he lived in Brooklyn on President Street and I'd walk to his house to get a lesson. This was, I guess, '59, '60. He'd say "Little Brother you play so hard, why do you blow so hard?" He felt I approached the instrument too hard—and I do. Over the years I've translated that hard blowing to the idea of a really wanting to express myself.
>
> I think he was the best trumpet teacher. He gave me that concept of playing the trumpet as far as telling me you have to be able to play top, bottom and the middle and you have to play it with feeling and that stuck with me today. You can play a lot of notes but what about the way that you feel, the feel. The artist must play what they feel more so than trying to be pitch perfect or pitch oriented. I'm more concerned about what I feel.[25]

Gale nicely summarizes a core component of Dorham's musicality, that technique works to serve feeling, not to make a display of itself. He also identifies Dorham's patience with developing musicians, a trait similarly extolled by John Eckert. In a similar vein, Dave Burrell recalled Dorham visiting him at his apartment on Bowery and Bond Streets: "I remember Kenny Dorham coming by and saying, 'You have to clean the place up and get a good piano and don't stop.'"[26] Sometimes Dorham's assistance would pay more tangible dividends; saxophonist Billy Harper remarked that Dorham helped him land a spot on a television show called *The Big Apple* which gave Harper some much needed media attention for his career: "Some of that had to do with Kenny Dorham, see, things work out don't they? Kenny heard one of the fellows who was in the producing side of it needed a jazz musician who was just into New York and he suggested me. Isn't that funny? It worked out beautifully didn't it?"[27] In other moments, Dorham's guidance erred on the side of the abstract. Trumpeter Marcus Belgrave described getting an unexpected sort of advice from Dorham:

> I didn't get a chance to spend a whole lot of time with Kenny [Dorham] but he would come by Cecil's [Belgrave's cousin] all the time. And Cecil would tell him, "Say, this is my cousin. He's going to be a great trumpet player," and Kenny would say, "Yeah, and I'll box him on his nose . . ." I said, "Kenny, when you going to show me something?" He said, "Come over the house, come on over the house . . ."
>
> I went to the house one time—he took me to the gym (laughter).[28]

Unfortunately for this generation, being in proximity to Dorham in his lifetime also meant feeling his loss all the more painfully. Free jazz trumpeter Roy Campbell Jr. described seeing Dorham when he was ill, and also his admiration for Dorham's continued commitment to playing and teaching:

> Now Kenny Dorham, I used to see him play at Minton's on Monday nights. He was a brave guy, but he was underrated and a little more introspective than Lee. What saddened me was that he was on dialysis, until the day before he passed—he was a dedicated man. Even though he was sick, and all that, he was still teaching the Jazz Mobile workshops and he was telling me how to hold my horn: you have to do this and you have to do that. You have to learn the scales and you have to learn the changes. That day I went to the class before he passed, it was very serious because, [*sic*] I could see that he was getting ready to go. It was just like an air, you could see it. And I think the next day we had a benefit for him at Town Hall and then he passed about 4:00 a.m. That experience and Lee Morgan's death stopped me, I just didn't want to go to the Jazz Mobile anymore. It wasn't the same for me after that, you know, two deaths close together.[29]

For these musicians, Dorham's death marked the end of an era of collaboration and mentorship, as well as the loss of a musical idol.

After Dorham's death, a third generation grappled with the musical legacy of an artist who died before they were born, or else when they were very young. Trumpeter and composer David Weiss (born 1964) is part of that third generation. Speaking about Dorham's influence on today's players, Weiss says that while people focus on capturing his tone, they fail to appreciate the depth of his harmonic concept:

> That's the interesting thing. . . . I don't really like how people talk about K. D. To me, K. D.'s harmonic stuff is unique. And very influential on me. I transcribed nothing but Kenny Dorham's solos pretty much through college. His tone is unique, and I guess that, to other people, is more readily identifiable. So when somebody compares some trumpet players today to Kenny Dorham, I don't hear it because I don't hear the harmonic conception, and I think that's what defines Dorham or what makes him unique and important. I mean, the sound is personal, tone is personal, and people can be more attracted to that tone. It's a matter of taste and that's all fine, but for me, for better or worse, it's not my first consideration, considering all the immensely important stuff he did. I don't really hear any trumpet player doing that.[30]

He clarifies that the influence is present today, but not in the way people might think. He says, "If it is [there], it's disguised. Like, if I do it at this point, because I don't play that much bebop anymore, it's disguised. But it's there."[31] He continues to say that another essential aspect of Dorham's playing was his obvious command on the bandstand, in both feel and sound: "Another thing that strikes me about him is that when you look at the Freddie Hubbards and Lee Morgans in the world, we don't look at Kenny Dorham as [that] a strong of a trumpet player, you know, physically on the instrument. But if you've ever watched those really grainy videos of him playing quartet with Swedish guys, his authority on those . . . I mean, he's really a commanding presence without being a superstar trumpet player per se. He plays with such authority. He's in command of the language and he's a true bebopper."[32] Weiss adds that Dorham's approach is uniquely hard to emulate; he says that modern trumpeters struggle to integrate his substitutions: "Maybe their tone and approach might be closer to K. D., but I don't hear the turnarounds. I don't hear the tritone subs in that way. Even if they play the notes, I don't hear it as part of a conception they understand. I mean if you really understand the conception and how to do it. Then you would expand upon it or use it in different ways."[33] Laughing at himself a bit, Weiss expands on how this has shaped his playing: "Here's the bragging part. I'd like to think that's what I do. I don't think it might be as immediately recognizable because I don't phrase [like Dorham]. But the harmonic conception, the tritone sub stuff, is the jumping-off point for me. That strongly influenced whatever harmonic stuff I try to do. I'm not really playing bebop that much anymore. If I started playing that stuff again . . . boy, I'd be leaning on that Kenny Dorham shit again."[34] Discussing a recent tribute to Dorham, the Kenny Dorham Centennial Celebration at Dizzy's Club Coca Cola, Weiss observes that he would name a surprisingly modern player as a Dorham acolyte:

> They just had a thing at Jazz at Lincoln Center for Dorham's birthday. Here's the interesting thing. I would bet that Josh Evans has more Kenny Dorham in their playing than guys who are known for trying to play like him because he learned the vocabulary and took it somewhere. I mean, Josh Evans, I would speculate, out of any of them he would be the guy. But again, Kenny Dorham's turnarounds can work in a total bebop context and stay there, or it can be a jumping off point of how you approach any kind of harmonically adventurous thing. I think Josh can go outside the chords and do whatever he wants, but if you have the grounding of a Kenny Dorham, it makes more sense. It has more direct ties to where this shit started.[35]

When asked about who was Dorham's clearest stylistic exponent in the following generation, Weiss says, that he thinks it was Woody Shaw:

> I mean the guy who I hear doing it the most is Woody Shaw. I listened to that *Setting Standards* record that came out when I was in college [1983]. I was all the way with Kenny Dorham and I was like, "It's in here too." Listen to "There Is No Greater Love," a couple of his turnarounds on that are . . . I can't say Kenny Dorham played that exact lick but it's totally based on that. To me, it's thirty years ago now, but there's your connection. Maybe you need to hear Woody playing "There Is No Greater Love" instead of "Kill A Brick" or one of his originals to get the lineage.[36]

Listening to "There Is No Greater Love," what becomes apparent is that Shaw extends Dorham's substitution concept into the territory of John Coltrane's harmonic innovations, pushing his use of diminished hinges into full-on superimpositions of clashing scales, outlining nonfunctional harmonic sequences. Shaw would later pay more overt tribute on *Double Take* (1985), his joint album with Hubbard, playing and recording the Dorham original, "Lotus Blossom."[37]

Weiss concludes that he is grateful for Dorham's legacy, as Dorham played a key role in his development: "I think he started the journey for a lot of guys. I know for me, for sure. I won't say I'm the most expansive player on earth, but I would say he put me on that journey away from [being] a standard bebop guy."[38] Dorham's influence, along with that of Shaw and Freddie Hubbard, is evident on Weiss's most recent release as a bandleader, *Auteur* (2024).[39] Weiss zigzags in and out of the changes on heady originals like "Too Little, Too Late" and "The Other Side of the Mountain," rarely sounding overtly like Dorham, but carrying the same lateral approach that Dorham defined, Shaw expanded, and trumpeters like Evans continue to develop.

Another member of that third generation is trumpeter Joe Magnarelli (born 1960). He is often held up as one of the most prominent players in Dorham's lineage on the scene today. When asked about how to recognize Dorham's imprint on a trumpeter's playing, Magnarelli points to two factors: "Well, obviously the sound is the first thing, you know you can hear it in the sound in the certain way that cats bend notes . . . and then the second thing is the harmonic concept and the time feel, which kind of go together. Both are coming from Charlie Parker. . . . One thing I know about Kenny Dorham is that before he joined Charlie Parker's band, he learned all of [his] solos that had been recorded up to that time. And that was very impressive to me . . . to go into a gig like that."[40] Magnarelli adds that he put in his time with Parker as well, in an effort to gain that same level of mastery. He acknowledges other factors, but said that Parker really cleared the way for Dorham's concept: "Now, he had a lot of blues in him, too, and he definitely loved Dizzy. But I think he tended more to play like Bird and Fats [Navarro]."[41]

Magnarelli lists a number of players who share, or shared, his appreciation for Dorham, bearing these trademarks in their respective sounds, including Tom Harrell, Bobby Shew, John Eckert, John Marshall, and Tommy Turrentine. He also mentions Freddie Hubbard. "Freddie Hubbard told me [that] when he came to town, he started studying with Kenny Dorham," Magnarelli says. "He was the cat, you wanted to play like him, you know? And you can hear it in early Freddie, and Dizzy Reece. Dizzy Reece was a perfect combination of Woody, who was a contemporary of his, and Kenny Dorham, who was probably ten or fifteen years older than him."[42]

Magnarelli says that, in the 1980s, the new generation of players shied away from Dorham, something Magnarelli attributes largely to tone: "There's a certain thing in Kenny Dorham's sound that trumpet players don't like. I love it. But certain trumpet players, they can't deal with it. Because it goes against the classical thing." Magnarelli adds that when he wants to hear classical music he listens to the Chicago Symphony, but for trumpet music he wants to hear "Elvin, Philly Joe" swing.[43] What Magnarelli says about Dorham logically follows what is prized in modern jazz conservatory trumpet playing: muscular technique, post-bop harmonic flexibility, and a bright tone. Dorham's vocabulary doesn't provide the same keys to modal playing as a Woody Shaw or a Freddie Hubbard, nor does it unlock the same discursive path through free playing as a Don Cherry or a Roscoe Mitchell. What Dorham had (and what studying his records may yield after thoughtful listening) is something more intangible, something that arrives at a different sonic place altogether. As Magnarelli says:

> What you have to understand is that he also played the saxophone. He also was a singer. So his sound had more dynamics to it than just trumpet.... His sound could touch you in many ways. He knew what a tenor felt like, the flow of a tenor saxophone. He understood the voice... so his sound, to me, has a lot of depth. When I hear Clifford's sound, of course as a trumpet player, it's amazing and I, at certain times, wish I could have that sound. But as far as what I'm attracted to it's totally Kenny Dorham.[44]

Magnarelli has a similarly haunted tone, mellow and rich, in contrast to the quicksilver brightness of many of his peers. While Dorham's playing might move in and out of the spotlight, players like Magnarelli show that he will always have acolytes, searching for that measure of vulnerability and poise.

Magnarelli remains intrigued by Dorham's compositions. He recorded the Dorham blues tune "Buffalo" on an early record of his own. Regarding the twists and turns of Dorham's writing, Magnarelli states: "That just speaks to the depth of his musicianship. It's all in his playing.... His compositions are very off the beaten track, very modern-sounding for where he came from." Magnarelli has listened to Dorham for a long time. In fact, *Showboat*, he says, "is the record that I kind of learned how to play the trumpet off," while "*Una Mas* might be his best record," but ultimately feels that "who's to say. There are so many!"[45]

Magnarelli's encounter with Dorham's legacy was transmitted directly to the fourth generation of Dorham-influenced musicians when he took on Freddie Hendrix as one of his graduate students. Hendrix represents perhaps the youngest group of jazz trumpeters to attain musical maturity, as Kenny Dorham would have put it. Currently at the peak of his powers, Hendrix has worked with Dorham contemporary Jimmy Heath, The Jazz at

Lincoln Center Orchestra, The Count Basie Orchestra, Mulgrew Miller, Roy Hargrove, Aretha Franklin, and Alicia Keys, among many other artists. He has also recorded under his own leadership and teaches at The New School and the University of Hartford. Hendrix recalls first hearing Dorham on the 1963 *Page One* recording. "All aspects of his playing stood out to me," Hendrix recalls. "He had a bright tone though the attacks in his notes have a roundness to them. He's a very melodic player as well as a great chord changes player. In all of the legacy of great trumpet players, he's one of the few who uses lots of staccato (short notes with a point) articulation as well as bending of the notes."[46]

Hendrix learned Dorham's solos through transcriptions, but also by listening and singing back the solo lines. Their melodic aspect makes the solo lines attractive to a student seeking to play musical ideas that will sound good over a given chord or song. "Lotus Blossom" (sometimes called "Asiatic Raes") is a favorite Dorham composition that Hendrix often performs. It is expressive and conducive to soloing. Hendrix also recalls an experience he had while recording with Jimmy Heath that connected him to Dorham: "Mr. Heath loved Kenny's improvised ideas so much that in one of his big band compositions 'Gingerbread Boy' in the shout chorus where the trumpet players play, he wrote a specific improvised line that KD played for us (the trumpet section) to play. . . . I played something over one of Mr. Heath's turnarounds in a KD kind of way and he said, 'Man, did you hear Freddie? Man, you was snaking through those chord changes!'"[47] This is a reference to Kenny Dorham's signature use of turnarounds or turnbacks, the ideas played over the last few bars of a musical form to anticipate the beginning of the form that is about to come around again. The comparison to Dorham was high praise for Hendrix, especially coming from Dorham's old friend.

In addition to acknowledging his own musical debt to Kenny Dorham, Hendrix notes the ways his contemporaries were also influenced. The late bassist Dwayne Burno wrote a song—"KD"—in Dorham's honor. The late trumpeter Roy Hargrove, born just an hour from Fairfield in nearby Waco, Texas, displayed a Dorham influence as well. He recorded Dorham's "Afrodisia" on a Latin jazz album called *Habana Cristal*. Discussing Dorham's Latin-inflected compositions brings Hendrix around to talking about the changes in Latin jazz that have occurred since Dorham's passing. For Hendrix, Dorham's Afro-Latin recording for Blue Note records "is one of my primary awarenesses of Afro Latin music on an introductory level." At the same time, Hendrix feels that Dorham only "scratched the surface in his explorations of Afro Latin rhythms."[48]

In the ensuing fifty or so years, many complexities have developed. For instance, Hendrix says, there are so many claves (repetitive melodic-rhythmic phrases) that create variation, not to mention specific song forms. One wonders what Dorham would have done with those new possibilities had he lived to hear them. In any case, Dorham deserves credit, along with Dizzy Gillespie and others, for exploring Latin rhythms in jazz and contributing to their "infusion," as he once put it. Contemporary trumpeter Brian Lynch, who profusely acknowledges a musical debt to Dorham, is a current leader in the melding of jazz and Latin rhythms as well.[49]

Dorham's influence on a fifth generation of jazz trumpet players can still be felt. Kal Ferretti, an up-and-coming trumpeter at Manhattan School of Music who has shared the stage with modern greats like Christian McBride and Joe Farnsworth, performed in the second half of Dorham's centennial celebration in 2024. Ferretti says that she first "fell in love with" Dorham's music when she heard his solo on "This Love of Mine" from *Jazz Contemporary*. She explains: "His sweet sound and melodic approach have been so instrumental to my process. Studying his material has taught me so much. He is one of the true masters of the utilization of the tritone substitution. Dorham was known for being such a sweet and kind person and that projects right into his playing."[50]

Ferretti adds that "La Mesha" and "Fair Weather" are some of her favorite Dorham compositions to perform, both of which she played at the centennial. Reflecting on her experience, she says:

> I was a part of Jazz at Lincoln Center's Young Trumpet Summit at Dizzy's Late Night in August, celebrating Dorham's centennial. The Dorham family was present each night. For my feature, I chose to play "La Mesha" and after I played, I heard tears nearby, coming from LaMesha Dorham herself. Playing my hero's composition for the person he wrote it for goes down as one of my most important musical moments. I have learned so much about what it means to be a musician from studying the genius of McKinley Howard Dorham's music and life.[51]

While Dorham may have received little appreciation either from the press or from the record business, he was undeniably appreciated and beloved by the musical community. These testimonials evidence how the community took care of its own and discerned the quality of Dorham's music right away. Across these generations, his talent, work ethic and kindness have always been seen clearly.

A MEASURE OF THE PERSON

One purpose of this examination of Kenny Dorham's life has been to argue for a more prominent positioning of Dorham's creative output in the history of American music. To that end, much time has been spent here examining specific works for their innovation, distinctiveness, and powerful message. Even before research for the book was started, the Austin community had granted some measure of that recognition by including Dorham in the Austin Music Memorial, essentially a small and select Hall of Fame for the music hub city, in 2008.[52] And the litany of praise and affection from Dorham's musical peers documented here, together with all of the musical output and milestones we have recounted, should provide the groundwork for many more such honors.

But getting to the core of who Kenny Dorham was as a person may prove more elusive. What does the record of his life show beyond concrete details about musical artifacts? What emerged again and again that a reader might not glean from the discography printed at the end of this book alone? Two such intangibles bear mentioning and were emphasized by Dorham's family, friends, and colleagues. First was his keen intelligence and deep intellectual curiosity. Jazz music requires intelligence in order to practice its musical language and balance one's expression with the rhythmic energy that drives the music, so intelligence is a prerequisite possessed by all the great jazz artists. But Dorham was always probing, inside and outside of music, to learn about all sorts of things and depict them musically: a passenger train, a fox, a Brazilian city. Voracious reading habits supported that quest, and a fondness for Scrabble was a manifestation of it.[53] Dorham dedicated an entire album to multifaceted depictions of spring. He could write in intricate and lucid detail about how to dig a board well or about how one of his complex compositions was structured. When interviewed for liner notes, he seemed to have difficulty stopping, as if his thought processes would always outstrip the allotted space.

As well as seeking knowledge, Kenny Dorham wanted to share it. Although his ultimate goal of a teaching career eluded him through his untimely passing, he found outlets to teach during his entire adult life by working with Harlem teens, aspiring musicians, and with colleagues who couldn't read music or couldn't compose. He would give his time and open his home to anyone who wanted to talk music or solve a musical problem. He would even allow people to live there, as George Coleman reveals.[54] As Phil Schaap said, Dorham "ran the scene" of jazz education by discovering and encouraging a number of the musicians who have been interviewed for this book, and also many others who weren't.[55] Dorham's weekly sessions at Minton's (right up until the last night of his life) were devoted to nurturing new talent. The institutionalization of that scene in schools, colleges, and conservatories is yet another overlooked aspect of Dorham's legacy, with incalculable benefit to and influence on the music world. Those words (about Dorham as mentor) were spoken at his eulogy in 1972, and they are even more accurate fifty years later.

But will anyone ever truly know him? Saxophonist Benny Golson, known as a member of Art Blakey and The Jazz Messengers, as well as the composer of numerous jazz standards, first met Kenny Dorham in the early 1950s. He would go on to record with Dorham on *The Modern Touch*, a smoothly arranged sextet album. In his autobiography, he characterizes Dorham as a practitioner of a mysterious, cryptic style on the trumpet: "Kenny perfected a particularly hip way of weaving in and out of chords that I loved but I could never figure out how he did it."[56]

Golson recounts asking Dorham about it directly, as noted above in chapter 9. Golson never got a clear answer, but upon further reflection, he found that this opacity perfectly encapsulated Dorham's whole essence, from his approach to improvisation to his manner of conversation:

> I realized that Kenny played with the same indirectness and obliquity I had just heard when he talked. His playing always offered something allusive, unexpected, and endlessly interesting. He developed a habit of teasing anticipation that had become an earmark of his virtue as a trumpeter. Without recognizing it, I had always been delighted by that "sideways" quality in his music. Now, in conversation, I saw that he *spoke* sideways as well, in a manner vague, teasing, figurative. A habit of irony or poetic approximation was rooted in the man's psyche. He searched for back doors and side entrances for his utterances, ducking inside musical and verbal expressions from odd angles. He may have been protecting himself from direct emotional exposure, unexpected dance-like movements misdirecting or obscuring his aims. The simple thing to account for Kenny's playing was its tonal allure, a firm but gentle, prowling quality. He gathered chords as if they held secrets that too much sunlight or attention might destroy.[57]

The magic of Dorham's playing, and perhaps of his personality, in Golson's eyes, was its inherent elusiveness, the sense that Dorham was holding out, never moving through the chords head-on, but always finding subterranean shortcuts through a song form. What Golson likely means is that Dorham did not play the chord changes of a song overtly, but instead used substitution harmonies to elegantly link his ideas together from measure to measure. The most common example of this would be his use of the diminished scale over a dominant chord. Perhaps the most interesting part of Golson's remark is his description of Dorham's fear that too much attention might ruin the subtle darkness of his playing. It suggests that this concealment was an essential element of his sound.

While Golson remembers Dorham very fondly, he notes that he never felt like he fully knew Dorham as a person: "No one I knew ever broke the 'Kenny' code. He was engaging and hip, a term that fit Kenny better than anyone else I could name. . . . I never figured out his technical or improvisational tricks, and I seldom had an inkling what he would say or do, musically or otherwise. To this very day I miss Kenny Dorham."[58]

Golson's understanding of Dorham seems to hinge on Dorham's essentially being uncrackable, a person who could not be reduced to one simple descriptor. In Golson's estimation, Dorham's personality was shrouded in as much mystery as his lateral approach to chord scales. While the affection Golson felt for Dorham seems deeply genuine, he could not claim a total understanding of Dorham. This impression appears elsewhere in other people's remarks, as people remember Dorham as being at big-hearted and warm in some moments and a sly joker in others. While Golson doesn't put it in these terms, this might account, in some regard, for the fact that Dorham was the same person who might twist through an intricate bebop run in one chorus and sting a single blue note in the next.

What is harder to explain is the divergence between Dorham's standing among musicians and the lack of recognition he received from many critics. The interviews and written comments presented here establish a deep and wide respect for Dorham as a trumpeter and composer, spanning generations from the 1940s to the present and crossing into numerous styles and eras. Jazz great Sonny Rollins knew Dorham from the early days of bebop through his modal period, and spoke of him as someone he looked up to. Ronald Shannon Jackson and Charles Tolliver went on to explore genres beyond bebop and hard bop, but cited Dorham as a profound influence. Joe Magnarelli and Freddie Hendrix are prominent on today's jazz scene and acknowledge a deep debt to Dorham, and so on. Why, then, have critical appraisals, often from nonmusicians, lagged behind peer appreciation and recognition? Some have pointed to Dorham's tone as being less classically-oriented than that of some other trumpeters. As Joe Magnarelli put it above, some people "can't deal with it." That may be so, but it cannot by itself explain the critical responses to Dorham's work. After all, Dizzy Gillespie and Chet

Baker did not play trumpet with a classical tone, but they attained more critical and popular acclaim than Dorham did.

Critical attention (or lack of it) tends to be self-reinforcing, and over time it became more difficult for Dorham to break through the ever-hardening barrier of critical neglect beginning in the 1950s after he left Charlie Parker's group. Critics, in turn, mediate artists' exposure to the public, and so they wield a powerful influence over the arc of a career. In the 1969 radio interview quoted earlier, Dorham offered his own explanation of the gap between jazz critics and musicians in their ability to understand the music. "It has to do," he said, "with a guy writing about something he's never really been a part of." He went on to describe the difference further, as not being on the "inside" of the music but rather approaching it "outside-in."[59] Listening to the interview, one feels Dorham's frustration at the "outside-in" critical perspective and how he had been weighed down by it for two decades.

Kenny Dorham struggled in the 1960s to make ends meet, to outpace destructive habits, and to maintain a presence on the jazz scene. He did not promote himself—perhaps, as some thought, because it was not in his personality. But it is also possible that Dorham had by the 1960s assumed that the critical and popular recognition others enjoyed could no longer be expected for him. We will never know for sure what Dorham hoped for in the last decade of his life or how his life might have been different if critical recognition had come earlier. It remains only to preserve Dorham's legacy today.

KENNY DORHAM'S BACKYARD

The efforts by Don Sickler and others to sustain Dorham's legacy in the jazz world represent one avenue to seeking belated recognition for him. At the same time, there is an energetic effort underway to preserve, celebrate, and transmit Kenny Dorham's influence on American music in the Austin neighborhood where he first learned to play trumpet. Harold McMillan, a musician, activist, and historian living in East Austin, is at the forefront of that effort. Two decades ago, McMillan obtained the right to use a vacant lot on East Eleventh Street, around the corner from the former Dorham home, as a performance venue. He calls it "Kenny Dorham's Backyard," which is quite literally what it is. McMillan often plays there, and he also books other artists from Austin's vibrant music scene. Some play jazz and blues and some branch out into less traditional forms. In any case, McMillan seeks simultaneously to revive the East Austin neighborhood into some semblance of the vibrancy and creative ferment that was seen in the 1950s, 1960s, and 1970s. He also wants people locally and nationally to know about the neighborhood's most famous son. In this effort, McMillan is contending against the urban renewal efforts that began in the 1970s and that wrought profound changes to the neighborhood.[60] These changes can best be summarized by the graffiti scrawled across one of the wooden placards that encircle Kenny Dorham's Backyard. Among messages like "Black Lives Matter" and "Celebrate the Arts," one placard asks, "What Do You Miss About East Austin?" In response, someone has spray-painted "The Brown People" across that sign.

Black-owned businesses in East Austin have mostly been replaced by white-owned ones. Some of the houses, including one that the Dorhams once occupied, have been extensively renovated. Others, like the 1218 East Twelfth Street house, have been bulldozed and replaced by slick-looking condominiums. The neighborhood is no longer segregated, which is a mixed blessing, at once indicating diversity and gentrification. This story is a familiar one, having played out across the country as longtime neighborhood residents in Brooklyn, New York (where Kenny Dorham lived with his wife and daughters), and elsewhere are priced out of their dwellings in the name of redevelopment. The redevelopment process has multiple drivers, with the profit motives of developers and city officials prominent among them. McMillan hopes to continue to fight for the soul of the neighborhood. He has obtained numerous extensions of the city lease of the property, and hopes one day to erect a permanent structure on the site. For now, Caribbean food trucks and two local bar and grills draw visitors even when music is not happening.

A stroll around Eleventh and Twelfth Streets reveals a complex reality. Some buildings are undoubtedly the same ones that were standing when Kenny Dorham lived there in the 1930s and early 1940s; others are gone. Historic sites are preserved. Anderson High burned down and is now the site of Kealing Middle School. The George Washington Carver Museum is around the corner, a celebration of African American history in general that houses an exhibit on the old Anderson High. Texas Sausage, the King-Tears Mortuary, and a couple of old cafés are still there. One of them displays a mural on its street-side wall dedicated to famous African Americans: Thurgood Marshall, Prince, Biggie Smalls, Jimi Hendrix. Kenny Dorham is not pictured. University of Texas sports facilities sprawl across from the west side of I-35 to creep eastward into the neighborhood. Innovative restaurants have popped up along Twelfth Street, right alongside historic landmark homes.

The Evergreen Cemetery lies a ways up Twelfth Street. It is fairly large and under renovation, with new pavement being laid in several sections. It is generally well-tended. McKinley Sr. died in 1969 and is buried at the front of the cemetery next to his wife, Minnie, who passed in 1992. Kenny

Dorham's grave is in a back corner. He has a flat gravestone that the Veterans Administration provides to all who served. Crows gather in an oak tree adjacent to the gravesite, scolding visitors to this quiet corner at the setting of the sun. Freeway traffic is a somewhat distant hum. Kenny Dorham could have been laid to rest in Freestone County, or in New York, but somehow East Austin seems more appropriate. It was where he discovered the trumpet, and he embarked from there to the music world. In death, he came back to join his parents. Austin is also the center of the state of Texas that was in turn central to Dorham's identity as an artist and a person. Histories are continually being updated and replaced. Someday, as materials accumulate and public awareness dawns, Dorham's rightful place in the stories of Texas and American music will be secure.

AFTERWORD

On a warm evening in early October, the Freestone County Fairgrounds are still hot and dusty from a day of Texas sun. A few bats are already flitting about, and the crickets are starting. The last of the doves leave the ground for their nighttime roosts. Beyond a picnic grove and the football field, the main building of Fairfield High sits on the Post Oak road, just before the road winds out of town. The high school marching band is practicing out on the field, drum cadences and horn parts drifting over to the fairgrounds. The marchers sound tired. Kenny Dorham would have lent some energy to the outfit, but in his teen years he would not have been allowed on the field of the then-all-white school. Today the school is no longer segregated, and Kenny Dorham has been gone fifty years. Some of the other Manning descendants live in the countryside beyond Fairfield, on much smaller plots of land than their ancestors held. Lignite and gas are still extracted from the county's lands on lease terms favorable to the energy companies. There is yet some farming and ranching activity, evidenced by a few sweat-soaked ranch hands filing into fast-food joints on Highway 84, but that way of life is mostly gone.

Kenny Dorham's life began in Post Oak, and we finished writing about him in the same place. The old fairgrounds are a place to think about this story of an artist and a family who trace their roots to a rural Texas community and who then dispersed around the country, and in Kenny Dorham's case, around the world. For us, the idea for this book began as a solo undertaking and then became a shared experience between father and son. One of us first heard Kenny Dorham in the 1980s, long before the other of us came into the world. For a trumpet student first discovering jazz, there was something different about Kenny Dorham's playing. So many trumpeters to learn from—Clifford Brown, Miles Davis, Lee Morgan, Donald Byrd—but Dorham could convey things with a unique sound and musical language while maintaining an unflagging rhythmic pulse seemingly without effort. One album led to another, and the liner notes left intriguing clues, like breadcrumbs, that explained some of the associations suggested by his playing and composing, thereby deepening the mystery. It seemed important both to transcribe Dorham's solos and to try and find the story of his life that was quoted in album notes. It took a year to track down that text, and that document turned out to be incomplete. Kenny Dorham never got to finish writing his autobiography, but only had time to submit an essay to *DownBeat*. It is a beautiful essay, but only five pages long. And no one else had written the story of his life as they had for Thelonious Monk and others. A long poem existed, but no biography.[1] As other book projects came to completion, the idea of writing about Dorham's life tugged at the mind, suggesting itself from time to time.

Twenty years later, there were two of us interested in jazz. And as a trumpeter and a pianist (and as father and son), we could share the experience of playing Dorham's music. His most famous composition, "Blue Bossa," is performed a lot, especially at jam sessions, but we wanted to go deeper into Dorham's catalogue. Fortunately, by that time Don Sickler had long been publishing arrangements of Kenny Dorham's work, and we used those meticulously faithful scores to play the music as originally envisioned. Sickler himself has said that one gains a deeper appreciation for Dorham's work by playing it, and it is natural to want to do justice to the composer's vision.

From there, it was but a short step to taking on a biographical project. We brought different backgrounds to the undertaking: the experience of an academic and a musician/musicologist.

We were often asked two questions in the process of writing this book: Why write about Dorham? And why we were writing this together? The first one was often easier to answer. We share a love for Dorham's music and an admiration for the subtleties of his craft. We also saw the massive gap between the scholarship surrounding his music and the reverence with which musicians spoke of his artistry. Outside of the music, or perhaps as a natural extension of it, Dorham's story spoke to a broader experience of being Black in America, with his family having roots in Texas and eventually migrating to New York and California, all the while bearing witness to cornerstone moments in American history, from Jackie Robinson winning the World Series for Brooklyn to the rise of the Black Panther party in Oakland. We wanted to speak to the enormity of Dorham's contribution to the music, while also shedding light on his extraordinary family. In doing so, we also hoped to reveal the ways in which their journey influenced his playing, like the Texas musical legacy reflected in his biting blues licks. We always had an appreciation for Dorham's albums, but in doing the work of examining his life, we found that there was so much more to the story than we could have anticipated.

As for the question of why we chose to do this together, it felt in many ways like a natural extension of our relationship. We spent long car rides listening to *Afro-Cuban* and *Una Mas*, talking about the tricky passages in solo forms or admiring the slickness of some of Dorham's turnarounds. Likewise, before shows, we would work out arrangements of these same songs, considering how to best navigate the sharp turns in a bridge section or stick the landing on rhythmic hits in the melody. This book was a comfortable offshoot of so many of these earlier conversations about Dorham's music. Additionally, our respective backgrounds, in music and political science, respectively, allowed us to move between the material purely about Dorham's music and the material in the more broadly historical sections. We agreed that the book wouldn't have been the same without both parts, and we couldn't have imagined writing it without each other.

Still, in many ways, beyond these practical concerns, this collaboration was also reflective of our trust in one another. This was not only a passion project about a musician we cared for deeply, but also a project we had been talking about long before so much as sketching an outline. As we conferred after interviews, listened to rare recordings or sent chapter drafts back and forth, we marveled at how much we were being given, and how much of this story had yet to be unearthed. To play in the Englewood Cliffs studio where Dorham recorded and to hear its hallowed acoustics, or to watch the sunset on a warm day in Dorham's hometown of Fairfield were moments we never would have imagined when we began our rough sketch of this book. To see the project come to fruition has been a joy that we could not have fully envisioned when we began, but has left us feeling so incredibly fortunate to write together.

APPENDIX: A SELECTED KENNY DORHAM DISCOGRAPHY

Below is our selected discography of Dorham's recorded work, including his dates as both a sideman and as a leader. The records are organized chronologically by the date they were recorded. In cases where they were released in a different year than they were recorded, we have made an additional note indicating that. When an album is described as having been recorded live, this means it was taped during a live performance, not at a studio date. For ease of access, in certain cases (particularly with Dorham's earliest recordings) we chose to list a compilation release with a more comprehensive collection of his work, rather than multiple piecemeal releases. We also opted not to include recordings that were not released or that were especially difficult to locate.

Source: The Jazz Discography Project. https://www.jazzdisco.org/kenny-dorham/discography/

1945

Ellington, Mercer. *Metronome All-Out/Pass Me By*. Musicraft 379, 1945.
Humphries, Frank. *After You've Gone/Lonesome Mood*. Pick-Up 1001, 1945.

1946

Dorham, Kenny. *Blues in Bebop*. Savoy SVY 17028, 1998, recorded in 1946 and originally released under Sonny Stitt's name.
Eckstine, Billy. *Billy Eckstine Sings*. Savoy SJL 1127, 1979, recorded in 1946.
Eckstine, Billy. *Mister B. and The Band: The Savoy Sessions*. Savoy SJL 2214, 1976, recorded in 1946.
Gillespie, Dizzy. *Dizzy Gillespie: In the Beginning*. Prestige P-24030, 1973.

Gillespie, Dizzy. *Dizzy Gillespie '46 Live at The Spotlite*. Hi-Fly H 01, 1946.

Navarro, Fats. *Fats Navarro—Fat Girl: The Savoy Sessions*. Savoy SJL 2216, 1976, recorded in 1946.

Various Artists. *The Be-Bop Era*. RCA Victor LPV-519, 1965, recorded in 1946 and originally released under Kenny Clarke's name.

1947

Art Blakey's Messengers. *New Sounds*. Blue Note CDP 7 84436 2, 1991, recorded in 1947.

Ellington, Mercer. *Al Hibbler With Mercer Ellington and Orchestra*. Sunrise SP 2007, 1947.

Ellington, Mercer. *Mercer Ellington and His Orchestra*. Sunrise SP 2003, 1947.

Hampton, Lionel. *One Night Stand*. Joyce LP 1055, 1947.

Hampton, Lionel. *Rock, Rock, Rock*. Golden Era GE 15038, 1947.

Williams, Mary Lou. *Mary Lou Williams and Her Orchestra*. Folkways FA 2996, 1947.

1948

Parker, Charlie. *Charlie Parker: Bird at the Roost/The Savoy Years Volume Two*. Savoy ZDS 4412, 1988, some tracks recorded live in 1948.

1949

Jackson, Milt. *Roll 'Em Bags*. Savoy MG-12042, 1956, recorded in 1949.

Johnson, J. J. *Looking Back*. Prestige PRLP 7253, 1963, recorded in 1949.

Moody, James. *James Moody—,In the Beginning: Jazz Legacy 47*. Jazz Legacy (F) JL 97, 1949, subsequently reissued under Max Roach's name in several rereleases.

Parker, Charlie. *Charlie Parker—Bird at the Roost/The Savoy Years Volume Two*. Savoy ZDS 4412, 1988, some tracks recorded live in 1949.

Parker Charlie. *Charlie Parker—Bird at the Roost/The Savoy Years Volume Three*. Savoy ZDS 4413, 1988, recorded live in 1949.

Parker, Charlie. *Charlie Parker—Bird at the Roost/The Savoy Years Volume Four*. Savoy ZDS 4414, 1988, recorded live in 1949.

Parker, Charlie. *Charlie Parker in France, 1949*. Jazz O.P. (F) OMS 7004, 1949.

Parker, Charlie. *Charlie Parker—Jazz Perennial: The Genius of Charlie Parker #7*. Verve MGV-8009, 1956, recorded in 1949.

Parker, Charlie. *Bird in Paris*. Spotlite (E) LP 118, 1971, recorded in 1949.

Parker, Charlie. *Charlie Parker: Visa/Passport*. Mercury 11022x45, 1949.

1950

Parker, Charlie. *Charlie Parker: Ballads and Birdland*. Klacto (E) MG 101, 1950.

Parker, Charlie. *Charlie Parker: Just Friends*. S.C.A.M. JPG 4, 1950.

Parker, Charlie. *Charlie Parker: Ultimate Bird 1949–50*. Grotto 495, 1950.

1952

Monk, Thelonious. *The Complete Blue Note Recordings of Thelonious Monk*. Mosaic MR4-101, 1983, recorded in 1952.

Monk, Thelonious. *Genius of Modern Music Volume Two*. Blue Note BLP 1511, 1956, recorded in 1952.

1953

Dorham, Kenny. *Kenny Dorham Quintet*. Original Jazz Classics OJCCD-113-2, 1953.

1954

Donaldson, Lou. *Lou Donaldson Sextet Vol. 2*. Blue Note BLP 5055, 1954.

Horace Silver and The Jazz Messengers. *Horace Silver and The Jazz Messengers*. 1956, recorded in 1954.

Rollins, Sonny. *Moving Out*. Prestige PRLP 7058, 1956, recorded 1954.

1955

Dorham, Kenny. *Afro-Cuban*. Blue Note BLP 1535, 1957, recorded in 1955.

The Jazz Messengers. *The Jazz Messengers at The Café Bohemia Volume 1*. Blue Note BLP 1507, 1956, recorded live in 1955.

The Jazz Messengers. *The Jazz Messengers at The Café Bohemia Volume 2*. Blue Note BLP 1508, 1956, recorded live in 1955.

The Jazz Messengers. *The Jazz Messengers at The Café Bohemia Volume 3*. Blue Note (J) DY-5805-01, 1983, recorded live in 1955.

1956

The Birdland Stars. *The Birdland Stars on Tour Vol. 1*. RCA Victor LPM-1327, 1956.

The Birdland Stars. *The Birdland Stars on Tour Vol. 2*. RCA Victor LPM-1328, 1956.

Dameron, Tadd. *Fontainebleau*. Prestige PRLP 7037, 1956.

Dorham, Kenny. *The Complete 'Round About Midnight at The Café Bohemia*. Blue Note CDP 7243 8 33576 2 8, 1995, recorded live in 1956.

Gee, Matthew. *Jazz By Gee!* Riverside RLP 12-221, 1956.

Henry, Ernie. *Ernie Henry: Last Chorus*. Riverside RLP 12-266, 1958, recorded in 1956.

Henry, Ernie. *Presenting Ernie Henry*. Riverside RLP 12-222, 1956.

Kenny Dorham and The Jazz Prophets. *Kenny Dorham and The Jazz Prophets Vol. 1*. ABC-Paramount ABC-122, 1956.

Melle, Gil. *Gil's Guests*. Prestige PRLP 7063, 1956.

Mobley, Hank. *Mobley's 2nd Message*. Prestige PRLP 7082, 1957, recorded in 1956.

Payne, Cecil. *Cecil Payne Quartet & Quintet*. Signal S 1203, 1957, recorded in 1956.

Roach, Max. *Max Roach + 4*. EmArcy MG-36098, 1956.

Rollins, Sonny. *Rollins Plays for Bird.* Prestige PRLP 7095, 1957, recorded in 1956.
Woods, Phil. *Pairing Off.* Prestige PRLP 7046, 1956.

1957

Dorham, Kenny. *Jazz Contrasts.* Riverside RLP 12-239, 1957.
Dorham, Kenny. *2 Horns/2 Rhythm.* Riverside RLP 12-255, 1958, recorded in 1957.
Geller, Herb. *Fire in the West.* Jubilee JLP 1044, 1957.
Golson, Benny. *The Modern Touch.* Riverside RLP 12-256, 1958, recorded in 1957.
Lincoln, Abbey. *Abbey Lincoln with the Riverside Jazz Stars.* Riverside RLP 12-251, 1958, recorded in 1957.
Pettiford, Oscar. *Oscar Pettiford and His Birdland Band: Jazz Off the Air Vol. 6.* Spotlite (E) SPJ 153, 1982, recorded live in 1957.
Roach, Max. *The Complete Mercury Max Roach Plus Four Sessions.* Mosaic MD7-201, 2000, recorded in 1956 and 1957.
Roach, Max. *Jazz in 3/4 Time.* EmArcy MG-36108, 1957.
Roach, Max. *The Max Roach 4 Plays Charlie Parker.* EmArcy MG-36127, SR-80019, 1959, recorded in 1957 and 1958.
Salim, A. K. *Pretty for the People.* Savoy MG-12118, 1957.

1958

Carter, Betty. *Out There with Betty Carter.* Peacock PLP 90, 1958.
Coltrane, John. *Coltrane Time.* United Artists UAJ 14001, 1963, recorded in 1958 and originally released under Cecil Taylor's name.
Dorham, Kenny. *This is the Moment!* Riverside RLP 12-275, 1958.
Lincoln, Abbey. *It's Magic.* Riverside RLP 12-277, 1958.
Merrill, Helen. *You've Got a Date with the Blues.* Metrojazz E1010, 1958.
Roach, Max. *Max!* Argo LP-623, 1958.

1959

Bey, Andy. *Andy and The Bey Sisters.* Fontana 464451, 1959.
Coleman, Ornette, Don Cherry, and Kenny Dorham. *Lenox School of Jazz*, Royal Jazz (D) SOJ ½, 1959.
Dorham, Kenny. *Blue Spring.* Riverside RLP 12-297, 1959.
Dorham, Kenny. *Quiet Kenny.* New Jazz NJLP 8225, 1960, recorded in 1959.
Lincoln, Abbey. *Abbey Is Blue.* Riverside RLP 12-308, 1959.
Mehegan, John. *Casual Affair with the John Mehegan Quartet.* TJ TJLP-A1, 1959.
Nelson, Oliver. *Meet Oliver Nelson*, 1960, recorded in 1959.
Weston, Randy. *Live at The Fivespot.* United Artists UAL 4066, 1959, recorded in 1960.
Wilen, Barney. *Barney.* RCA (F) 430.053, 1959.
Wilen, Barney. *Un témoin dans la ville.* Fontana (F) 660 226 MR, 1959.

1960

Dorham, Kenny. *The Arrival of Kenny Dorham*. JARO International JAM-5007, 1960.
Dorham, Kenny. *Jazz Contemporary*. Time 52004, 1960.
Dorham, Kenny. *Showboat*. Time 52024 1960.
Jazz Artists Guild. *Various Artists: The Jazz Life!* Candid CJM 8019, 1961, recorded in 1961.
Land, Harold. *Eastward Ho!* Jazzland JLP 33, 1961, recorded in 1960.

1961

Bailey, Dave. *Bash!* Jazzline JAZ 33-01, 1961.
Boyd, Rocky. *Ease It*. Jazztime JT 001, 1961,
Dorham, Kenny. *Hot Stuff from Brazil*. West Wind (G) LP 015, 1990, recorded live in 1961.
Dorham, Kenny, and Jackie McLean. *Inta Somethin'*. Pacific Jazz PJ-41, 1962, recorded live in 1961.
Dorham, Kenny. *Osmosis*. Black Lion (G) BLCD 760146, 1961, an expanded reissue of recordings from Bailey's *Bash!* Sessions.
Dorham, Kenny. *Whistle Stop*. Blue Note BLP 4063, 1961.
Jordan, Clifford. *Starting Time*. Jazzland JLP 52, 1961.

1962

Dorham, Kenny. *Matador*. United Artists UAJ 14007, 1962.
Jackson, Milt. *Invitation*. Riverside RM 446, 1963.
McLean, Jackie. *Hipnosis*. Blue Note BN-LA483-J2, 1978, recorded in 1962.
McLean, Jackie. *Vertigo*. Blue Note 7243 5 22669 2 0, 2000, recorded in 1962.

1963

Dorham, Kenny. *The Flamboyan, Queens, NY, 1963*. Uptown UPCD 27.60, 2009, recorded live in 1963.
Dorham, Kenny. *Scandia Skies*. SteepleChase (D) SCC 6011, 1980, recorded live in 1963.
Dorham, Kenny. *Short Story*. SteepleChase (D) SCC 6010, 1979, recorded live in 1963,
Dorham, Kenny. *Una Mas*. Blue Note BLP 4127, 1963.
Henderson, Joe. *The Complete Joe Henderson Blue Note Studio Sessions*. Mosaic MD5-271, 2021, recorded in 1963.
Henderson, Joe. *Page One*. Blue Note BLP 4140, 1963.

1964

Dorham, Kenny. *Blowin' From New York 1964 Vol. 1*. Raretone (It) 5021-FC, 1988, recorded live in 1964.
Dorham, Kenny. *Trompeta Toccata*. Blue Note BLP 4181, 1965, recorded in 1964.
Henderson, Joe. *In 'n Out*. Blue Note BLP 4166, 1965, recorded in 1964.

Hill, Andrew. *The Complete Blue Note Andrew Hill Sessions (1963–66).* Mosaic MR10-161, 1995, recorded 1964.

Hill, Andrew. *Point of Departure.* Blue Note BLP 4167, 1965, recorded in 1964.

1965

Various Artists. *Charlie Parker 10th Memorial Concert Recorded Live at Carnegie Hall.* Limelight LM-82017, 1965.

Various Artists. *A Trumpet Tribute to Fats Navarro, Clifford Brown and Booker Little.* Trip Jazz TLX-5036, 1965.

1966

Dorham, Kenny. *The Shadow of Your Smile.* West Wind (G) WW 2049, 1990, recorded live in 1966.

Ellington, Duke, Thad Jones, Kenny Dorham, and Howard McGhee. *Europa Jazz.* Europa Jazz (It) EJ-1039, 1981.

1967

Dorham, Kenny. *Blue Bossa in the Bronx (Live from The Blue Morocco).* Resonance Records HLP-9072, 2025, recorded live in 1967.

Walton, Cedar. *Cedar!* Prestige PRST 7519, 1967.

1968

Akiyoshi, Toshiko. *Toshiko at Top of the Gate.* Nippon Columbia (J) XMS-10008-CT, 1968.

Harris, Barry. *Bull's Eye!* Prestige PRST 7600, 1968.

Payne, Cecil. *Zodiac.* Strata-East SES-19734, 1971, recorded in 1968.

1969

Jordan, Clifford. *In the World.* Strata-East SES-19721, 1972, recorded in 1969.

1970

Various Artists. *Charlie Parker Memorial Concert.* Cadet 2CA 60002, 1970.

NOTES

INTRODUCTION

1. Kenny Dorham, "Fragments of an Autobiography," *DownBeat*, Yearbook special issue, December 1970, 30, 34.

2. Kenny Dorham, *Round About Midnight at the Café Bohemia*, Blue Note 1524, 1956, 33 1/3 rpm.

3. Don Awalt, interview by Robert Pallitto, September 17, 2021.

4. The creation of a new Texas county was often the result of a political favor as it gave to an enterprising resident the equivalent of a fiefdom that became more financially rewarding as the population grew.

5. US Census Bureau, 1870 US Census, via Ancestry, https://www.ancestry.com.

6. Brian Hosmer, "Quanah Parker," Texas State Historical Association, updated January 7, 2021, https://www.tshaonline.org/handbook/entries/parker-quanah.

7. US Census Bureau, 1870 US Census.

8. Don Awalt, interview with Robert Pallitto, September 17, 2021.

9. For example, Henry Manning to Trustees of Methodist Episcopal Church of Pine Top, warranty deed, church site, Butler, Texas, 1879, page 451, Freestone County Clerk deed records (C. Y. Manning, witness); C. Y. Manning to Henry Manning, warranty deed to certain property in Freestone County, Texas, 1883, page 493, Freestone County Clerk deed records (grantor) https://kofilequicklinks.com/Freestone/.

10. B. J. Parker to Henry Manning, warranty deed to "Gorman Place," Butler, Texas, 1899, page 453, Freestone County Clerk deed records, https://kofilequicklinks.com/Freestone.

11. US Census Bureau, 1890 US Census, via Ancestry, https://www.ancestry.com.

12. "Texas Reports of Murder and Outrages: Affidavit of Mark Walker (colored) of Freestone, Texas," *The Freedmen's Bureau Online*, https://www.freedmensbureau.com/texas/texaffidavit2.htm.

13. Eric Foner, "Black Reconstruction Leaders at the Grass Roots," in *Black Leaders of the Nineteenth Century*, ed. Leon Litwack and August Meier (University of Illinois Press, 1991), 221.

14. US Census Bureau, 1920 US Census, via Ancestry, https://www.ancestry.com.

15. US Census Bureau, 1900 US Census, via Ancestry, https://www.ancestry.com.

16. Death certificate of Jasper Dorham, July 20, 1919, Freestone County Texas Vital Statistics, via Ancestry https://www.ancestry.com.

17. US Census Bureau, 1920 US Census, via Ancestry, https://www.ancestry.com.

18. Death certificate of McKinley Howard Dorham Sr., November 6, 1969, Travis County Texas Vital Statistics, via Ancestry, https://www.ancestry.com.

19. Henry Manning to Trustees of Methodist Episcopal Church of Pine Top, warranty deed.

20. Death certificate of Sarah Manning, January 2, 1920, Freestone County Texas Vital Statistics, via Ancestry, https://www.ancestry.com.

CHAPTER 1: POST OAK

1. Kenny Dorham, "Fragments of an Autobiography," Yearbook special issue, *DownBeat*, December 1970, 30.

2. Phil Schaap recalled the provenance of Kenny Dorham's name in an interview with Evette Dorham. Evette Dorham, interview by Phil Schaap, *Bird Flight*, WKCR-FM, December 5, 2018.

3. Linda English, *By All Accounts: General Stores and Community Life in Texas and the Indian Territory* (University of Oklahoma Press, 2013),10.

4. Monte Akers, *Flames After Midnight: Murder, Vengeance, and the Desolation of a Texas Community* (University of Texas Press, 2011), 209.

5. Kenny Dorham, "Fragments of an Autobiography," 30.

6. Greg Brown, "Whippoorwill," on *The Evening Call*, Red House Records, 2000, compact disc.

7. W. C. Handy, *Father of the Blues: An Autobiography* (Da Capo Press, 1969), 2.

8. Dorham, "Fragments," 30.

9. Dorham, "Fragments," 31.

10. Dorham, "Fragments," 30.

11. Dorham, "Fragments," 30.

12. Dorham, "Fragments," 30.

13. Kenny Dorham, "Fragments of an Autobiography (original draft)," on Lewis Porter, "Kenny Dorham: Unknown Audio Interviews (+Bonus Autobiography)," *Playback with Lewis Porter!*, February 10, 2024, https://lewisporter.substack.com/p/kenny-dorham-unknown-audio-interviews.

14. Woody Guthrie, *Bound for Glory* (Plume Books, 1983), 19.

15. Dorham, "Fragments," 30.

16. US Census Bureau, 1940 US Census, via Ancestry, https://www.ancestry.com.

17. Dorham, "Fragments," 30.

18. Dorham, "Fragments," 30.

19. Dorham, "Fragments," 30.

20. Sara Massey, ed., *Black Cowboys of Texas* (Texas A&M University Press, 2004).

21. Massey, *Black Cowboys*, 3.

22. Dorham, "Fragments," 30.

23. Kenny Dorham, "Whistle Stop," *Whistle Stop*, Blue Note 84063, 1961, 33 1/3 rpm.

24. Kenny Dorham, "I'm an Old Cowhand" by Johnny Mercer, track 2 on *The Arrival of Kenny Dorham*, Jaro Records JAM 5007, 1960, 33 1/3 rpm .

25. Dorham, "Fragments," 31.

26. Nat Hentoff, liner notes to *Trompeta Toccata*, Blue Note BST 84181 1965, 33 1/3 rpm.

27. Dorham, "Fragments," 31.

28. Dorham, "Fragments," 31.

29. Blind Lemon Jefferson, "One Dime Blues," single, Paramount Records 12578, 1927, 78 rpm.

30. Dorham, "Fragments," 32.

31. Joel Dorham, interview with Robert Pallitto, various dates in 2021.

32. *Birth of the Cool*, directed by Stanley Nelson (Firelight Media, 2019), Blu-ray.

33. David Brand, "Jazz Pioneer Cannonball Adderley Made Tallahassee Proud," *Tallahassee Democrat*, October 19, 2019, https://www.tallahassee.com/story/life/2019/10/19/jazz-pioneer-cannonball-adderley-made-tallahassee-proud/4013428002/.

34. *American Masters*, season 4, episode 5, "Celebrating Bird: The Triumph of Charlie Parker," PBS, directed by Gary Giddens, aired August 17, 1989 on PBS, https://www.pbs.org/wnet/americanmasters/charlie-parker-documentary/15474/; "Max Roach Biography and Career Timeline," *PBS American Masters*, September 22, 2023, https://www.pbs.org/wnet/americanmasters/max-roach-biography-and-career-timeline/29310/; Aidan Levy, *Saxophone Colossus: The Life and Music of Sonny Rollins* (Hachette, 2022), 6; Robin Kelley, *Thelonious Monk: The Life and Times of An American Original* (Simon and Schuster, 2009), 2.

35. "John Birks 'Dizzy' Gillespie: Trumpeter, Composer, Bandleader," National Endowment for the Arts, https://www.arts.gov/honors/jazz/john-birks-dizzy-gillespie, accessed March 4, 2024.

36. David Oliphant, *Texan Jazz* (University of Texas Press, 1996).

CHAPTER 2: LAND LOSS AND SHARECROPPING: "FARMING ON THE HALVES"

1. Quoted in Arthur Taylor, *Notes and Tones* (Da Capo Press, 1993), 231.

2. Quoted in Taylor, *Notes and Tones*, 236.

3. Kenny Dorham, "Fragments of an Autobiography," *DownBeat*, Yearbook special issue, December 1970, 32.

4. Joel Dorham, interview with Robert Pallitto, various dates in 2021.

5. Quoted in Taylor, *Notes and Tones*, 231.

6. Quoted in Taylor, *Notes and Tones*, 231.

7. Austin telephone directory for 1940, Austin Historical Museum, Austin, Texas.

8. C. Y. Manning to Henry Manning, warranty deed to certain property south of Butler, Texas, 1883, page 493, Freestone County Clerk deed records, https://kofilequicklinks.com/Freestone/.

9. B.J. Parker to G.W. Manning, warranty deed to certain property near Butler, TX, 1904, pages 414-15, Freestone County Clerk deed records, https://kofilequicklinks.com/Freestone

10. Deed Map, Freestone County, 1910, on file with authors.

11. Compare the deed cited in note 10 in the introduction above with the following: B. J. Parker to Henry Manning, warranty deed for "Gorman Place," near Butler, TX, 1906, page 297, Freestone County County Clerk deed records, https://kofilequicklinks.com/Freestone/.

12. Will Manning to F. E. Hill, warranty deed for certain property in Freestone County, 1913, page 397, Freestone County Clerk deed records, https://kofilequicklinks.com/Freestone.

13. This description excludes farm laborers, who worked in the fields for a wage.

14. Linda English, *By All Accounts: General Stores and Community Life in Texas and Indian Territory* (University of Oklahoma Press, 2013), 54.

15. Dorham, "Fragments," 32.

16. English, *By All Accounts*, 54.

17. Robert Pallitto, interview with W. King Mott, July 12, 2021.

18. Workers of the Writers' Program of the Work Projects Administration of the State of Texas, *Texas: A Guide to the Lone Star State* (Hastings House, 1940), 569.

19. WPA Writers' Program, *Texas*, 90.

20. WPA Writers' Program, *Texas*, 91.

21. WPA Writers' Program, *Texas*, 81.

22. Dorham, "Fragments," 32.

23. E. Henderson Lawson and R. T. Kennedy, *Colored Rivers: The Untold Story of the Great Land Theft Conspiracy in Freestone County, Texas* (pub. by authors, 2018).

24. Annette Gordon-Reed, *On Juneteenth* (Liveright Publishing, 2021), 33.

25. Bob Baker, "Descendants of Slave Charge Swindle by Texas Whites: Long Quest Harvests a Tale of Lost Land," *Los Angeles Times*, March 30, 1987, https://www.latimes.com/archives/la-xpm-1987-03-30-mn-564-story.html.

26. 6. Bob Baker, "Descendants of Black Settler to Appeal Ruling by Texas Judge," *Los Angeles Times*, September 16, 1987, https://www.latimes.com/archives/la-xpm-1987-09-16-me-5391-story.html.

27. Henderson Lawson and Kennedy, *Colored Rivers*, 83.

28. Henderson Lawson and Kennedy, *Colored Rivers*, 28 and 83.

29. Williford et al. v. Manning et al., No. 20325-B (Texas 87th District Court, 1934).

30. Lott v. Manning et al., No. 8628-B (Texas 87th District Court, 1934).

31. Lott v. Manning et al.

32. Lott v. Manning et al.

33. Lott v. Manning et al.

34. Lott v. Manning et al.

35. See note 11 above.

36. See note 11 above.

37. Lott's name and title appear many times in deed records from this period.

38. Joel Dorham interview, October 21, 2021.

39. We are indebted to Lily Goren for this insight. Personal communication, October 1, 2021.

40. However, as Frederick Douglass pointed out in 1852 in a speech titled "What to the Slave Is the Fourth of July?" this negation of legal personhood did not extend to criminal law. Enslaved Black Americans were tried and punished under the criminal laws of the states even more severely than whites. This was an acknowledgment of some degree of

humanity, otherwise they could not have been held responsible. The text of Douglass's speech is available at The National Constitution Center, https://constitutioncenter.org/the-constitution/historic-document-library/detail/frederick-douglass-what-to-the-slave-is-the-fourth-of-july-1852, accessed March 10, 2024.

41. W. E. B. Du Bois, *The Souls of Black Folk*, Penguin Classics edition (Penguin, 1996), 1–2.

42. Edward Ayers, *The Promise of the New South: Life After Reconstruction* (Oxford University Press, 1992), 145.

43. Peter Irons, *Jim Crow's Children: The Broken Promise of the Brown Decision* (Penguin Random House, 2002), 173, 189, 203, 205.

44. "History of Lynching in America," NAACP, https://naacp.org/find-resources/history-explained/history-lynching-america, accessed March 10, 2024.

45. Dorham, "Fragments," 32.

46. Quoted in Alan Govenar, *Texas Blues: The Rise of a Contemporary Sound* (Texas A&M Press, 2008), 47.

47. 170 U.S. 213 (1898).

48. *The African Americans: Many Rivers to Cross*, episode 3, "Into the Fire (1861 to 1896)," written by Henry Louis Gates Jr., aired November 5, 2013, on PBS.

49. Quoted in Ayers, *Promise of the New South*, 428.

50. Death certificate of McKinley Howard Dorham Sr., November 6, 1969, Travis County Texas Vital Statistics, via Ancestry, https://www.ancestry.com.

51. Joel Dorham interview, January 25, 2022.

CHAPTER 3: TEXAS BLUES

1. Quoted in Arthur Taylor, *Notes and Tones* (Da Capo Press, 1972), 237.

2. Quoted in Taylor, *Notes and Tones*, 237.

3. Alan Govenar, *Texas Blues: The Rise of a Contemporary Sound* (Texas A&M Press, 2008), 1.

4. Kenny Dorham, "No Bells and Beads," *DownBeat*, September 19, 1968, 20.

5. Govenar, *Texas Blues*, 3.

6. Govenar, *Texas Blues*, 3.

7. Govenar, *Texas Blues*, 6.

8. Govenar, *Texas Blues*, 6.

9. Edward Ayers, *The Promise of the New South: Life After Reconstruction* (Oxford University Press, 1992), 368.

10. Ayers, *Promise of the New South*, 368.

11. Ayers, *Promise of the New South*, 384.

12. Ayers, *Promise of the New South*, 390.

13. David Oliphant, *Texan Jazz* (The University of Texas Press, 1996), 29.

14. Oliphant, *Texan Jazz*, 35.

15. Ayers, *Promise of the New South*, 388.

16. Govenar, *Texas Blues*, 13.

17. Ayers, *Promise of the New South*, 383.

18. Ayers, *Promise of the New South*, 398.

19. Oliphant, *Texan Jazz*, 376n6.

20. Texas swing, or western swing, grew out of the early blues and did use fuller instrumentation as well.

21. W. C. Handy described a 1903 encounter with a country blues singer who was playing "the weirdest music I had ever heard" (quoted in Ayers, *Promise of the New South*, 387). Playing with a knife pressed against the guitar strings, the stranger sang one specific verse again and again: "Goin' where the Southern cross the Dog." He told Handy it was a reference to the intersection of two rail lines (quoted in Ayers, *Promise of the New South*, 387). This chance meeting inspired Handy to build blues elements into his written compositions, and thus changed the course of American music. And it was such an essential, typical moment in blues music: with a shared or borrowed verse that had probably been passed around by different singers for years, the longing to wander by rail, and the practice of changing the guitar's tuning and creating new sounds with an object pressing and sliding against the strings.

22. Quoted in Govenar, *Texas Blues*, 37.

23. Huddie "Leadbelly" Ledbetter, "Boll Weevil," track 15 on *Leadbelly: The Smithsonian Folkways Collection*, Smithsonian Folkways 40201, 2015, compact disc.

24. Quoted in Oliphant, *Texan Jazz*, 50.

25. John Coltrane, *Blue Train*, Blue Note 95236, 1958, 33 1/3 rpm. That Coltrane album actually contains a track titled "Locomotion" as well.

26. Oliphant, *Texan Jazz*, 39.

27. Oliphant, *Texan Jazz*, 38.

28. Oliphant, *Texan Jazz*, 42.

29. Samuel Charters, *The Blues Makers* (Springer, 1991), quoted in Oliphant, *Texan Jazz*, 42.

30. Govenar, *Texas Blues*, 8.

31. Govenar, *Texas Blues*, 36.

32. Quoted in Govenar, *Texas Blues*, 44.

33. Kenny Dorham, "Blue Spring," track 1 on *Blue Spring*, Riverside Records RLP 1139, 1959, 33 1/3 rpm.

34. Govenar, *Texas Blues*, 23.

35. W. C. Handy, *Father of the Blues: An Autobiography* (Da Capo Press, 1969), 34.

36. Oliphant, *Texan Jazz*, 36.

37. Ayers, *Promise of the New South*, 390.

38. Blind Lemon Jefferson, "Matchbox Blues," on *Black Snake Moan/Match Box Blues*, Okeh Records 80524-B, 1927, 78 rpm.

39. Jimmy Rushing, "How Long, How Long Blues," track 4 on *The Essential Jimmy Rushing*, Vanguard VSD 65/66, 1991, compact disc.

40. Govenar, *Texas Blues*, 20.

41. W. King Mott, interview with Robert Pallitto, July 12, 2021.

42. Ironically, "Relaxing at Camarillo" makes reference to Parker's time at Camarillo State Mental Hospital. Parker apparently did not choose the title. Edward Komara,

"Historical Narrative," in Michael Gray, ed., *The Dial Recordings of Charlie Parker: A Discography* (Greenwood Press, 1998), 27.

43. Freddie Hendrix to Robert Pallitto and John Melendez, October 9, 2022.

44. Clifford Brown and Max Roach Quintet, "Parisian Thoroughfare," track 2 on *Clifford Brown and Max Roach*, EmArcy 26043, 1954; compact disc rerelease, Jazz Plaza Music 123499, 1990.

45. Max Roach Quintet, with Kenny Dorham, "Just One of Those Things," track 3 on *Max Roach Plus Four*, Emarcy 36098, 1956; compact disc rerelease, EmArcy, 822 673-2, 1990. Dorham had been tapped to replace Clifford Brown in the Max Roach group after Brown died in a tragic car accident. Dorham praised Brown in "Fragments," 34. And on his only vocal album, Dorham sang "I'll Remember Clifford" in tribute to Brown. "I'll Remember Clifford," track 2 on *This Is the Moment: Kenny Dorham Sings and Plays*, Riverside, RLP 12-275, 1958, 33 1/3 rpm.

46. If you want to imagine how fast that is, try patting your hand on the table in front of you as fast as you can. If you are able to do it for more than a few seconds, you are too slow, slower than they are playing. This experiment gives some measure of the difficulty of playing a flawless improvised solo, created on the spot, at that speed.

47. Ayers, *Promise of the New South*, 389.

48. Ayers, *Promise of the New South*, 383.

49. Ayers, *Promise of the New South*, 383.

50. Ayers, *Promise of the New South*, 383.

51. Ayers, *Promise of the New South*, 383.

52. Oliphant, *Texan Jazz*, 54.

53. Like Sippie Wallace, Ma Rainey also recorded with Armstrong in the 1920s, creating another early link between blues and jazz. And of course blues music from its beginnings included improvised solos, as jazz did.

54. Oliphant, *Texan Jazz*, 89.

55. Oliphant, *Texan Jazz*, 85.

56. Oliphant, *Texan Jazz*, 85.

57. Oliphant, *Texan Jazz*, 94.

CHAPTER 4: AUSTIN

1. Arthur Taylor, *Notes and Tones* (Da Capo Press, 1993), 230.

2. Austin telephone directory, 1940, Austin Historical Museum, Austin, Texas.

3. Opened the day World War II ended, the Victory Grill was a café and nightclub intended to provide a place to eat and hear music for people in the segregated East Austin community. It became one among several lively night spots in the neighborhood, and over the years the Grill hosted music legends Billie Holiday, Etta James, B. B. King, James Brown, and many others. It is an historic landmark today.

4. Harold McMillan, interview by Robert Pallitto, October 9, 2022.

5. Austin telephone directory, 1940. 1965.

6. McMillan interview.

7. Rebekah Dobrasko, "Losing a Community Catalyst: The Closure of L.C. Anderson High School," *Preservation Austin*, https://www.preservationaustin.org/news/2021/7/8/losing-a-community-catalyst-the-closure-of-lc-anderson-high-school; "Wilhelmina Delco: L. C. Anderson, Education and Desegregation," YouTube, May 12, 2015, https://www.youtube.com/watch?v=wxnzhJx2-Tc&t=906s.

8. Quoted in Taylor, *Notes and Tones*, 230.

9. Quoted in Taylor, *Notes and Tones*, 230.

10. Quoted in Taylor, *Notes and Tones* 231.

11. Alvin Patterson, quoted in Michael Corcoran, "East End Stories: The L. C. Anderson High Yellowjackets," http://www.eastendculturaldistrict.org/cms/culture-art-music/east-end-stories-lc-anderson-high-yellowjackets.

12. Patterson, quoted in Corcoran, "East End Stories."

13. William Grant Still (1895–1978) was an exception, given the performance of his works by symphony orchestras as early as the 1930s. Still also worked in commercial music during his career, and collaborated with major figures in the Harlem Renaissance. "William Grant Still, 1895–1978," Library of Congress, accessed April 15, 2024, https://www.loc.gov/item/ihas.200186213.

14. Lou Donaldson, interview by Ted Panken, June 20 and 21, 2012, Smithsonian Jazz Oral History Project, https://americanhistory.si.edu/explore/projects/smithsonian-jazz/collections-and-archives/smithsonian-jazz-oral-history-program.

15. Corcoran, "East End Stories."

16. Corcoran, "East End Stories."

17. Patterson, quoted in Corcoran, "East End Stories."

18. Quoted in Gene Feehan, "Durable Dorham," *DownBeat*, September 27, 1962, 16.

19. Quoted in Feehan, "Durable Dorham," 16.

20. Sonny Rollins, quoted in Kahron Spearman, "Trumpet Colossus Kenny Dorham Towers Alongside the Jazz Gods," *Austin Chronicle*, September 14, 2018, https://www.austinchronicle.com/music/2018-09-14/trumpet-colossus-kenny-dorham-towers-alongside-the-jazz-gods/.

21. One of us happened to be at a community event in Paterson, New Jersey in 2000. A group of talented young musicians from the renowned jazz program at nearby William Paterson University had been hired to play at the event, and the trumpeter was arresting in his Dorham-like navigation of the chord changes. The influence was unmistakable, and confirmed by the musician himself with a broad smile. He was not yet as well-known then as he is now, but Freddie Hendrix talked enthusiastically that night about what Kenny Dorham meant to him as a college student and a developing musician. He was doing what Dorham himself had done six decades earlier: forging his own style through absorbing the influences of his predecessors.

22. Dorham, "Fragments of an Autobiography," *DownBeat*, Yearbook special issue, December 1970, 33.

23. *The African Americans: Many Rivers to Cross*, episode 3, "Into the Fire (1861 to 1896)," written by Henry Louis Gates Jr., aired November 5, 2013, on PBS.

24. David Oliphant, *Texan Jazz* (The University of Texas Press, 1996), 19.

25. McKinley H. Dorham, Jr., service record, US Army records 1890–1945, https://www.va.gov/records/.

26. Dorham, "Fragments," 32.

27. Taylor, *Notes and Tones*, 232.

28. Kenny Dorham, interview by Jim Toman, August 1969, link in Lewis Porter, "Kenny Dorham: Unknown Audio Interviews (+Bonus Autobiography)," *Playback with Lewis Porter!*, February 10, 2024, https://lewisporter.substack.com/p/kenny-dorham-unknown-audio-interviews.

29. Dorham, "Fragments," 33.

30. Other musicians at this session included alto saxophonist Sonny Stitt, tenor saxophonist Morris Lane, baritone saxophonist Eddie DeVerteuil, pianist Bud Powell, bassist Al Hall, and drummer Kenny Clarke. Fats Navarro, Fat Girl—The Savoy Sessions,

31. Feehan, "Durable Dorham," 16.

32. Evette Dorham, interview by Phil Schaap, *Bird Flight*, WKCR-FM, December 5, 2018.

33. Keturah Dorham-Holley, interview by Robert Pallitto, October 1, 2021.

34. Dorham-Holley interview.

35. Dorham-Holley interview.

36. Dorham-Holley interview.

37. Evette Dorham interview.

38. Feehan, "Durable Dorham," 17. Pianist Cedar Walton once said of Dorham, "I used to love to hear people who played other instruments play the piano because they weren't like a piano player; they were like a horn player. . . . Kenny Dorham, on the other hand uh, was a person who was very proficient at the piano. He'd uh been close to Bud Powell and learned so much. . . ." Cedar Walton, interview by William Brower, October 2 and 3, 2010, Smithsonian Jazz Oral History Project, https://americanhistory.si.edu/explore/projects/smithsonian-jazz/collections-and-archives/smithsonian-jazz-oral-history-program.

39. Evette Dorham interview.

40. Please refer to the discography at the end of the book.

41. Tammy L. Kernodle, *Soul on Soul: The Life and Music of Mary Lou Williams* (University of Illinois Press, 2020), 113.

42. Kernodle, *Soul on Soul*, 75.

43. Mary Lou Williams, Interview. *Melody Maker*. April—June, 1954 https://www.ratical.org/MaryLouWilliams/MMiview1954.html.

44. Kernodle, *Soul on Soul*, 113.

45. Dorham, "Fragments," 32.

46. Dorham, "Fragments," 32.

47. Robin D. G. Kelley, *Race Rebels: Culture Politics and the Black Working Class* (The Free Press, 1994), 165.

48. Benny Golson and Jim Merod, *Whisper Not: The Autobiography of Benny Golson* (Temple University Press, 2016), 261.

49. Bernard Drayton, interview by Robert Pallitto, October 26, 2022.

50. Dorham, "Fragments," 33.

51. Dorham, "Fragments," 33.

52. Dorham, "Fragments," 33.

53. Dorham, "Fragments," 34.

54. There is a similar story (with multiple versions) about Charles Mingus's dismissal from the Ellington band after a fight involving a large ax with trombonist Juan Tizol. See, for example, "This Cat Needs No Pulitzer Prize," *New York Times Magazine*, September 12, 1965, 64–66.

55. Colin Fleming, "Remembering Bob Dylan's Infamous 'Judas' Show," *Rolling Stone*, May 17, 2016, https://www.rollingstone.com/music/music-news/remembering-bob-dylans-infamous-judas-show-203760/.

56. Gene Feehan, "Durable Dorham," 16.

57. W. C. Handy, *Father of the Blues: An Autobiography* (Da Capo Press, 1969), 56, 60.

58. Quoted in Nat Hentoff, liner notes to Kenny Dorham, *Una Mas*, Blue Note BST 84127, 1964, 33 1/3 rpm.

CHAPTER 5: AN INVITATION FROM CHARLIE PARKER

1. Arthur Taylor, *Notes and Tones*, (Da Capo Press, 1973), 232.

2. Quoted in Taylor, *Notes and Tones*, 232.

3. Guthrie P. Ramsey, *The Amazing Bud Powell: Black Genius, Jazz History, and the Challenge of Bebop* (University of California Press, 2013), 56.

4. Ramsey, *Amazing Bud Powell*, 128.

5. Kahron Spearman, "Trumpet Colossus Kenny Dorham Towers Among the Jazz Gods," *Austin Chronicle*, September 14, 2018, https://www.austinchronicle.com/music/2018-09-14/trumpet-colossus-kenny-dorham-towers-alongside-the-jazz-gods/.

6. Quoted in Taylor, *Notes and Tones*, 232.

7. Ramsey, *Amazing Bud Powell*, 28.

8. Dan Morgenstern, *Living with Jazz: A Reader*, ed. Sheldon Meyer (Knopf Doubleday Publishing Group, 2009), 487.

9. Morgenstern, *Living with Jazz*, 660.

10. Richard Cook and Brian Morton, *The Penguin Guide to Jazz* (Penguin, 2004), 453.

11. Quoted in Morgenstern, *Living with Jazz*, 220–21.

12. Tenor saxophonist Hank Mobley once expressed a similar wish: for "somewhere to play where people aren't just comparing you to someone else. Where they have a brochure on the table telling you all about the musician." Quoted in Pannonica de Koenigswarter, *Three Wishes: An Intimate Look at Jazz Greats* (Abrams Image, 2008), 75.

13. The Gershwin chord progression became commonly known as "rhythm changes."

14. Kenny Dorham, liner notes to *Whistle Stop*, Blue Note BST 84063, 1961, 33 1/3 rpm.

15. Phil Schaap, *Bird Flight*, WKCR, May 17, 2023.

16. Schaap, *Bird Flight*, May 17, 2023.

17. Schaap, *Bird Flight*, May 17, 2023.

18. Charlie Parker, liner notes to *Bird in Paris*, Spotlite, RLR 88658, 1971, 33 1/3 rpm.

19. "Max Roach," *La revue du jazz: Organe officiel du Hot Club de France* 1, no. 7 (August 1949): 25.

20. Quoted in Taylor, *Notes and Tones*, 233.
21. Quoted in Taylor, *Notes and Tones*, 233.
22. Quoted in Taylor, *Notes and Tones*, 233.
23. Quoted in Taylor, *Notes and Tones*, 233.
24. Schaap, *Bird Flight*, May 17, 2023.
25. Peter Losin, "Charlie Parker session details: May 8–15, 1949, Salle Pleyel," Miles Ahead: A Miles Davis Website, https://www.plosin.com/milesahead/BirdSessions.aspx?s=490508b.
26. Parker, liner notes to *Bird in Paris*.
27. Boris Vian, "Lundi 9," *Jazz News: Blue Star Revue* 1, no. 6 (June 1949): 9.
28. André Hodeir, "Le Festival 1949," *Jazz Hot* 34 (June 1949): 7–10.
29. Hodeir, "Le Festival 1949," 7–10.
30. Quoted in Gene Feehan, "Durable Dorham," *DownBeat*, September 1962, 17.
31. Quoted in Feehan, "Durable Dorham," 17.
32. Quoted in Feehan, "Durable Dorham," 17.
33. Quoted in Feehan, "Durable Dorham," 17.
34. Quoted in Taylor, *Notes and Tones*, 233.
35. Quoted in Feehan, "Durable Dorham," 17.
36. Quoted in Feehan, "Durable Dorham," 17.
37. Tom Herrick, "Diggin the Discs with Tom," *DownBeat*, November 4, 1949, 1.
38. Quoted in Taylor, *Notes and Tones*, 232.
39. Spearman, "Trumpet Colossus Kenny Dorham."
40. Ramsey, *Amazing Bud Powell*, 110, quoting Eric C. Schneider, *Smack: Heroin and the American City* (University of Pennsylvania Press, 2008), 17.
41. Ramsey, *Amazing Bud Powell*, 110, quoting Schneider, *Smack*, 31.
42. Ramsey, *Amazing Bud Powell*, 110, quoting Schneider, *Smack*, 27.
43. Gary Bartz, interview by John Moultrie, "Gary Bartz Talks About Drug Use Among Jazz Greats," iRock Jazz, September 28, 2013, https://www.youtube.com/watch?v=8KL1pbN9Gjo.
44. Bartz interview.
45. Leonard Feather, "Parker Finally Finds Peace," *DownBeat*, April 20, 1955, 8.
46. "The First 10 Years of Birdland," *DownBeat*, December 10, 1959, 21.

CHAPTER 6: THE UNCROWNED KING

1. Keturah Dorham-Holley, interview by Robert Pallitto, October 1, 2021.
2. Kenny Dorham, "Fragments of an Autobiography," *DownBeat*, Yearbook special issue, December 1970, 34.
3. Dorham, "Fragments," 34.
4. Dorham, "Fragments," 34.
5. Paul Berliner, *Thinking in Jazz: The Infinite Art of Improvisation* (University of Chicago Press, 2009), 238.
6. Horace Silver, *Let's Get to the Nitty Gritty: The Autobiography of Horace Silver* (University of California Press, 2007), 25.

7. Silver, *Let's Get to the Nitty Gritty*, 79.

8. Dorham, "Fragments," 34.

9. Silver, *Let's Get to the Nitty Gritty*, " 88.

10. Gene Seymour, "Hard Bop," in *The Oxford Companion to Jazz*, ed. Bill Kirchner, (Oxford University Press, 2005), 337.

11. This club was named after Parker's nickname, "Bird."

12. George E. Pitts, "After Twelve with George E. Pitts," *Pittsburgh Courier*, July 23, 1955, p. 19, col. 1.

13. Dom Cerulli, "Strictly Ad Lib," *DownBeat*, November 30, 1955, 53.

14. Nat Hentoff, "Jazz-In-High-Schools Project Under Way," *DownBeat*, November 16, 1955, 7.

15. *Gene Lees' Jazzletter* 9, no. 4 (April 1990): 6.

16. *Jazzletter*, 6.

17. *Jazzletter*, 6.

18. Sam Lacy, "Theatrical Whirl," *Afro-American*, November 24, 1956, p. 7, col. 1.

19. "Birdland Stars Here Feb. 18 for 2 Concerts," *Daily Defender*, February 7, 1956, ProQuest Black Studies page 21, https://www.proquest.com/historical-newspapers/birdland-stars-here-feb-18-2-concerts/docview/493556331/se-2.

20. Les Matthews, "Mr. 1-2-5 Street," *New York Amsterdam News*, October 31, 1959, p. 11, col. 6.

21. Stanley Robertson, "Sentinel Platter Parade: Ten Most Popular Records of The Week MAX REPLIES," *Los Angeles Sentinel*, April 18, 1957, p. B10, col. 1.

22. George Pitts, "After Twelve: Small Talk," *Pittsburgh Courier*, June 9, 1956, ProQuest Black Studies page 23, https://www.proquest.com/historical-newspapers/after-twelve/docview/202306604/se-2.

23. Jimmy Rivers, "Jazz in Review," *Philadelphia Tribune*, May 9, 1959, ProQuest Black Studies page 6, https://www.proquest.com/historical-newspapers/jazz-review/docview/532352677/se-2.

24. Larry Greene, "Fight on Two Fronts: Black GIs in World War II and Ollie Stewart's Reporting in the *NJ Afro-American*," lecture at Newark Public Library, May 23, 2023.

25. Photo standalone 28—no title, *Pittsburgh Courier*, February 18, 1956, ProQuest Black Studies page A20, https://www.proquest.com/historical-newspapers/photo-standalone-28-no-title/docview/202297254/se-2.

26. "Birdland Stars Invade West; Boss Suit Minded: Asks Chicago Nightery Drop Copyrighted Name," *Chicago Defender*, February 11, 1956, ProQuest Black Studies page 15, https://www.proquest.com/historical-newspapers/birdland-stars-invade-west-boss-suit-minded/docview/492981165/se-2.

27. Quoted in Aidan Levy, *Saxophone Colossus: The Life and Music of Sonny Rollins*, (Hachette Books, 2022), 80.

28. Sonny Rollins, interview by John Melendez, January 10, 2023.

29. Rollins interview.

30. Rollins interview.

31. Kenny Dorham, *Lotus Blossom*, arr. Kenny Dorham (unpublished), 10, m. 131.

32. Dorham, "Fragments," 34.

33. Rollins interview.

34. Levy, *Saxophone Colossus*, 544.

35. Nick Catalano, *Clifford Brown: The Life and Art of the Legendary Jazz Trumpeter* (Oxford University Press, 2000), 185.

36. Matt Schudel, "50 Years Later, Unmuted Awe for Clifford Brown," *Washington Post*, June 25, 2006, www.washingtonpost.com/archive/lifestyle/2006/06/26/50-years-later-unmuted-awe-for-clifford-brown/c535e301-a8f8-4c44-9fb6-878392d4b722/.

37. "More Than 1000 At Powell Benefit," *DownBeat*, October 31, 1956, 9.

38. Liner notes for Max Roach, *Max Roach + 4*, recorded September 1956, EmArcy MG 36098, 33 1/3 rpm.

39. Rollins interview.

40. Dorham, "Fragments," 34.

41. Greg Henderson, "George Morrow," *Cadence* 7, no. 1 (January 1981): 7.

42. Elliott Bratton, "Art Davis," *Cadence* 12, no. 9 (September 1986): 14.

43. Nat Hentoff, "Caught in The Act," *DownBeat*, February 6, 1957, 10.

44. Photo standalone 20—no title, *Daily Defender*, February 13, 1957, ProQuest Black Studies page 14, https://www.proquest.com/historical-newspapers/photo-standalone-20-no-title/docview/493725057/se-2.

45. John Tynan, "Strictly Ad Lib," *DownBeat*, May 16, 1957, 8.

46. Al Cottman, "Strictly Ad Lib," *DownBeat*, July 25, 1957, 58.

47. Dom Cerulli, "Heard in Person," *DownBeat*, October 3, 1957, 49.

48. Ralph J. Gleason, "Strictly Ad Lib," *DownBeat*, December 12, 1957, 14.

49. "Jazz in Chicago Schools," *DownBeat*, October 31, 1957, 10.

50. "It's Swingland, Man," *DownBeat*, February 20, 1958, 10.

51. "Strictly Ad Lib," *DownBeat*, March 20, 1958, 10.

52. J. H. Walker, "Theatricals," *New York Amsterdam News*, March 8, 1958, ProQuest Black Studies page 12, https://www.proquest.com/historical-newspapers/theatricals/docview/225564668/se-2.

53. "Strictly Ad Lib," *DownBeat*, April 17, 1958, 10.

54. Don Gold "Max Roach," *DownBeat*, March 20, 1958, 15.

55. "Strictly Ad Lib," *DownBeat*, June 12, 1958, 8.

56. Dave Bittan, "Concert Review," *DownBeat*, December 11, 1958, 52.

57. Kenny Dorham, interview by Jim Toman, August 1969, link in Lewis Porter, "Kenny Dorham: Unknown Audio Interviews (+Bonus Autobiography)," *Playback with Lewis Porter!*, February 10, 2024, https://lewisporter.substack.com/p/kenny-dorham-unknown-audio-interviews.

58. Leonard Feather, "Durable Dorham," *DownBeat*, May 15, 1958, 33. Surprisingly, this is a second article with the title "Durable Dorham," along with the piece bearing the same name written by Gene Feehan and cited above.

59. Feather, "Durable Dorham," 33.

60. Feather, "Durable Dorham," 33.

61. Kenny Dorham, "Fragments," 34.

62. "Dorham Prophets Ink with ABC-Paramount," *DownBeat*, May 30, 1956, 26.

63. "Band Routes," *DownBeat*, May 30, 1956, 40.

64. "Jazz Greats Here in Birdland Show of '55," *Cleveland Call and Post*, February 11, 1956, p. 7A, col. 4.

65. Nat Hentoff, "Kenny Dorham's Jazz Prophets: Basin Street," *DownBeat*, June 27, 1956, 8.

66. Hentoff, "Kenny Dorham's Jazz Prophets: Basin Street," 8.

67. John Tynan, "Strictly Ad Lib," *DownBeat*, March 21, 1956, 6.

68. John Tynan, "Strictly Ad Lib," *DownBeat*, June 13, 1956, 6.

69. Vernon Duke, "Autumn in New York," on Kenny Dorham, *The Complete 'Round About Midnight at the Cafe Bohemia*, recorded May 31, 1956, Blue Note Records, BLP 1524, 1956, 33 1/3 rpm.

70. Quoted in Arthur Taylor, *Notes and Tones* (Da Capo Press, 1993), 237.

71. Harvey Husten, "Strictly Ad Lib," *DownBeat*, July 11, 1956, 32.

72. Tom Tomlinson, "Strictly Ad Lib," *DownBeat*, August 22, 1956, 6.

73. Miles Davis and Quincy Troupe, *Miles: The Autobiography* (Simon & Schuster Press, 1990), 212. Perhaps more consistent with his reputation, Davis claims to have outplayed Dorham the following night, when he returned to sit in once again.

74. *Third stream* is the genre designation given to jazz with classical inflections. Saxophonist Stan Getz's *Focus* and the work of composers Gunther Schuller and Ran Blake are commonly cited examples of its sound.

75. Ron Dyke, "Abbey Sings About Men and Love," *Metronome Magazine* 75, no. 7 (July 1958): 14.

76. Abbey Lincoln, interview by Sally Plaxson, December 17–18, 1986, Smithsonian Jazz Oral History Project, available at https://americanhistory.si.edu/explore/projects/smithsonian-jazz/collections-and-archives/smithsonian-jazz-oral-history-program.

77. Richard Cook and Brian Morton, *The Penguin Guide to Jazz* (Penguin, 2004), 393.

78. Not to be confused with the Billy Strayhorn original of the same name.

79. Paul Berliner, *Thinking in Jazz: The Infinite Art of Improvisation* (University of Chicago Press), 545.

80. Quoted in Berliner, *Thinking in Jazz*, 69.

81. Jeremy Yudkin, *The Lenox School of Jazz: A Vital Chapter in the History of American Music and Race Relations* (Farshaw Pub., 2006), 54.

82. Quoted in Yudkin, *Lenox School*, 54.

83. Article 5 (untitled), *Daily Defender*, November 15, 1958, https://www.proquest.com/historical-newspapers/article-5-no-title/docview/493772777/se-2.

84. Bill Coss, "The School of Jazz, Part II: A Practical Approach to Music Education," *Metronome* 75, no. 11 (November 1958), 38.

85. Yudkin, *Lenox School of Jazz*, 78n75.

86. Yudkin, *Lenox School of Jazz*, 78.

87. John Eckert, interview by John Melendez, December 18, 2024.

88. Eckert interview.

89. Eckert interview.

90. Eckert interview.

91. Tom Everett, "Ran Blake Interview," *Cadence* 2, no. 8 (April 1977): 4.

92. Quoted in "The Lenox School of Jazz 1959," *The Music Aficionado: Quality Articles About the Golden Age of Music*, June 13, 2018, https://musicaficionado.blog/2018/06/13/the-lenox-school-of-jazz-1959/.

93. W. Jones, "Willie's Happenings," *Philadelphia Tribune*, March 7, 1959, ProQuest Black Studies page 7, https://www.proquest.com/historical-newspapers/willies-happenings/docview/532328150/se-2.

94. R. Johnson, "Germantown Highlights," *Philadelphia Tribune*, March 14, 1959, ProQuest Black Studies page 13, https://www.proquest.com/historical-newspapers/germantown-highlights/docview/532195074/se-2.

95. "Strictly Ad Lib," *DownBeat*, April 30, 1959, 46–47.

96. J. Porter, "'Sax-ist' Jimmy Heath Playing at 'Horseshoe.'" *Philadelphia Tribune*, June 13, 1959, ProQuest Black Studies page 16, https://www.proquest.com/historical-newspapers/sax-ist-jimmy-heath-playing-at-horseshoe/docview/532191644/se-2.

97. Pete Welding, "The Return of Jimmy Heath," *DownBeat*, March 2, 1961, 17.

98. J. Rivers, "Jazz in Review," *Philadelphia Tribune*, May 9, 1959, ProQuest Black Studies page 6, https://www.proquest.com/historical-newspapers/jazz-review/docview/532352677/se-2.

99. Rivers, "Jazz in Review."

100. Frederick A. Douglass, "Jazz Pianist of the Future," *New York Amsterdam News*, March 3, 1979.

101. A. B. Spellman, *Four Lives in the Bebop Business* (Limelight Editions, 1994), 69.

102. Spellman, *Four Lives*, 69.

103. Buell Neidinger, "Bob Rusch," *Cadence* 12, no. 6 (June 1986): 9.

104. Louis Hayes, interview by John Melendez, December 13, 2024.

105. Hayes interview.

106. Hayes interview.

107. Hayes interview.

108. Hayes interview.

109. Hayes plays regularly at the jazz club Smoke and released an album titled *Artform Revisited* in 2024.

110. Hayes interview.

111. Israels is white.

112. Chuck Israels, *Bass Notes: Jazz in American Culture: A Personal View* (Rowman & Littlefield Publishers, 2023), 42–43.

113. Israels, *Bass Notes*, 44.

114. Dorham, "Fragments," 34.

115. Dorham, "Fragments," 34.

116. Rollins interview.

117. Art Blakey and the Jazz Messengers, *At the Café Bohemia*, vol. 1, Blue Note BLP 1507, 1956, compact disc rerelease, Blue Note 5321482, 2001.

CHAPTER 7: CALIFORNIA

1. Langston Hughes, *One-Way Ticket* (Alfred A. Knopf, 1949), 60.

2. Joel Dorham, interview by Robert Pallitto, October 6, 2021.

3. Joel Dorham, interview by Alisa Clancy, KCSM Radio, San Mateo, California, November 16, 2018 (copy on file with authors).

4. Joel Dorham, interview by Robert Pallitto.

5. Kenny Dorham, "Fragments of an Autobiography," Yearbook special issue, *DownBeat*, December 1970, 30.

6. A copy of Eva Lois McIlveen's MA thesis is on file at the Freestone County Historical Museum. Eva Lois McIlveen, "An Analysis of Some Moral Ideals as Reflected in Milton's Major Poems" (master's thesis, Texas Southern University, 1955).

7. Carolyn Yarbro Smith, interview by Robert Pallitto, January 27, 2022.

8. Dorham, "Fragments," 30.

9. Dorham, "Fragments," 30.

10. Grave marker, Eva Lois McIlveen, Fairfield Cemetery, recorded at https://www.findagrave.com/memorial/47108386/eva-lois-mcilveen, accessed March 19, 2024.

11. Yarbro Smith interview.

12. "Local Musician Bobby Cooper a Music Legend," *Freestone County Times*, July 3, 2018, https://freestonecountytimesonline.com/local-musician-bobby-cooper-a-music-legend/.

13. Don Awalt, interview by Robert Pallitto, September 15, 2021.

14. Historian Annette Gordon-Reed notes that one of the paradoxes accompanying desegregation was a shift in role for Black teachers. Gordon-Reed's mother taught in East Texas schools as desegregation unfolded, and she noted on the one hand that many Black teachers were removed from classrooms that now contained white students and given administrative tasks instead. Some, like Gordon-Reed's mother and Eva Lois McIlveen, were sought out for their teaching ability and retained in the classroom. Annette Gordon-Reed, *On Juneteenth* (Liveright, 2021), 51. Even then, however, they sensed a difference: "[I]t was harder to address Black students in the classroom, and talk openly about their common mission of moving the Black community ahead." Gordon-Reed, *On Juneteenth*, 51. Regarding Eva Lois McIlveen's contribution to the desegregation cause, see "First Integrated Class Commemorated as School Milestone," *Freestone County Times*, December 1, 2017, https://freestonecountytimesonline.com/first-integrated-class-commemorated-as-school-milestone/.

15. Obituary for James Milford McIlveen, https://www.mooresangelicfuneralhome.com/obituary/4912490, accessed March 20, 2024.

16. Yarbro Smith interview.

17. Joel Dorham, interview by Robert Pallitto.

18. Joel Dorham, interview by Robert Pallitto.

19. Joel Dorham, interview by Robert Pallitto.

20. Joel Dorham, interview by Robert Pallitto.

21. Ronald Dellums and H. Lee Halterman, *Lying Down with Lions: A Public Life from the Streets of Oakland to the Halls of Power* (Beacon Press, 2000), 45.

22. Hon. Ronald V. Dellums, "Congressional Record: Extensions of Remarks," May 17, 1988, 11358, https://www.congress.gov/100/crecb/1988/05/17/GPO-CRECB-1988-pt8-5-3.pdf.

23. "Stroll the Walk of Fame at West Oakland," *BARTable*, https://bartable.bart.gov/featured/stroll-walk-fame-west-oakland, updated September 13, 2016, accessed March 21, 2024.

24. The timbales are a percussion instrument closely related to the timpani, which is featured in symphonic music. Timbales are usually played with a pair of sticks, though sometimes the *timbalero* uses their hands as well.

25. Joel Dorham, KCSM interview.

26. Joel Dorham, interview by Robert Pallitto.

27. The Oakland Walk of Fame is a series of plaques on Seventh Street commemorating influential musical artists associated with the city. See The West Coast Blues Society, "The Music They Played," https://www.westcoastbluessociety.org/the-music-they-played-on-7th-street.

28. Joel Dorham, interview by Robert Pallitto.

29. The Back Room, concert announcement for Joel Dorham and his Latin Jazz Octet held on March 19, 2019, Facebook, https://www.facebook.com/events/the-back-room/joel-dorham/270822616921053/.

30. Joel Dorham, KCSM interview.

31. Hon. William (Bill) Clay, "Congressional Record: Extension of Remarks," November 3, 1977, 37051–52, https://www.congress.gov/95/crecb/1977/11/03/GPO-CRECB-1977-pt28-6-3.pdf, accessed February 9, 2022.

32. Clay, "Extension of Remarks," November 3, 1977, 37051–52.

33. Clay, "Extension of Remarks," November 3, 1977, 37051–52.

34. Clay, "Extension of Remarks," November 3, 1977, 37051–52.

35. Clay, "Extension of Remarks," November 3, 1977, 37051–52.

36. Hon. William (Bill) Clay, "Congressional Record: Extension of Remarks," September 23, 1988, 25271, https://www.congress.gov/100/crecb/1988/09/23/GPO-CRECB-1988-pt17-6-3.pdf, accessed February 9, 2022.

37. Clay, "Extension of Remarks," September 23, 1988, 25271.

38. Interestingly, Kenny Dorham appeared on *The Tonight Show* in 1957 along with other guests, but not as a house bandleader or band member. J. H. Walker, "Theatricals," *New York Amsterdam News*, June 29, 1957, ProQuest Black Studies page 16, https://www.proquest.com/historical-newspapers/theatricals/docview/225563615/se-2.

39. Quoted in Gene Feehan, "Durable Dorham," *DownBeat*, September 27, 1962, 17.

40. Kenny Dorham, interview by Claes Dahlgren, November 23,1962, link in Lewis Porter, "Kenny Dorham: Unknown Audio Interviews (+Bonus Autobiography)," *Playback with Lewis Porter!*, February 10, 2024, https://lewisporter.substack.com/p/kenny-dorham-unknown-audio-interviews.

41. Quoted in Arthur Taylor, *Notes and Tones* (Da Capo Press, 1993), 235.

42. The travails of jazz composers related to unscrupulous business adversaries goes back at least to W. C. Handy, who chronicled the way he was cheated out of royalties for his first best-selling composition, "Memphis Blues." That experience led him to form his

own publishing company. W. C. Handy, *Father of the Blues: An Autobiography* (Da Capo Press, 1969), 125.

43. Taylor, *Notes and Tones*, 233.

44. Quoted in Taylor, *Notes and Tones*, 234.

45. Quoted in Taylor, *Notes and Tones*, 33.

46. Guthrie P. Ramsey, *The Amazing Bud Powell: Black Genius, Jazz History, and the Challenge of Bebop* (University of California Press, 2013), 133.

47. Ramsey, *The Amazing Bud Powell*, 133.

48. Taylor, *Notes and Tones*, 234, 237.

49. Joel Dorham interview, January 25, 2022.

50. Joel Dorham interview, January 25, 2022.

CHAPTER 8: ONE MORE TIME

1. Bernard Drayton, interview by Robert Pallitto, October 26, 2022.

2. Drayton interview.

3. Drayton interview

4. Drayton interview.

5. Kenny Dorham, *Jazz Contemporary*, Time, S/2004, 1960, 33 1/3 rpm. Warren recorded on February 11 and Garrison on February 12, each playing on about half of the tracks.

6. Bob Rusch, "Steve Kuhn," *Cadence* 19, no. 1 (January 1993): 8.

7. Rusch, "Steve Kuhn," 9.

8. Quoted in Michael Cuscuna, liner notes to *Whistle Stop*, Blue Note Records BST 84063, 1961, 33 1/3 rpm.

9. Brent Hayes Edwards, *Epistrophies: Jazz and the Literary Imagination* (Harvard University Press, 2017), 186.

10. Edwards, *Epistrophies*, 187.

11. Kenny Dorham, "Fragments of an Autobiography," Yearbook special issue, *DownBeat*, December 1970, 30–34.

12. Cobb was referring to the time period when Davis was selected by Charlie Parker to join his group. Jimmy Cobb, interview by William Brower, July 26 and 27, 2010, Smithsonian Jazz Oral History Project, https://americanhistory.si.edu/explore/projects/smithsonian-jazz/collections-and-archives/smithsonian-jazz-oral-history-program.

13. Untitled display ad 53, *New York Amsterdam News*, July 30, 1960, ProQuest Black Studies page 15, https://www.proquest.com/historical-newspapers/display-ad-53-no-title/docview/225476650/se-2.

14. "Jazz Concerts 7 Nights a Week," *New York Amsterdam News*, August 20, 1960, ProQuest Black Studies page 15, https://www.proquest.com/historical-newspapers/jazz-concerts-7-nights-week/docview/225471483/se-2.

15. Untitled display ad 24, *Chicago Daily Defender*, November 16, 1960, ProQuest Black Studies page 23, https://www.proquest.com/historical-newspapers/display-ad-24-no-title/docview/493839988/se-2.

16. Jesse H. Walker, "Theatricals" *New York Amsterdam News*, March 5, 1960, p. 15, col. 1; "Strictly Ad Lib," *DownBeat*, March 31, 1960, 38.

17. "Strictly Ad Lib," *DownBeat*, April 14, 1960, 47.

18. "Strictly Ad Lib," *DownBeat*, October 13, 1960, 50.

19. "DownBeat's Combo Directory," *DownBeat* June 23, 1960, 43.

20. George Palmer, "Tavern Topics," *New York Amsterdam News*, May 21, 1960, p. 16, col. 1.

21. "Coffee Concerts to Close with 'The Barrier,'" *New York Amsterdam News*, March 26, 1960, p. 15, col. 3.

22. Jesse H. Walker, "Theatricals," *New York Amsterdam News*, April 22, 1961, p. 19, col. 1.

23. H. A. Woodfin, "Kenny Dorham," *The Jazz Review* 3, no. 7 (August 1960): 7, 8, 9.

24. "Strictly Ad Lib," *DownBeat*, November 20, 1960, 10.

25. Untitled display ad 51, *New York Amsterdam News*, May 13, 1961, ProQuest Black Studies page 17, https://www.proquest.com/historical-newspapers/display-ad-51-no-title/docview/225436423/se-2.

26. Untitled display ad 75, *New York Amsterdam News*, June 24, 1961, ProQuest Black Studies page 23, https://www.proquest.com/historical-newspapers/display-ad-75-no-title/docview/225447709/se-2.

27. Kenny Dorham, *Hot Stuff from Brazil*, West Wind, WW 015, 1988, 33 1/3 rpm.

28. Bob Rusch, "Curtis Fuller," *Cadence* 2, no. 6 (March 1977): 5–6.

29. "Kenny Dorham Playing at Riverside Pk," *New York Amsterdam News*, City edition, August 19, 1961, http://www.proquest.com/newspapers/classified-ad-2-no-title/docview/225448845/se-2?accountid=10226.

30. Untitled display ad 117, *Los Angeles Sentinel*, August 24, 1961,ProQuest Black Studies page C3, https://www.proquest.com/historical-newspapers/display-ad-117-no-title/docview/564603017/se-2.

31. Untitled display ad 111, *Los Angeles Sentinel*, November 16, 1961, ProQuest Black Studies page C2, https://www.proquest.com/historical-newspapers/display-ad-111-no-title/docview/564594146/se-2.

32. "Strictly Ad Lib," *DownBeat*, February 1, 1962, 45.

33. "Strictly Ad Lib," *DownBeat*, January 18, 1962, 38.

34. "Strictly Ad Lib," *DownBeat*, January 18, 1962, 38.

35. Leonard Feather, "All That Jazz," *New York Amsterdam News*, March 17, 1962, p. 17, col. 3.

36. Kenny Dorham, *Inta Somethin'*, Pacific Jazz, STEREO-41, 1962, 33 1/3 rpm.

37. Jackie Mclean, *Vertigo*, Blue Note, KT-1085, 1980, Vinyl; *Hipnosis*, Blue Note, BN-LA483-J2, 1978, 33 1/3 rpm.

38. Ira Gitler, "Caught in the Act," *DownBeat*, August 30, 1962, 34.

39. "Strictly Ad Lib," *DownBeat*, June 7, 1962, 10.

40. "DownBeat's Annual Combo Directory," *DownBeat*, June 21, 1962, 35.

41. "Combo Directory," June 21, 1962, 35.

42. "Combo Directory," June 21, 1962, 35.

43. "Strictly Ad Lib," *DownBeat*, July 5, 1962, 43.

44. "Strictly Ad Lib," *DownBeat*, August 30, 1962, 42.

45. "Strictly Ad Lib," *DownBeat*, January 3, 1963, 10.

46. Kenny Dorham, "Kenny's Lament," *DownBeat*, March 14, 1963, 9.

47. "Strictly Ad Lib," *DownBeat*, March 28, 1963, 54.

48. "Strictly Ad Lib," *DownBeat*, May 23, 1963, 12.

49. "Strictly Ad Lib," *DownBeat*, June 20, 1963, 44.

50. "Strictly Ad Lib," *DownBeat*, June 20, 1963, 13.

51. "Strictly Ad Lib," *DownBeat*, June 6, 1963, 45.

52. Michael Cuscuna, interview by Robert Pallitto, September 8, 2022.

53. Cuscuna interview.

54. Cuscuna interview.

55. Cuscuna interview.

56. Cuscuna interview.

57. Dolphy was known for playing bass clarinet and flute in addition to alto saxophone.

58. Nat Hentoff, liner notes to Andrew Hill, *Point of Departure*, Blue Note Records, BLP 4167, 1964, 33 1/3 rpm.

59. Phyl Garland, "Pick of the Year's Crop," *Pittsburgh Courier*, August 14, 1965, p. 17, col. 1.

60. David Woods, "Joe Henderson," *Jazz Journal International*, December 1991, 7.

61. Quoted in Nat Hentoff, liner notes to *Point of Departure*, Blue Note Records 7243 4 99007 2 1, 1999, compact disc.

62. Joe Henderson, *Page One*, Blue Note, BST 84140, 1963, 33 1/3 rpm; *Our Thing*, Blue Note BST 84152, 1963, 33 1/3 rpm; *In 'n Out*, Blue Note BST 84166,1963, 33 1/3 rpm.

63. Nathaniel Mackey, *Blue Fasa* (New Directions 2015), 81.

64. Kenny Dorham, *Live at the Flamboyan*, Uptown Records, UPCD 27.60, 2009, compact disc.

65. rarejazzvideos3, "Kenny Dorham Quartet—Stockholm 1963," YouTube, September 23, 2013, https://www.youtube.com/watch?v=h_Afv2mQs6s, accessed October 20, 2022.

66. Kenny Dorham, *Short Story*, Steeplechase, SCC6010, 1979, 33 1/3 rpm.

67. Kenny Dorham, *Scandia Skies*, Steeplechase, SCC-6011, 1980, 33 1/3 rpm.

68. Larry Smith, "T. S. Monk," *Cadence* 24, no. 7 (July 1998): 9.

69. Quoted in Nat Hentoff, liner notes to *Una Mas*, Blue Note Records BST 84127, 1963, rpm; rereleased as Recording Company 5212282, 1999, compact disc.

70. Quoted in Bob Blumenthal, liner notes to *Trompeta Toccata*, Blue Note BST 84181, 1964, rpm, rereleased as Records 62635, 2006, compact disc.

71. Quoted in Woods, "Joe Henderson," 7.

72. "Brooklyn Apollo Gets Jazz," *New York Amsterdam News*, December 10, 1966, ProQuest Black Studies page 23, https://www.proquest.com/historical-newspapers/brooklyn-apollo-get-jazz/docview/226704059/se-2.

73. Untitled display ad 17, *Philadelphia Tribune*, July 25, 1967, ProQuest Black Studies page 17, https://www.proquest.com/historical-newspapers/display-ad-17-no-title/docview/532487674/se-2.

74. Rossy Mendez, "Harlem Youth Opportunities Unlimited," NYC Department of Records and Information Services, June 1, 2018, https://www.archives.nyc/blog/2018/6/1/harlem-youth-opportunities-unlimited.

75. Kenny Dorham, "Thanks From K.D." *DownBeat*, December 30, 1965, 6.

76. William Robinson, "HARYOU-ACT Youngsters Score With Arts Festival: Amateurs Perform in Professional Manner," *New York Amsterdam News*, October 3, 1964, ProQuest Black Studies page 14, https://www.proquest.com/historical-newspapers/haryou-act-youngsters-score-with-arts-festival/docview/226691058/se-2.

77. "Dance Group Sets First '64 Concert, *New York Amsterdam News*, November 7, 1964, ProQuest Black Studies page 17, https://www.proquest.com/historical-newspapers/dance-group-sets-first-64-concert/docview/226800746/se-2.

78. "HARYOU ACT at Library," *New York Amsterdam News*, August 19, 1967, ProQuest Black Studies page 43, https://www.proquest.com/historical-newspapers/haryou-acts-at-library/docview/226617901/se-2.

79. "Brooklyn Kids Hear Museum Jazz Concert," *New York Amsterdam New*, October 27, ProQuest Black Studies page 20, 1962, https://www.proquest.com/historical-newspapers/brooklyn-kids-hear-museum-jazz-concert/docview/226825447/se-2.

80. "Children's Home Scene of Jazz Concert," *New York Amsterdam News*, February 10, 1962, ProQuest Black Studies page A16, https://www.proquest.com/historical-newspapers/childrens-home-scene-jazz-concert/docview/2293397782/se-2.

81. "Children's Home Scene of Jazz Concert."

82. "Penthouse Jazz Party on May 20," *New York Amsterdam News*, May 19, 1962, ProQuest Black Studies page 19, https://www.proquest.com/historical-newspapers/penthouse-jazz-party-on-may-20/docview/226793931/se-2.

83. "Jazz Arts Society on the Move," *New York Amsterdam News*, January 27, 1962, ProQuest Black Studies page 19, https://www.proquest.com/historical-newspapers/jazz-arts-society-on-move/docview/2293400255/se-2.

84. "Jazz Concerts 7 Nights a Week," *New York Amsterdam News*, August 20, 1960, ProQuest Black Studies page 15, https://www.proquest.com/historical-newspapers/jazz-concerts-7-nights-week/docview/225471483/se-2.

85. "Garden Jazz," *New York Amsterdam News*, July 28, 1962, ProQuest Black Studies page 16, https://www.proquest.com/historical-newspapers/garden-jazz/docview/226810886/se-2.

86. E. Cunningham, "Sugar Ray Robinson Takes on Sinatra, Cole, Mathis," *Pittsburgh Courier*, July 14, 1962, ProQuest Black Studies page 22, https://www.proquest.com/historical-newspapers/sugar-ray-robinson-takes-on-sinatra-cole-mathis/docview/202467735/se-2.

87. "'Jazz giants' in Brooklyn," *New York Amsterdam News*, July 13, 1963, ProQuest Black Studies page 16, https://www.proquest.com/historical-newspapers/jazz-giants-brooklyn/docview/226728807/se-2.

88. Jimmy Heath, *I Walked with Giants* (Temple University Press, 2007), 133.

89. Heath, *I Walked with Giants*, 133.

90. "Chronological Listing of Concerts Sponsored by the Left Bank Jazz Society," *Baltimore Jazz Scene* 1 (January 1967): 38.

91. "Concerts Sponsored by the Left Bank Jazz Society," 38.

92. "Concerts Sponsored by the Left Bank Jazz Society," 38.

93. "Live 1965 at Murphy Fine Arts Center, Morgan State College—Baltimore," *Sonny Red*, https://sonnyredmusic.com/audio-archive/.

94. Kenny Dorham, interview by Claes Dahlgren, link on Lewis Porter, "Kenny Dorham: Unknown Audio Interviews (+Bonus Autobiography)," *Playback with Lewis Porter!* February 10, 2024, https://lewisporter.substack.com/p/kenny-dorham-unknown-audio-interviews.

95. Dorham, interview by Dahlgren.

96. Dorham, interview by Dahlgren.

97. Dorham, interview by Dahlgren.

98. Dorham, interview by Dahlgren.

99. Quoted in Arthur Taylor, *Notes and Tones* (Da Capo Press, 1973), 237.

100. Kahron Spearman, "Trumpet Colossus Kenny Dorham Towers Among the Jazz Gods," *Austin Chronicle*, September 14, 2018, https://www.austinchronicle.com/music/2018-09-14/trumpet-colossus-kenny-dorham-towers-alongside-the-jazz-gods/.

101. Taylor, *Notes and Tones*, 233.

102. Taylor, *Notes and Tones*, 233; Spearman, "Trumpet Colossus."

103. Ira Gitler, "WBAI at the Gate," *Sounds and Fury* 1, no. 5 (April 1966): 29; Jesse H. Walker, "Theatricals," *New York Amsterdam News*, December 11, 1965, p. 23, col. 3.

104. Kenny Dorham, *Live at the Half Note*, Magnetic, MRCD 129, 1992, compact disc; Gitler, "WBAI at the Gate"

105. "Newport '66 All Star Trumpet Jam," YouTube, March 2, 2024, uploaded by JJ Martin, https://youtu.be/v1CpFSDV5ao?si=pfD5BSg3ExUuzKh2.

106. "Newport Trumpet Jam."

107. "Newport Trumpet Jam."

108. Ashawnta Jackson, "The Newport Rebels and Jazz as Protest" *JSTOR Daily*, July 23, 2020, https://daily.jstor.org/the-newport-rebels-and-jazz-as-protest/.

109. Lewis Porter, "Kenny Dorham Unknown Audio Interviews," *Playback with Lewis Porter* (Introductory text), https://lewisporter.substack.com/p/kenny-dorham-unknown-audio-interviews.

110. Quoted in Taylor, *Notes and Tones*, 234, 237.

111. "Newport Jazz Festival Stars Named: Rhode Island Meet Is Set," *Chicago Daily Defender*, April 19, 1966, ProQuest Black Studies page 10, https://www.proquest.com/historical-newspapers/newport-jazz-festival-stars-named/docview/494243784/se-2. As noted in this later article, the unruliness of crowds continued to be controversial in the years following the 1960 festival.

112. Michael Corcoran, "Longhorn Jazz Festival 'Lost Money on the Good Ones' During Its Five-Year Run," *Michael Corcorans's Overserved*, Michael.corcoran.substack.com.

113. "Anderson Musicians to Serve as Ushers," *Austin American Statesman*, April 2, 1966, https://library.austintexas.gov/digital/austin-american-statesman.

114. Quoted in Jim Langdon, "Nightbeat," *Austin American Statesman*, April 9, 1966, https://library.austintexas.gov/digital/austin-american-statesman.

115. Quoted in Langdon, "Nightbeat."

116. Quoted in Langdon, "Nightbeat."

117. George Wein, Clippings folder, box 8, George Wein Papers. Rutgers Institute of Jazz Studies, Rutgers University, Newark, New Jersey.

118. "Promoter Repaying Musicians," *New York Amsterdam News*, February 6, 1965, https://www.proquest.com/historical-newspapers/promoter-repaying-musicians/docview/226738349/se-2.

119. "Garner Plays New Jersey," *New York Amsterdam News*, July 24, 1965, ProQuest Black Studies page 24, https://www.proquest.com/historical-newspapers/garner-plays-new-jersey/docview/226708651/se-2.

120. Untitled display ad 72, *New York Amsterdam News*, December 4, 1965, ProQuest Black Studies page 22, https://www.proquest.com/historical-newspapers/display-ad-72-no-title/docview/226754846/se-2.

121. J. H. Walker, "Theatricals," *New York Amsterdam News*, February 12, 1966, ProQuest Black Studies page 18, https://www.proquest.com/historical-newspapers/theatricals/docview/226734647/se-2.

122. "At Slugs," *New York Amsterdam News*, October 1, 1966, ProQuest Black Studies page 11, https://www.proquest.com/historical-newspapers/at-slugs/docview/226687681/se-2.

123. Fred Jung, "Fireside Chat With: Ronald Shannon Jackson," *Jazz Weekly*, March 31, 1999, https://www.jazzweekly.com/1999/03/fireside-chat-with-ronald-shannon-jackson/.

124. Quoted in Paul Berliner, *Thinking in Jazz: The Infinite Art of Improvisation* (University of Chicago Press, 2009), 367–68.

125. Quoted in Taylor, *Notes and Tones*, 234.

126. Brent Hayes Edwards, *Epistrophies: Jazz and the Literary Imagination* (Harvard University Press, 2017), 46. And while there is evidence to support Armstrong's choices about where and when to speak out, he did in fact speak publicly to criticize President Eisenhower's initial handling of the 1957 violent resistance to desegregation in Little Rock, Arkansas. See Ricky Riccardi, "I'm Still Louis Armstrong–Colored: Louis Armstrong and the Civil Rights Era," That's My Home: Louis Armstrong House Museum Virtual Exhibits, May 11, 2020, https://virtualexhibits.louisarmstronghouse.org/2020/05/11/im-still-louis-armstrong-colored-louis-armstrong-and-the-civil-rights-era/.

CHAPTER 9: IF EVER I WOULD LEAVE YOU: LOST YEARS

1. Simon Anekwe, "Bud Powell Plays Final Performance," *New York Amsterdam News*, August 13, 1966, p. 1, col. 1.

2. Jazz n Bossa, "Dorham Date Blue Bossa in the Bronx: Live from the Blue Morocco Bows as Two-LP Set from Resonance Records," *Puerto Rico Jazz*, February 15, 2025, https://prjazz.blogspot.com/2025/02/dorham-date-blue-bossa-in-bronx-live.html?m=1.

3. Rocky Boyd, *Ease It*, Jazztime, JT001, 1961, 33 1/3 rpm.

4. Ron Carter, interview by John Melendez, December 11, 2024.

5. Lew Tabackin, interview by John Melendez, June 25, 2021.

6. Tabackin interview.

7. Tabackin interview.

8. Tabackin interview.

9. Tabackin interview.

10. Jimmy Owens, interview by Maxine Gordon, September 10 and 11, 2011, Smithsonian Jazz Oral History Project, available at https://americanhistory.si.edu/explore/projects/smithsonian-jazz/collections-and-archives/smithsonian-jazz-oral-history-program.

11. "The Lenox School of Jazz 1959," *The Music Aficionado*, June 13, 2018, https://musicaficionado.blog/2018/06/13/the-lenox-school-of-jazz-1959/.

12. Evette Dorham, interview by Phil Schaap, *Bird Flight*, WKCR-FM, December 5, 2018.

13. Nat Hentoff, liner notes for *Trompeta Toccata*, Blue Note BST 84181, 1965, 33 1/3 rpm.

14. Barry Harris, *Bull's Eye*, Prestige, PRST 7600, 1968, 33 1/3 rpm.

15. Cecil Payne, *Zodiac*, Strata-East, SES-19734, 1973, 33 1/3 rpm.

16. Jesse H. Walker, "Theatricals," *New York Amsterdam News*, March 30, 1968, p. 40, col. 4.

17. Clifford Jordan, *In the World*, Strata-East 19721, 1972, 45 rpm.

18. Jim Toman, interview with Kenny Dorham, August 1969, link at Lewis Porter, "Kenny Dorham: Unknown Audio Interviews (+Bonus Autobiography," *Playback with Lewis Porter!*, https://lewisporter.substack.com/p/kenny-dorham-unknown-audio-interviews.

19. Kenny Dorham, *Blue Bossa in the Bronx: Live from the Blue Morocco*, Resonance Records, HCD-2072, 2025, compact disc.

20. Dorham, *Blue Bossa in the Bronx*.

21. Bob Rusch, "Frank Strazzeri," *Cadence* 21, no. 9 (September 1995): 16, 17.

22. Kenny Dorham, Woody Shaw, Bill Hardman, Blue Mitchell, Richard Williams, Walter Kelly, *Trumpet Summit: Live at Club Ruby 1968*, Fresh Sound Records, FSRCD 382, 2015, compact disc.

23. Owen Cordle, "Various Artists: Trumpet Summit: Live at Club Ruby 1968," *JazzTimes: America's Jazz Magazine*, September 1, 2005, updated April 25, 2019, jazztimes.com/archives/various-artists-trumpet-summit-live-at-club-ruby-1968/.

24. "Chronological Listing of Concerts Sponsored by the Left Bank Jazz Society," *Baltimore Jazz Scene* 1, no. 3 (January 1969): 48.

25. Untitled display ad 34, *New York Amsterdam News*, February 21, 1970, p. 17, col. 2.

26. Quoted in Al Young, liner notes to *Kenny Dorham, But Beautiful*, Milestone M-47036, 1976, 33 1/3 rpm.

27. Jesse H. Walker, "Theatricals," *New York Amsterdam News*, July 18, 1970, p. 18, col. 1.

28. "Strictly Ad Lib," *DownBeat*, July 22, 1971, 12.

29. "Peace," *Expansions*, May 10, 1971, 8.

30. "Collective Black Artists' Members," *Expansions*, June 10, 1971, 19.

31. Hank Mobley, *Mobley's Second Message*, Prestige, PRLP 7082, 1957, 33 1/3 rpm.

32. Walter Bishop Jr., interview by Larry Ridley, July 23, 1996, video recording, Schomburg Center, New York, New York. Dorham helped other musicians who lacked his reading and composition training, but he also held them to his own standard. Dorham's friend Jackie McLean recalled him chiding him as he struggled with written charts. Jackie McLean, interview by William Brower, July 20 and 21, 2001, Smithsonian Jazz Oral History Project, https://americanhistory.si.edu/explore/projects/smithsonian-jazz/collections-and-archives/smithsonian-jazz-oral-history-program.

33. Larry Hollis, "Bobby Shew," *Cadence* 15, no. 9 (September 1989): 7.

34. Bishop interview.

35. Bishop interview.

36. Bishop interview.

37. Bishop interview.

38. Bishop interview.

39. Bishop interview.

40. Charles Davis, interview by Larry Ridley, June 25, 1996, video recording, Schomburg Center, New York, New York, .

41. Ronnie Matthews, interview by Larry Ridley, video recording, June 25, 1996, Schomburg Center, New York, New York.

42. Matthews interview.

43. Matthews interview.

44. Dan Morgenstern, interview by Michael Steinman, "Dan Morgenstern Recalls Kenny Dorham (Dec. 14, 2018)." YouTube, June 20, 2019, uploaded by swingyoucats, https://www.youtube.com/watch?v=411W-cjz5aQ.

45. Morgenstern interview.

46. "K.D. – Famous Initials," *DownBeat*, June 3, 1965, 25.

47. Kenny Dorham, "Record Reviews", *DownBeat*, August 25, 1966, 31.

48. Kenny Dorham, "Record Reviews", *DownBeat*, April 21, 1966, 34–35.

49. Kenny Dorham, "Two Views of Three Outer Views," *DownBeat*, July 15, 1965, 29.

50. Dorham, "Two Views," 29.

51. Dorham, "Two Views," 30.

52. Dorham, "Two Views," 29.

53. Kirk Silsbee, "Bobby Bradford," *Cadence* 22, no. 1 (January 1996): 11.

54. Kenny Dorham, "Record Reviews", *DownBeat*, January 13, 1966, 22-–23.

55. Joe Maita, "Conversations with Gary Giddins: On Underrated Jazz Musicians, Part One," *Jerry Jazz Musician*, January 5, 2004, https://www.jerryjazzmusician.com/conversations-with-gary-giddins-on-underrated-jazz-musicians-part-one/.

56. Benny Golson and Jim Merod, *Whisper Not: The Autobiography of Benny Golson* (Temple University Press, 2016), 259.

57. Golson and Merod, *Whisper Not*, 259.

58. James Brown, "Dorham's Delight," *DownBeat*, September 9, 1965, 10.

59. Peter R. Farmer, "K.D. Pro," *DownBeat*, March 10, 1966, 6.

60. Kenny Dorham, "Record Reviews," *DownBeat*, December 30, 1965, 34.

61. Dorham, "Record Reviews," December 30, 1965, 34.

62. Dorham, "Record Reviews," December 30, 1965, 34.

63. Kenny Dorham, "Record Reviews," *DownBeat*, July 1, 1965, 26.

64. Kenny Dorham, "Record Reviews," *DownBeat*, February 24, 1966, 26.

65. Dorham, "Record Reviews," February 24, 1966, 26.

66. Kenny Dorham, "Record Reviews," *DownBeat*, October 7, 1965, 34.

67. Kenny Dorham, "Record Reviews," *DownBeat*, January 27, 1966, 32.

68. Morgenstern interview.

69. Quoted in Brent Hayes Edwards, *Epistrophies: Jazz and the Literary Imagination* (Harvard University Press, 2017), 185. Brown's book is *Recollections: Essays, Drawings, Miscellanea* (Juergen A. Schmitt Publikationen, 1984).

70. "Women's Day at Shiloh," *New York Amsterdam News*, September 12, 1970, ProQuest Black Studies page 28, https://www.proquest.com/historical-newspapers/womens-day-at-shiloh/docview/226548785/se-2.

71. Quoted in Kahron Spearman, "Trumpet Colossus Kenny Dorham Towers Alongside the Jazz Gods," *Austin Chronicle*, September 14, 2018, https://www.austinchronicle.com/music/2018-09-14/trumpet-colossus-kenny-dorham-towers-alongside-the-jazz-gods/.

72. "Potpourri," *DownBeat*, November 9, 1972, 11.

73. Mark Harvey, interview by Robert Pallitto, July 2022.

74. Harvey interview.

75. Mark Harvey, "Final Chorus," *Boston After Dark*, December 12, 1972.

76. Stephen Davis, "Sounds of the City," *The Real Paper*, December 13, 1972.

77. Quoted in Bob Blumenthal, "Kenny Dorham: Tribute to a Trumpeter," *Boston Phoenix*, December 12, 1972.

78. Quoted in Paul Berliner, *Thinking in Jazz: The Infinite Art of Improvisation* (University of Chicago Press, 2009), 503.

79. "Kenny Dorham, Trumpeter; Early Exponent of Be-Bop," *New York Times*, December 6, 1972.

80. Harvey, "Final Chorus."

81. "Funeral for Jazz Star Kenny Dorham Now Set," *Austin American-Statesman*, December 9, 1972.

82. "Funeral for Jazz Star Kenny Dorham."

83. "Funeral for Jazz Star Kenny Dorham."

84. Richard Williams, "Dorham—One of the Best," *Melody Maker*, December 23, 1972, 14.

85. "Kenny Dorham—1924–1972, *DownBeat*, December 22, 1972, 10.

86. "In Memoriam," *Expansions* (March–April 1972): 2.

87. "College Fest Honors Jazz Great," *Austin American-Statesman*, March 25, 1973.

CHAPTER 10: LEGACY

1. https://www.jazzleadsheets.com.

2. Ratliff, "Kenny Dorham, from Be-Bop On," *New York Times*, August 27, 1999, https://www.nytimes.com/1999/08/27/movies/kenny-dorham-from-be-bop-on.html.

3. Ratliff, "Kenny Dorham, from Be-Bop On."

4. Don Sickler, *The Music of Kenny Dorham*, Reservoir RSR CD 111, 1984, compact disc.

5. Ratliff, "Kenny Dorham, from Be-Bop On."

6. Don Sickler, interview by Robert Pallitto, June 15, 2022.

7. Ratliff, "Kenny Dorham, from Be-Bop On."

8. *'Round Midnight*, directed by Bertrand Tavernier (1986).

9. Eric Siereveld, "Kenny Dorham, [*sic*] sings and plays Fairweather [*sic*]," YouTube, https://www.youtube.com/watch?v=xqvCDwKikGQ, accessed April 22, 2024.

10. Sickler interview.

11. Quoted in Kahron Spearman, "Trumpet Colossus Kenny Dorham Towers Alongside the Jazz Gods," *Austin Chronicle*, September 14, 2018, https://www.austinchronicle.com/music/2018-09-14/trumpet-colossus-kenny-dorham-towers-alongside-the-jazz-gods/.

12. Quoted in Nat Hentoff, liner notes to *Point of Departure*, Blue Note BLP 4176, 1965, 33 1/3 rpm.

13. Patricia Pratt, interview by Robert Pallitto, September 18, 2021.

14. Randy Sandke, "The Trumpet in Jazz," in *The Oxford Companion to Jazz*, ed. Bill Kirchner (Oxford University Press, 2005), 623.

15. Paul Berliner, *Thinking in Jazz: The Infinite Art of Improvisation* (University of Chicago Press, 2009), 136.

16. Jimmy Heath, *I Walked with Giants* (Temple University Press, 2007), 79.

17. Heath, *I Walked with Giants*, 79–80.

18. Heath, *I Walked with Giants*, 99.

19. Heath, *I Walked with Giants*, 123.

20. Heath, *I Walked with Giants*, 124; The Milt Jackson Sextet, "None Shall Wander" by Kenny Dorham, track 8 on *Invitation*, Riverside 9446, 1963, 33 1/3 rpm.

21. The provenance of the song's title is interesting. Dorham may have been alluding to his parents' biblical tutelage in selecting the title, as it appears to resemble closely Ezekiel 14:11, which reads, "so that the house of Israel may no longer go astray from me, nor defile themselves any more with all their transgressions. Then they shall be my people, and I will be their God, says the Lord God" (NRSV). In this passage, Ezekiel urges the Israelites, then in exile in Babylon, to restore themselves to God's favor. Parallels between the plight of the Israelites in antiquity and that of African Americans, whose ancestors were brought in captivity to a foreign land in early modernity, have long been invoked in song, worship, and activism.

22. Jimmy Owens and Charles Tolliver, interview by Art Farmer, 1 April 1993 "Oral History Interview with Charles Tolliver," Schomburg Center, New York, New York.

23. Owens and Tolliver interview.

24. Max Roach, *Members Don't Git Weary*, Atlantic 1510, 1968, 33 1/3 rpm.

25. Bob Rusch, "Eddie Gale," *Cadence* 15, no. 10 (October 1989): 13.

26. Ludwig Van Trikt, "Dave Burrell," *Cadence* 14, no. 7 (July 1988): 18.

27. Alwyn Lewis and Laurie Lewis, "Billie Harper," *Cadence* 19, no. 6 (June 1993): 7.

28. Alwyn Lewis and Laurie Lewis, "Marcus Belgrave," *Cadence* 26, no. 2 (February 2000): 7.

29. Ludwig Van Trikt, "Roy Campbell," *Cadence* 25, no. 12 (December 1999): 18–19

30. David Weiss, interview by John Melendez, December 24, 2024.

31. Weiss interview.

32. Weiss interview.

33. Weiss interview.

34. Weiss interview.

35. Weiss interview.

36. Weiss interview. Woody Shaw, *Setting Standards*, Muse, MR 5318, 1985, 33 1/3 rpm.

37. Freddie Hubbard and Woody Shaw, "Lotus Blossom" by Kenny Dorham, track 7 on *Double Take*, Blue Note 46294, 1986, compact disc.

38. Weiss interview.

39. David Weiss, *Auteur*, Origin, 82903, 2024, compact disc.

40. Joe Magnarelli, interview by John Melendez, September 7, 2021.

41. Magnarelli interview.

42. Magnarelli interview.

43. Magnarelli interview.

44. Magnarelli interview.

45. Magnarelli interview.

46. Freddie Hendrix to Robert Pallitto and John Melendez, October 9, 2022.

47. Hendrix to Pallitto and Melendez.

48. Hendrix interview.

49. Hendrix interview.

50. Kal Ferretti, interview by John Melendez, January 7, 2025.

51. Ferretti interview.

52. Laurie E. Jasinski, "Austin Music Memorial: Honoring Music Legends," Texas State Historical Association, updated February 25, 2021, https://www.tshaonline.org/handbook/entries/austin-music-memorial, accessed October 21, 2022.

53. Evette Dorham, interview by Phil Schaap, *Bird Flight*, WKCR-FM, December 5, 2018.

54. George Coleman, interview by Maxine Gordon, November 11, 2014, Smithsonian Jazz Oral History Project, available at https://americanhistory.si.edu/explore/projects/smithsonian-jazz/collections-and-archives/smithsonian-jazz-oral-history-program.

55. Coleman interview.

56. Benny Golson and Jim Merod, *Whisper Not: The Autobiography of Benny Golson* (Temple University Press, 2016), 259.

57. Golson and Merod, *Whisper Not*, 260.

58. Golson and Merod, *Whisper Not*, 261.

59. Kenny Dorham, interview by Jim Toman, August 1969, link at Lewis Porter, "Kenny Dorham: Unknown Audio Interviews (+Bonus Autobiography," *Playback with Lewis Porter!*, https://lewisporter.substack.com/p/kenny-dorham-unknown-audio-interviews.

60. Harold McMillan, interview by Robert Pallitto, October 9, 2022.

AFTERWORD

1. Dave Oliphant, *KD: A Jazz Biography* (Wings Press, 2012).

INDEX

ABOUT THE AUTHORS

ROBERT M. PALLITTO is professor of political science at Seton Hall University. His previous publications include four books and numerous scholarly and popular articles.

JOHN A. MELENDEZ is a writer and musician based in Brooklyn. His work has appeared in *Full Stop Magazine*, *On the Run*, and *Bluegrass Unlimited*.

*Photos courtesy of the authors